WRITING AGAINST

# WRITING AGAINST TIME

Michael W. Clune

STANFORD UNIVERSITY PRESS
STANFORD, CALIFORNIA

Stanford University Press
Stanford, California

©2013 by the Board of Trustees of the Leland Stanford Junior University. All rights reserved.

No part of this book may be reproduced or transmitted in any form or by any means, electronic or mechanical, including photocopying and recording, or in any information storage or retrieval system without the prior written permission of Stanford University Press.

Printed in the United States of America on acid-free, archival-quality paper

Library of Congress Cataloging-in-Publication Data

Clune, Michael W., author.
 Writing against time / Michael W. Clune.
    pages cm
 Includes bibliographical references and index.
  ISBN 978-0-8047-7081-1 (cloth : alk. paper)--ISBN 978-0-8047-7082-8 (pbk. : alk. paper)
 1. Literature, Modern--History and criticism. 2. Time in literature. I. Title.
 PN56.T5C56 2013
 809'.93384--dc23                                                    2012035993

Typeset by Bruce Lundquist in 10/14 Minion

## CONTENTS

Acknowledgments — vii

Introduction: Writing Against Time — 1
1  Imaginary Music — 23
2  The Addictive Image — 57
3  Big Brother Stops Time — 87
4  The Cultured Image — 115
Conclusion: From Representation to Creation — 139

Notes — 151
Bibliography — 171
Index — 185

# ACKNOWLEDGMENTS

MY THANKS GO FIRST TO AARON KUNIN, both for the example of his own work and for the gift of his intellectual friendship, which has so enriched the writing of this book. Amy Hungerford, Walter Benn Michaels, Kerry Larson, David Drewes, James Kuzner, and the two anonymous readers for the press offered valuable advice on various drafts. I'd also like to thank Frances Ferguson, Mark Pedretti, Jonathan Flatley, and the members of my Forms of Life seminars in 2009 and 2010. Emily-Jane Cohen has been a wonderful editor, and I am grateful for her support of this project. For their assistance with the scientific portions of this book I'd like to thank Rebecca Traynor, Mike Robinson, Nancy Campbell, Daniel Lende, John Sarneki, and Ming Li and the members of his lab. I've benefitted from the generous responses of the audiences who have heard parts of this project; I'd like to extend special thanks to Mary Esteve, James Narajan, William Marling, J. D. Connor, Garrett Stewart, Athena Vrettos, Oren Izenberg, Gary Stonum, Allison Carruth, and Andrew Hoberek. The Mellon Foundation provided crucial support in the early stages of this project, and the College of Arts and Sciences at Case Western Reserve University provided support during its completion. This book is dedicated to Colleen, with timeless love.

An early version of Chapter 3 appeared in *Representations* 107; and an element of the argument in Chapter 2 was published in *Behavioral and Brain Sciences* 31.4 as a brief piece coauthored with Rebecca Traynor and John Sarneki. Part of Chapter 4 appeared in *Criticism* 50.3 (Copyright 2008 Wayne State University Press, reprinted with permission of Wayne State University Press).

# WRITING AGAINST TIME

# INTRODUCTION: WRITING AGAINST TIME

IS ART DIFFERENT FROM LIFE? According to an emerging consensus, our experience of a description of a house, person, or landscape in a novel or poem, and our experience of an actual house, person, or landscape, are not essentially different. Critics and philosophers have drawn on recent neuroscientific research to argue that the brain processes the images prompted by literature in much the same way as it processes any other image. Thus Alvin Goldman describes a study in which subjects responded to a verbal description of a beach by robustly enacting vision, manifesting eye movements and neural signals as if they were examining the real thing ("Imagination," 42). Blakey Vermule and others have argued that we relate to literary characters using the same mechanisms deployed in our negotiation of actual social situations.[1] Timothy Schroeder and Carl Matheson, in a summary of the past two decades' work on aesthetics, write: "Insofar as the imagination causes the same feelings as the real, it does so by using the same structures in the brain as those used by the real world" (30). An event causes sensory stimulation; various mental representations are formed; signals are sent to affective centers. Thus "fictional stimuli entrain neural consequences similar to [those of] non-fictional stimuli" (28).

To say that our brains process fictional images in much the same way as they process actual images is not, however, to say that there are no differences. Three are particularly salient. First, the experience of a novelistic description of a thunderstorm, compared with the experience of an actual thunderstorm, requires a different kind of interpretation. The reader draws on various linguistic and cultural competences and assumptions in order to turn the marks on the page into the image he understands the author to intend to project.[2] The second obvious difference between real and literary experiences is that the latter do not typically entail the same kinds of actions as the former. I will not run even from Shirley Jackson's ghosts. This may be, as some speculate, because my belief that an image is fictional severs it from action consequences (running for my life) but not from affective consequences (I shiver, my hair stands on edge).[3] Or my failure to run may be due to the third difference between life and literature: literary images are less vivid than actual images.

This is Elaine Scarry's assumption in her classic study *Dreaming by the Book*, and recent neuroscience supports this intuition by suggesting that the impulses triggered by fictional images are similar, but less robust, that those triggered by actual images.[4] Scarry describes works of literature as containing "set[s] of instructions" for creating images (244). Beset by what Aristotle calls "the feebleness of images," writers struggle to copy those dynamics of actual perception muted by imaginary perception (4). This "counterfictional" drive gives rise to ingenious techniques designed to give literary images something of the vivacity of the flowers, skies, and faces we encounter in everyday life. Scarry illustrates some of these techniques by quoting a passage from Proust's *In Search of Lost Time*, where Marcel, describing the effect of the magic lantern on his bedroom wall, exclaims that "the anaesthetic effect of habit was destroyed" (11). Scarry comments: "But more fundamental than Proust's philosophical speculation on habit is what he does not openly remark on: the perceptual mimesis of the solidity of the room brought about by the 'impalpable iridescence'" of the magic lantern on the walls (11). A weakly imagined wall together with the equally weak, dreamlike image of magic lantern light combine to create an image of surprising solidity. Proust's "philosophical" ruminations about habit are merely a "distraction," something to draw our attention away from the trick by which two feeble images are folded on top of one another to give the effect of solidity.

Writers want to create vivid images. But is philosophy really so extrinsic to this work? I want to call this assumption into question by first questioning another of Scarry's assumptions. Is it true that everyday perception is vivid? The color of the sky on my way to work, the flowers in my neighbors' yard, my neighbors' faces—is this really what writers seeking vivacity seek to imitate? I don't often have a particularly vivid impression of the sky on my way to work. I couldn't say what colors my neighbors' flowers are. In fact, I'm not even sure that they have flowers. I will shortly present evidence that the feebleness of everyday perception is not my private tragedy. But if, as Scarry argues, the flowers in books are in constant danger of dying for want of the solidity of real flowers, then what is killing the real flowers? And what is the medicine? The analysts of literary effects from Edmund Burke through Viktor Shklovsky, from Scarry to the latest cognitive critics, have been distracted by formal features, structures, and techniques. The sickness of literary flowers may be a problem for literary technique. The sickness of living flowers is a problem for philosophy. And this philosophy, as I will argue, has been the constant practice of a literature that doesn't want to imitate life, but to transform it.

❃

Time poisons perception. No existing technique has proven effective at inoculating images against time. The problem is familiar. The more we see something, the duller and feebler our experience of it becomes. In a review of recent neuroscientific studies, David Eagleman describes strong evidence for a process that will be intuitively obvious to all readers. The first time we encounter an image, our perceptual experience tends to be richly vivid. Repeated exposure leads to a dramatic drop-off in vivacity. "With repeated presentations of a stimulus, a sharpened representation or a more efficient encoding is achieved in the neural network coding for the object" (132).[5] Once the brain has learned to recognize the image, it no longer requires the high "metabolic costs" of intense sensory engagement.

This efficiency has clear evolutionary advantages, but it means that we are subject to an incessant erasure of perceptual life. No sooner do we catch a glimpse of the shining colors of the world, than they begin to darken. Time's threat to perception may seem less pressing than the death and aging with which time menaces the organism. But from the first reflections on experience, writers have been consumed with how time poisons even the brief life we possess.

Sixteen centuries ago Augustine, in the first phenomenology of human time, describes time as introducing a fatal distortion into experience. Man is "stretched" between past and future; temporal succession means that we are denied the fullness of the present moment. "A person singing or listening to a song he knows well suffers a distension or stretching in feeling and in sense perception from the expectation of future sounds and the memory of past sound" (245).[6] The familiar object has become a cognitive whole practically sealed off from direct perceptual contact. Familiarity thins out sensory engagement nearly to the point of evaporation. The "stretching" of memory and anticipation replaces listening, seeing, touching. We are buried alive in time. "Who can lay hold of the heart and give it fixity," Augustine cries, "so that for some little moment it may be stable, and for a fraction of time may grasp the splendor of a constant eternity?" (228) Augustine does not long for the inorganic eternity of the statue or pyramid. He prays for the splendor of a heart stopped but not dead, for a "fraction of time" lifted out of succession.

But if humans lack the power to stop time, we can slow it. Time seems to slow when we perceive something for the first time. The moment of perception swells; the "fraction of time" expands. "Subjective duration," writes Eagleman, "mirrors the amount of neural energy used to encode a stimulus". The "first appearance" of an image seems to last out of all proportion to chronological time; a gap opens between the time of the clock and neurobiological time. "These dilations of perceived duration have been called a subjective expansion of time" (132). In such moments we get a glimpse of the splendor of eternal life, of unfading color, unerased sensation. But these dilations don't last. What if they could?

In his sonnet "Bright Star," Keats expresses the desire for the complete arrest of neurobiological time with the paradox its illogic demands.

> Bright Star! Would I were stedfast as thou art!
> Not in lone splendor hung aloft the night,
> And watching, with eternal lids apart,
> Like nature's patient, sleepless Eremite[ . . . ]
> No—yet still stedfast, still unchangeable
> Pillow'd upon my fair love's ripening breast,
> To feel for ever its soft swell and fall,
> Awake for ever in a sweet unrest,
> Still, still to hear her tender-taken breath,
> And so live ever—or else swoon to death—(338)

The poem's stark fusion of geologic and organic time scarcely mitigates the unimaginability of the desired state. How can one picture the stasis of the star fused with the beating of a living heart? The "soft swell and fall" of breath, the rhythm of circulation, the tingle of sensation: life is intertwined with time. To try to imagine disentangling them, to try to imagine introducing the stillness of the star into a living heart, is like trying to imagine a melody of one note.

Like Augustine's image of a hand laying hold of a heart, Keats's desired state is supernatural not just because its achievement seems beyond any technology known to him or to us. It is supernatural because it seems to require some greater mental force to make what is desired comprehensible. How can a heart be stopped without killing it? The beat is life itself. How can a heart be stopped without stopping? Such a state is unimaginable at every level. How can you even want to "feel for ever" the "soft swell and fall" of your lover's breast? Wouldn't your neck start to ache? Wouldn't you get bored? Wouldn't you soon simply stop noticing that regular rise and fall and start to daydream?

I doubt anyone reading this will claim never to have thought of some experience, "I wish this would last forever." But we seem to know instinctively this is a desire that does not bear reflection. If a genie suddenly appeared, ready to grant our wish, we would be wise, remembering the fate of the oracle, not to wish this. Would anyone really want any moment to last forever? But then what do we wish for when we wish it?

In the absence of clarity about what is wanted, Keats's wish for endless life collapses at the touch of a thought. But the desire for immortality is by no means condemned to the difficulties it faces in this sonnet. The history of religion shows the concept of a kind of consciousness that might slip free of the body to be a great help in fashioning comprehensible and attractive images of immortality. But Keats rigorously identifies consciousness with bodily sensation. To be "awake" is to "feel" and to "hear." Life is perception.

Keats wants a sensation that is exactly like the sensation of resting his head upon his lover's rising, falling breast. This ideal sensation is just like the actual sensation in every way but one: It is timeless. It is static. It is "unchangeable." What does this ideal sensation look like? The poem has no answer. The star and heart are not ultimately fused; they break up against each other. There is no object of desire here, no image for what is wanted. The poem ends in despair. Despair of life: What I most want I cannot have. And despair of thought and of language: I cannot even say what it is I want. This is the problem time represents for writing. Technique is powerless to solve it.

But perhaps this is going too far. Surely not all writers frame the problem of time in the extreme terms of this sonnet. In fact, we can't even take the paradoxes of this sonnet as representative of Keats's poetry. Several of the odes, for example, express confidence in the power of art to renew, prolong, and intensify life. Perhaps "Bright Star," like "When I Have Fears That I May Cease to Be," is emblematic less of art's relation to time than of the slowly dying Keats's mental state. No one can deny that some art successfully changes life and defeats time. What about Shakespeare?

"So long as men can breathe or eyes can see / So long lives this, and this gives life to thee" (19). Shakespeare's Sonnet 18, expressive of an abundantly justified confidence in the power of artistic form over time, is the antithesis of Keats's sonnet, and represents a tradition of artistic immortality that runs counter to the Romantic tradition explored by this book. As Aaron Kunin has shown, Shakespeare's sonnets are the central examples in English literature of the ancient tradition of the artwork as technology for defeating time. The poet creates a beautiful form. Its beauty is the hook that attracts generations of breathing, seeing readers, and the poem passes through them like a virus, its immortality parasitic on the mortal taste for beauty.

But what exactly is preserved in Sonnet 18? Not Shakespeare's life, nor the life of his subject.[7] Only that part of living bodies that can withstand translation into an unliving object survives. Simple logic animates this tradition. "That which is only living," as Eliot puts it, "can only die" (19). Therefore only that which can't die can be preserved. This tradition, which I will call the classical, is older than the one I explore, and it depends on three assumptions that the writers I study reject. The first is that the most valuable aspect of a person is the object that the person becomes in the public eye. That one's name shall be remembered, that one's deeds shall be celebrated: this is the ambition of ancient heroes and poets. Sensation is not subject to preservation. Hannah Arendt is perhaps the most powerful modern theorist of this tradition. "Nothing," she writes, "is less common and less communicable, and therefore more securely shielded against the visibility and audibility of the public realm, than what goes on within the confines of the body" (*The Human Condition*, 112). The evanescence of sensation is the source of its low value in the tradition. What lasts is valuable.

The second assumption is that lastingness is procured only at the cost of a sacrifice of life. The glorious death of Achilles is the western prototype of a tradition that has not disappeared from our literature. A modernist example, Yeats's "Sailing to Byzantium," gladly exchanges the sensual rhythms of life for "monuments of unaging intellect" (80). "Once out of nature I shall never take / My bodily form from any natural thing." The speaker envisions a golden bird as emblem of an artwork that preserves a version of the self purged of what "Byzantium" calls "the fury and the mire of human veins."[8]

Roberto Bolano's fiction is a particularly compelling recent example of and meditation on this tradition. At the end of *By Night in Chile*, the narrator, surveying the human wreckage strewn across his story of Chilean literature during the Pinochet regime, exclaims: "That is how literature is made, that is how the great works of Western literature are made. You better get used to it" (128). When Bolano associates the violence that nurtures literature with "time's giant meat-grinder," he makes explicit a dark secret implicit in Arendt (127). The immortality of art is not opposed to time at all. Time is not defeated. Art simply fashions human experience into a lasting form by performing time's work beforehand. Everything that goes on within the confines of the body is cut out. The action survives, the name, the durable form, the bone beneath the flesh. All else is burned away.

The refining violence that the work performs on human bodies is simply the violence of time itself. Earlier in Bolano's novel, the narrator relates the parable of the shoemaker who spends his life and fortune constructing an elaborate shrine for the heroes of the empire. Decades later, the soldiers who prize open the shrine's padlocked gate find the shoemaker's skeleton inside, "his jaw hanging open, as if he were still laughing after having glimpsed immortality" (48). Bolano's sense that art is a tomb that preserves a *dead* body finds pointed expression in a joke from the same novel. French archeologists visit the pope in Rome, saying they have good news and bad news. "The good news is that they have discovered the Holy Sepulchre . . . The pope is moved to tears. What's the bad news? he asks, drying his eyes. Well, inside the Holy Sepulchre we found the body of Christ. The pope passes out" (79).

Bolano's ambivalence about literary immortality in no way signals its rejection. We find the same ambivalence in the *Iliad*, in Achilles' hesitation at the prospect of exchanging life for immortality. The preservation art effects is tragic. It is always difficult to say whether the ultimate victor is the being whose name, words, or actions are preserved, or time, which takes everything else. Yeats's golden bird, after all, survives only as a plaything for "lords and ladies of Byzantium." Is it better to be an undying toy or a living, breathing, dying animal?

The third assumption of this classical tradition is that the beneficiary of the immortality conferred by art is the author or subject, not the audience. When the audience is visible at all, as in Sonnet 18, it is as the mortal engine that powers the work's immortality device. The eyes and lips wear out and are replaced; the name they pass on endures. Sylvia Plath's poem "Edge" represents a particularly interesting postwar example.

> The woman is perfected.
> Her dead
>
> Body wears the smile of accomplishment,
> The illusion of a Greek necessity
>
> Flows in the scrolls of her toga,
> Her bare
>
> Feet seem to be saying:
> We have come so far, it is over.
>
> Each dead child coiled, a white serpent [ . . . ]
> She has folded
>
> Them back into her body as petals
> Of a rose close (272–73)

The Greek imagery alerts us to the tradition which Plath's vision of deathly perfection develops and revises. But the force with which this poem draws life into lasting form is almost[9] without precedent; the effort requires the effacement of the speaking voice itself, the very essence of lyric. "Her bare / Feet *seem* to be saying." This concealment of living speech in the "seeming" expressiveness of mute sculpture has as its parallel the poem-statue-woman's fantasy of absolute withdrawal from any dependence on audience. If Shakespeare acknowledges that his sonnets' transcendence of mortality relies on attracting the interest of living generations, Plath imagines an immortality finally free of mortals.

The way Plath explicitly opposes her immortalization project to Shakespeare's first preservation technique—the biological reproduction he urges on the young man in the first sonnets of the sequence—suggests one motive for an interesting feature of the classical tradition's fate in recent English-language writing: its gendering. Women writers, from Gwendolyn Brooks and Sylvia Plath through Marilynne Robinson and Jennifer Moxley, have dominated the reworking of classical immortality into a vital contemporary literature.[10] Conversely, the male exponents of the Romantic tradition break from the conventional gender association of reproduced life, although, as we will see, not without surprising moments of cross-gender identification.

In contrast to the classical effort to preserve the person as object, the Romantic tradition that "Bright Star" represents is concerned with renewing and preserving sensation, and this effort is often described in terms of the effect the work produces on an audience. Nietzsche, for example, writes that art is "an excitation of the animal functions through the images and desires of intensified life;—an enhancement of the feeling of life, a stimulant to it" (422). We have now passed over into consideration of the Romantic tradition, but note that Nietzsche's statement has none of the doubt that tortures Keats's sonnet. Art produces excitation, enhancement, stimulation. Art serves a different end than in the classical tradition; these writers reject the effort to ensure the "survival" of a thing across gulfs of chronological time. For Nietzsche, art aims not to preserve an object but to enhance and prolong life. As Georges Poulet writes, in the Romantic vision "eternity is not endlessness." It is a "full and perfect possession of interminable life" ("Timelessness and Romanticism," 6). Yet Nietzsche and Poulet share Shakespeare's confidence in the ability of art to achieve its end. And they are hardly alone in their testimony of art's power to awaken sleeping senses. In "Richard Wagner and *Tannhäuser* in Paris," Baudelaire exclaims, "From that very moment, at that first concert . . . I had—or at least it seemed to me that I had—undergone a spiritual operation, a revelation. My thrill of pleasure had been so powerful and terrible that I could not prevent myself from ceaselessly wanting to return to it" (117).

For Baudelaire, the first encounter with Wagner produces a feeling of intensified life. The richness and vividness of the first experience figures prominently in the Romantic tradition. This tradition seeks to counter experiential time, and thus becomes involved in the paradoxes that Keats articulates with such painful clarity. By comparison to the relatively straightforward classical concern with lastingness, the desire to counter time's negative effects on ineluctably time-bound human experience creates deep conceptual and practical problems. There can be no question of simply cutting life free of time altogether. Rather, in Schiller's phrase, art's problem involves "annulling time within time" (97).

Romantic and post-Romantic writers discover in the peculiar temporal structure of first impressions a strategy for pursuing this paradoxical goal. Thus the effort to counter neurobiological time typically finds expression in an effort to achieve two experientially related but conceptually distinct states. The first is the felt slowing or stopping of time that accompanies an intensely vivid perception. The second is the persistence of this perceptual intensity across chronological time. Since in everyday life the most vivid perception of a thing tends to be the first impression, the persistence of the qualities of the first impression across the second, tenth, and hundredth impressions signals a countering of time's effect on the feeling of life. And in fact, as we shall see, a central criterion for artistic success within this tradition is the extent to which a work produces and preserves the effect of a first impression.

By inventing structures to prolong the first impression, the artists I study attempt to arrest the flow of neurobiological time, the tendency of the brain to reduce sensory engagement with repeated exposure. "Our failure is to form habits," Pater writes. "To burn always with this hard, gem-like flame, to maintain this ecstasy, is success in life" (152). Shelley claims that "poetry makes familiar objects be as if they were not familiar" (642). Coleridge argues that Wordsworth's poetic aim is "to give the charm of novelty to things of every day, and to excite a feeling analogous to the supernatural, by awakening the mind's attention from the lethargy of custom and directing it to the loveliness and wonders of the world before us" (313).

The theorists of this tradition typically associate the successful arrest of neurobiological time with specific techniques that, in Shklovsky's famous term, "defamiliarize," restore our perception of things to the vitality of the first sight. The founder of materialist aesthetics, Edmund Burke, invents the template for subsequent criticism. Aesthetic experience for Burke does not simply illustrate the natural workings of the brain but consists in the effort to suspend or override neural tendencies in pursuit of something unnatural.

"Knowledge and acquaintance make the most striking causes affect but little," Burke writes (57). "When we accustom our eyes" to an image, it ceases to affect us. And we become accustomed more rapidly to more clearly delineated images: "A great clearness . . . [is] an enemy to all enthusiasms whatsoever" (56). The introduction of fuzziness, vagueness, or shadow forestalls the familiarization that reduces impact. Thus verbal images are more effective for Burke because they are more obscure. As an ideal description of the encounter with an obscure image, Burke quotes the *Book of Job*: "It stood still, but I could not discern the form thereof; an image was before mine eyes" (58).

Vagueness thus operates to separate the image's affective impact from that aspect of the image—clear delineation of visual shape—that enables familiarity. Burke's aesthetic identifies an aspect of perception abundantly confirmed by recent research—the tendency of the brain to automatize the processing of familiar images—with a view to overcoming this tendency. He then identifies a particular artistic technique—obscurity—which forestalls familiarization and prolongs intense perceptual experience.[11] Subsequent materialist critics have added to the repertoire of habit-defeating techniques. Shklovsky, for example, alternately points to Tolstoy's use of the perspective of a horse to estrange familiar objects, and to the complexity of futurist poems that prolong and intensify the experience of reading itself (1–14).

But now, given Burke's, Coleridge's, and Shklovsky's confidence in the capacity of the artwork to renew our constantly decaying perceptual life, Keats's sonnet looks like an outlier. Is Keats's sense of the impossibility of freeing feeling from time simply an overly pessimistic, even hysterical view of the problem? Shakespeare promised the survival of an object; the object survives. But can art "lay hold of the heart and give it fixity?" Can art reliably return us to the intense duration of the first impression? This question transfixes Proust, and his reflections will help us decide whether to credit Coleridge's confidence or Keats's despair. Here is Proust's description of Swann's most profound experience of art.

> The year before, at an evening party, he had heard a piece of music played on the piano and violin. At first he had appreciated only the material quality of the sounds which those instruments secreted. And it had been a source of keen pleasure when, below the delicate line of the violin-part, slender but robust, compact and commanding, he had suddenly become aware of the mass of the piano-part beginning to emerge in a sort of liquid rippling of sound, multiform but indivisible, smooth yet restless, like the deep blue tumult of the sea, silvered and charmed into a minor key by the moonlight. But then at a certain moment, without being able to distinguish any clear outline, or to give a name to what was pleasing him, suddenly enraptured, he had tried to grasp the phrase or harmony—he did not know which—that had just been played and that had opened and expanded his soul. . . . Perhaps it was owing to his ignorance of music that he had received so confused an impression, one of those that are none the less the only purely musical impressions. . . . An impression of this order, vanishing in an instant, is, so to speak, *sine materia* . . . impossible to describe, to recollect, to name, ineffable—did not our memory, like a laborer who toils at the laying down of firm foundations beneath the tumult of the waves, by fashioning for us facsimiles of those fugitive phrases, enable us to compare and to contrast them with those that follow . . . when the same impression suddenly returned, it was no longer impossible to grasp. He could picture to himself its extent,

its symmetrical arrangement, its notation, its expressive value; he had before him something that was no longer pure music, but rather design, architecture, thought, and which allowed the actual music to be recalled. (I, 204–5)

The phrase recurs a third time, "bringing him, indeed, a pleasure less profound." This artwork seems constructed according to the exacting technical specifications of Burke and Shklovsky: it is both obscure and difficult. And at first it does indeed "enrapture" Swann. Yet the work stops working almost at once. As the phrase becomes more familiar, he gradually discovers in it "some disenchantment" (214).[12] At a certain moment, "a phrase or harmony—he did not know which" took ecstatic possession of his senses, of his being. But as the form of the work becomes clear, the magic dies.

Swann has discovered something quite simple: repeated exposure to a work of art operates just like repeated exposure to anything else. The achievement of cognitive mastery over form, the ability to recognize the object, simultaneously causes a precipitous drop-off in sensory intensity. The experience of art is not immune to the relentless erosive force of neurobiological time, but is simply another instance of it. Eventually Swann's sensory engagement with the phrase drains utterly away; it becomes a "token of his love" for Odette, a love which has the same structure as his experience of art: an initial, mysterious, formless beauty, followed by disenchantment (214). The phrase stands for Odette, who stands for the decay of life and love. Art has become mere meaning. Music has become writing. It has died.

Music, as we shall see, occupies a special place in the tradition that concerns us. But for Proust it is simply the most striking instance of a phenomenon that corrodes all artistic objects, as it corrodes all other objects. Consider, for example, the narrator's reflections on how the works of his favorite writer, Bergotte, have lost their magic. After long familiarity, Bergotte's "sentences stood out as clearly before my eyes as my own thoughts, the furniture in my room and the carriages in the street. All the details were easily visible, not perhaps precisely as one has always seen them, but at any rate as one was accustomed to see them now ... from then onwards I felt less admiration for Bergotte" (II, 603).

Of course not everyone feels as Proust does; not everyone prefers the first time listening to a symphony or reading a poem to the result of further acquaintance, when experience is illuminated by understanding. In fact, one way of determining whether a writer belongs to the particular Romantic tradition considered by this book is to ask how he evaluates the initial experience of a work of art. Contrast the following statement by Winckelmann from 1764 with the passages from Proust above. "The first view of beautiful statues is . . . like the first glance over the open sea; we gaze on it bewildered, and with undistinguishing eyes, but after we have contemplated it repeatedly the soul becomes more tranquil and the eye more quiet, and capable of separating the whole into its particulars" (Cited by Nehamas, 16).

Interestingly, Proust and Winckelmann do not disagree about the phenomenology of the initial exposure to the work of art; they both compare it to the formless dynamism of the ocean. (To Swann the music is "multiform but indivisible, smooth yet restless, like the deep blue tumult of the sea.") But whereas Winckelmann values the knowledge of form, the "quiet" eye that accompanies the ability to grasp structure is for Proust precisely the symptom of perception's sickness that art must counter.

The juxtaposition of Proust and Winckelmann might suggest that the tradition I am describing is roughly coextensive with a period: traditional Romanticism, extended into the modern. But things aren't so simple. Consider the contemporary philosopher Alva Noe's description of the phenomenology of music:

> You play a record through. The music is unfamiliar, strange; the album exhibits a kind of opacity. As you become familiar with the music, you begin more fully to experience it. Your experience becomes richer. Where the songs were thin and meaningless before, they are now structured, complex and motivated. . . . Without acquaintance with the music itself, you were, in effect, unable to hear it. ("Experience," 31)[13]

For Noe, as for Winckelmann, the richness of aesthetic experience is bound up with the ability to decipher the relations of the work's parts. To hear music, for Noe, is to know it. But to say that Noe and Winckelmann value the understanding of the art object while Swann values raw sensation would be wrong. Proust shows Swann straining to understand the "phrase or melody." Indeed, as the studies surveyed by Eagleman suggest, this straining is precisely what produces the heightened sensory intensity. Winckelmann and Proust pick out two points on a continuum as the ne plus ultra of aesthetic experience, but it is the same continuum, and the points are related as before and after. Proust's ideal listener is inexorably becoming Winckelmann's ideal listener.

And yet, with only a little inventiveness, Swann could surely expose himself to a music or noise so utterly devoid of pattern that it would completely frustrate his effort to make sense of it. The absurdity of this suggestion to anyone familiar with *In Search of Lost Time* shows how little the desired experience consists of raw sensation. Proust's listeners, viewers, and readers seek out recognizable forms in which novelty is in tension with a familiarity that provides some foothold for understanding. No one in this tradition is drawn to cacophony, and they tend not be drawn to the overwhelming alterity of the objects associated with the sublime.[14] Without seeing how Proust's listener strains toward understanding we will miss the tragic paradox of his conception of artistic experience. The effort to grasp the work's form triggers the intense sensory engagement that the success of that effort destroys.

If the Romantic listener is always being carried from enrapturing intensity towards quiet Winckelmannian comprehension, then all that distinguishes him is the desire, fast turning into nostalgia, for the former state over the latter. And yet even this desire betrays him. Baudelaire, in the passage on Wagner I quoted earlier, supplies an instance. After describing his ecstasy at the first time he hears *Tannhäuser*, he writes: "The experience that I had had doubtless contained much of what Weber and Beethoven had already taught me, but there was also something new which I was incapable of defining, and this incapacity caused me a rage and a curiosity mingled with a strange delight . . . I resolved . . . to transform my pleasure into knowledge" (117). Possessed by this raging curiosity, he roams Paris looking for anyone who will play him some Wagner.

There are two ways of reading this passage. We might say that for Baudelaire the knowledge of the music's form is the antidote to an experience the intensity of which he finds intolerable. The disturbing ecstasy brings a longing for tranquility, and knowledge is the tranquilizer. This sentiment is not hard to sympathize with. Imagine you are suddenly struck with a feeling of intense pleasure. It is likely that a desperate anxiety to know why—did I just have a stroke? did someone slip me something?—would snuff the desire to remain in the mysteriously pleasurable state.

On this reading, Baudelaire's intense joy inspires a longing for soothing knowledge. But there is another interpretation. The passage suggests that Baudelaire's "rage and curiosity" are in fact identical with the "strange delight" the new music inspires. Perhaps the desire for knowledge doesn't succeed the pleasure; perhaps to feel the delight is just to be driven to understand the form. *Intensity of perception is what desire for knowledge feels like.* The prospect of prolonging this intensity introduces another form of Keats's paradox, pitched now in the key of desire. How can one want the feeling of wanting knowledge without wanting knowledge? How can one even imagine arresting a process that is essentially teleological without destroying what it is?

John Dewey, whose *Art as Experience* remains the most sophisticated account of experiential aesthetics, believes that one cannot, and one should not, arrest this process. In terms very like Proust's, Dewey describes how in the encounter with art "the total overwhelming impression comes first . . . the effect upon us of entrance into a cathedral when dim light, incense, stained glass and majestic proportions fuse in one indistinguishable whole. . . . There is an impact that precedes all definite recognition of what it is about" (145). Quoting Delacroix on first seeing a painting, he writes, "Before knowing what the picture represents you are seized by its magical accord" (145).

And yet Dewey warns us not to be seduced by the magic. "Not only, however, is it impossible to prolong this stage of aesthetic experience indefinitely, but it is not desirable to do so" (145). The "impact" is only the first step in the temporal unfolding of the work's form. To wish to prolong it is alien to art, and belongs rather to "such things as narcotics, sexual orgasms, and gambling indulged in for the sake of the immediate excitement of sensation" (124). In artistic experience, as in everyday experience, "a sensory quality is related to other qualities in such ways as to define an object" (124). We want to understand the object, to grasp its parts and their interrelations. This understanding "takes time" (55). He is insistent on this point, writing that some readers may think that he "exaggerate[s] the temporal aspect of perception. . . . But in no case can there be perception of an object except in a process developing in time. Mere excitations, yes" (175).

Yet the dismissal of "mere excitation" conceals an ambiguity in Dewey's account. After all, he writes with feeling and longing of the first impression. Maybe an element of psychological self-protection enters into his theory. Perhaps his belief that prolonging the magical moment of perception is impossible dictates his belief that such a prolongation is also undesirable. As we shall see, other writers will not shrink from an impossible desire, nor will they hesitate to send art to the school of "narcotics, sexual orgasms, and gambling" in hope of achieving it.

But to return to the problem of periodization, the contrast between Noe/ Dewey/Winckelmann and Proust/Keats suggests that the period in question is rather small. It is a question of preferring the beginning or the end of a process of aesthetic attention that seems to have neurobiological, rather than historical, determinants. The "classical" writer prefers the end, when knowledge of the enduring form has been achieved; the "Romantic" prefers the beginning, when subjective time swells and slows, and the senses are enraptured. As support for this view, one might point to the example of a contemporary writer like Bolano, who clearly sees himself extending the classical tradition of literary immortality as the persistence of form across time. At the other end, Arendt's picture of classical antiquity as indifferent to inner experience has been complicated by the work of Pierre Hadot, who has written persuasively of the effort to intensify the experience of the present moment in ancient philosophy (217–37), and Martha Nussbaum, who has excavated the complex attitudes towards mortality in the Epicurean tradition (192–239). Finally, in *Romantic Poets and the Culture of Posterity*, Andrew Bennet has shown the extent to which the classical concern with the immortality of the text persists in Keats and Shelley, suggesting that both impulses might be found within a single authorship.[15]

Perhaps, then, it is better to think of the opposition "classical" and "Romantic," as I have been referring to these two distinct efforts to defeat time, as attitudes equally present in all periods, roughly analogous to Nietzsche's "Apollonian" and "Dionysian" dyad. But this would be to distort both the contents of this book—which draws all of its examples from after 1800, and most from after 1900—and the tradition it analyzes. I do not think it can be denied that artistic efforts to stop experiential time multiply exponentially around the dawn of what has been traditionally identified as the Romantic era, even as they expand into the modern and postmodern. But these efforts are by no means definitive of any of these periods. Many, and perhaps most, nineteenth- and twentieth-century writers are unconcerned with the obsessions of the tradition I delineate here.

For these reasons, I use the terms *classical* and *Romantic* as pragmatic markers of two distinct ways of thinking about literary immortality. These terms are appropriate because generations of critics have associated the desire to preserve a person's name and image most strongly with Homer and Horace, while the desire to preserve and intensify sensation has been most strongly linked with the British Romantic poets. But while in the pages that follow I will welcome some additional senses of *Romantic*—its association with excessive claims for the power of literature, its association with virtual, unactualizable form—I do not intend any broad characterization of Romanticism as period or movement, nor any redescription of the work of writers like Orwell or Ashbery as Romantic in any sense other than the orientation to literary immortality they share with writers like Keats and Coleridge.

My reluctance to make broad periodizing claims should not, however, be taken to imply that I think that no significant historical context links the exponents of the Romantic tradition I analyze. The clustering of examples after 1800 undoubtedly has historical causes. Scholars looking for such causes might start with the consolidation of consumer capitalism, the rise of medical science, or the waning of traditional religion in the educated classes along with the version of eternal life it promised.[16] But this book is concerned with describing the key features of the Romantic quest to defeat time, in the hope that its most powerful examples can teach us something new about art and life. While the chapters that follow attend to social, political, and economic contexts when necessary to make sense of a given work's dynamics, this is not a historicist study, and I make no attempt to enumerate and analyze the historical causes of the impulses animating the tradition as a whole. Nor, for the pragmatic reasons I elaborate in my conclusion, do I think such an investigation is especially urgent. At this moment in the history of the disciplines, literary criticism's best opportunity for creating new knowledge lies not in the description of art's embeddedness in contexts recognizable to historians or sociologists, but in the description of the forces by which art attempts to free itself of such contexts and such recognitions.

※

We have begun to see how art is not immune to the temporality of perceptual experience. What do we make, then, of the confidence expressed by Nietzsche, Shklovsky, Shelley, or Coleridge? These writers celebrate the techniques by which poets, painters, and composers renew our fading senses. But they are not ignorant of the process described by Proust, whereby the perceptual vitality of the first encounter with the work quickly cools into understanding. In fact, the proponents of art's efficacy at renewing and transforming our experience are acutely aware of this problem. The solutions they propose fall into two general categories: reasonable and unreasonable. While I will be primarily interested in the latter, we must first survey the reasonable response to art's entanglement with time.

Proust's unreasonable solution will in part serve as the subject of my first chapter, but he can also be reasonable. Immediately following the passage in which the narrator reflects on his disenchantment with Bergotte, he describes the new writer who has succeeded Bergotte in his admiration. This writer "had recently begun to publish work in which the relations between things were so different from those that connected them for me that I could understand hardly anything of what he wrote. . . . Only I felt that it was not the sentence that was badly constructed but I myself that lacked the strength and agility necessary to reach the end. I would start afresh, striving tooth and nail to reach the point from which I would see the new relationships between things" (II, 603). Through the process of struggling with the new writer, he discovers "a charm similar to those which I had found long ago in reading Bergotte" (604).

Marcel concludes these reflections by declaring that "Art was in this respect like science" (604). He shifts the burden of renewing our senses from the individual artwork to the history of art, which tirelessly discovers new forms. Even the most powerful works become old. We might discover new significance in our twentieth reading of Macbeth or our thirtieth examination of "View of Delft," but the "magic accord" of the early encounter will have fled. So from Shakespeare we proceed to Ibsen and Beckett, from Vermeer to Monet and Matisse, from Beethoven to Wagner and Debussy. "Art is like science" in its constant invention of new techniques. But art runs to stand still. It is simply the case that to keep our perceptual clock at first sight requires continual innovation. A narrower and more precise analogy might be to the project of countering the tendency of bacteria to develop immunity to antibiotics. Like artists, chemists search for new formulas that will produce the effect the old formulas no longer can.

Many of the strongest theorists of art's experiential value reproduce Marcel's logic. Shklovsky's "Art as Device," for example, also deploys the scientific metaphor, and envisions ceaseless formal innovation as necessary to the project of defamiliarization. Michael Fried, who in "Art and Objecthood" famously praises the "grace" of "presentness" achieved in the viewer's absorption by great art (168), in the trilogy that begins with *Absorption and Theatricality* describes the history of French painting as driven by the inevitable decay of the techniques that produce this absorption. What works for Chardin will no longer work for Courbet, and so the artist must try something new. Even Dewey, who, as we have seen, is more ambivalent about the value of presentness, has a version of the reasonable solution. "Advances in technique occur," he writes, "in connection with efforts to solve problems that are not technical but that grow out of the need for new modes of experience" (141).

These solutions are reasonable because they accept that perceptual vitality, the subjective expansion of the present moment, is a consequence of the mind's attempt to grasp form, and vanishes at the conclusion of that process. So one has two sensible choices. The first option is to seek art's value in understanding rather than in experience. This has the great advantage of preserving the shelf life of old works, since, as the history of criticism shows, there seems to be no limit to the new *ideas* one can get from writers like Shakespeare or Baudelaire.[17] If, however, you are committed to art as a technology for the renewal of human life, then you are condemned to read new books, see new paintings, listen to new music. Once you have understood one work, you must start over with a new artifact in which the interplay between novelty and familiarity will once again strike the senses with the "magic accord."

All reasonable criticism holds the tacit belief that the experience of art is subject to the same temporal limits as all other experience. Art is not different from life. Recent work in experiential aesthetics has tended to rely on models drawn from the cognitive sciences to specify these limits. In their different ways, critics like Mark Turner, Lisa Zunshine, Gabrielle Starr, and Blakey Vermule apply scientific models of everyday cognition and perception to describe literature and literary experience.[18] Science tells us what the brain can do, and the critics show how literature does it. Here reasonableness shades into disciplinary modesty. Literary scholars take models from the sciences, but have little to give back. Zunshine, for instance, describes this new work as "applying insights from cognitive science to cultural representations" (*Introduction to Cultural Studies*, 1).

One problem with some of this criticism, as both the critic Jonathan Kramnick and the scientist Paul Bloom have recently pointed out, is that the science applied by these critics is often dated and inaccurate, and the critics represent models as authoritative without acknowledging the scientific debates. But for my immediate purposes a more serious problem is that this critical approach lacks the capacity to describe literature's unreasonable efforts to do something the brain can't do. And yet, as I will attempt to show, it is by attending to this effort that a truly interdisciplinary relation between literature and science becomes possible.

This book examines the unreasonable approach to the problem of stopping time. The reasonable Romantics respect the temporal constraints of perception. They transfer the desire to enhance life through art from the individual work to the historical succession of forms. The unreasonable Romantics seek the creation of a work that will permanently arrest perception at the moment of the first encounter.

By now we have some sense of the scale of this problem, enough at least to know that Scarry's attempt to explain the literary effort to achieve vivacity by cordoning off philosophical speculation from technical innovation is untenable. To even imagine what a life undimmed by time would look like requires no ordinary philosophy. Literary form can do many things, but it can't do this.[19] The writers I examine invent virtual techniques, imaginary forms for arresting neurobiological time by overcoming the brain's stubborn boundaries.[20] The mode is ekphrastic. These writers create images of more powerful images; they fashion techniques for imagining better techniques. Poems by Keats and Ashbery, novels by Proust, Orwell, and Nabokov are not works so much as workshops in which the shape of an ideal artwork is pieced together from blueprints and models. Fragments of the real world are brought inside and scrutinized for any hint, any insight. Like an airplane designer examining a bird's wing, the artist studies life to overcome its limits.

My hope is that this study, by reading central works of the past two centuries in the light of their shared ambition, will produce a revisionary understanding of some of our most important writing. But I have another aim. These writers, voracious in their appetite for any knowledge that will further their goal, find help in unlikely places. Totalitarian regimes, addiction, and global commodity exchange furnish them with tools and models. By attending to the thinking animated and distorted by literature's extreme ambition, literary criticism might fulfill its ambition to produce new knowledge of its own.

Each chapter considers a different method, a different research strategy for imagining and then constructing the perfect technique. The first chapter, "Imaginary Music," examines the image of ideal, always-new music in Keats and Proust. A neglected dimension of Kant's aesthetics illuminates the mental structures that these virtual melodies are designed to engage. The second chapter, "The Addictive Image," shows how the addictive object provides a model for the effective time-killing image in De Quincey's *Confessions of an English Opium Eater* and Nabokov's *Lolita*. This chapter engages with recent neuroscientific research on addiction to test the ability of unreasonable literature to produce scientifically interesting knowledge.

"Big Brother Stops Time," the third chapter, shows how Orwell draws the principle of a total artwork from the historical existence of totalitarian regimes. Shklovsky's "reasonable" aesthetics turns out to provide a useful guide to how permanent defamiliarization operates in Orwell's fictional world. In its exploration of Orwell's mixed reaction to the prospect of a truly effective victory over experiential time, this chapter also identifies a Romantic analogue to the ambiguity characteristic of the classical effort to defeat chronological time. My fourth chapter, "The Cultured Image," examines how the line in John Ashbery's late poetry exploits a previously undiscovered power of the science fiction sentence. The resulting image mimics the form of the global commodity. Curious perceptual properties of the artifact from another culture power a virtual object absolutely resistant to habituation. Finally, in my conclusion I abstract from the procedures of this study to describe a viable place for literary criticism among the knowledges of the twenty-first century.

# 1   IMAGINARY MUSIC

IMAGINARY MUSIC is the first weapon Romantic writing deploys in its war against time. Immanuel Kant, John Keats, Friedrich Nietzsche, Henri Bergson, and Marcel Proust all imagine musical forms that resist neurobiological time's erosive force. But why imaginary music? Time is a great enemy. One wouldn't bring an imaginary knife to a gunfight. These writers' interest in virtual forms thus immediately raises a fundamental question. Does the imagination of time-resistant music represent some kind of victory or an admission of complete defeat? Can the creation of imaginary music really count as an achievement?

A simple experiment will decide the issue. Close your eyes. Pick a familiar song, one that once gave you intense joy, and that now gives you a milder pleasure or none. Try to remember what the song sounded like when you first heard it. Recall what it sounded like the last time you heard it. Now imagine a different kind of song. This song will sound just as fresh after several hundred listenings as it did on first hearing. Imagine listening to this song. How do you feel? What is the song like? Describe the features that imbue it with unfading freshness.

My intuition is that the mental operations this experiment elicits will provoke little resistance until the subject is asked to imagine the different song. At that point, I suspect, most people will find it very difficult to imagine this new, habit-resistant music in anything but the most general terms. If my intuition is justified, then a piece of writing that makes it possible to imagine what such music is like with any detail will have achieved something significant.

What resistance does such writing have to overcome? Why is it hard to imagine music that stays new? I will approach these questions through a different one. Why is it hard to imagine seeing with our ears? This is the question Thomas Nagel poses in his 1974 essay "What Is It Like to Be a Bat?" Nagel posits an "explanatory gap" between everything we can learn about a bat from a third-person perspective and the subjective experience, the "feel," of actually being a bat. The bat's sonar, a mode of perception unlike any human capacity, lends the example its particular salience. We know about sonar. Science can describe the mechanism by which the bat creates an image of space through the emission and reception of sound waves in abundant detail. But to know what it is like to experience the world through sonar, we need to imaginatively place ourselves in the bat's position. And imagination, Nagel argues, is simply not powerful enough to do this.

> Our own experience provides the basic material for our imagination, whose range is therefore limited. It will not help to try to imagine that one has webbing on one's arms, which enables one to fly around at dusk. . . . Insofar as I can imagine this (which is not very far), it tells me only what it would be like for *me* to behave as a bat behaves. But that is not the question. I want to know what it is like for a *bat* to be a bat. (520–21)[1]

For Nagel, our past experience imposes a limit on our perceptual imagination. To the extent we are able to robustly imagine new perceptions, we do so by piecing together familiar perceptions. I may never have eaten pineapple ice cream, but if I have had pineapples and ice cream I can do a good job of imagining what this would be like. If I love pineapples, however, it might be difficult to imagine what pineapple ice cream would taste like to someone who hates them. It might not be as hard as imagining what it's like to have sonar, but it wouldn't be easy. Perception, after all, is not just raw sensation, but sensation filtered through a set of capacities, memories, associations, and desires. It might even be hard to specify exactly what the pineapple lover's taste perception shares with the pineapple hater's. Does the hater register the same precise mixture of sweet and tart as I do before she spits it out? Or does the recognition—this isn't peach ice cream, it's pineapple!—blot out everything else?

How can I imagine the world from the perspective of a different perceptual organization? The first step would be to eradicate my own habitual associations. Nagel reasonably doubts our ability to do this. But we can imagine such an imaginative ability. Bruce Sterling, in his 1985 science fiction novel *Schizmatrix*, writes about a technology that closes the explanatory gap by showing you exactly what it is like to be a giant insect equipped with a very inhuman sensory apparatus. And as soon as one plugs in, the technology "render[s] everything novel" (176). The device that answers Nagel's question—what is it like to have a different sense?—also answers the question with which we began—what kind of object can defeat habit? Here is a fuller excerpt of Sterling's description of the experience of the character transformed by "The Shatter."

> He could see time lying on the world like a sheen, a frozen blur of movement chopped out of context and painted onto the surface of the cold stone like alien shellac. Walls became floors, balustrades cold barricades. He realized then that he had too many legs. . . . He became aware of fine detail within the stone, the surface suddenly no more than frozen smoke, a hard fog petrified by captive eons. (176)

Through some organ unknown to us, the alien sensorium enables the character to "see time." Time is fully spatialized. Thus the effect of plunging a person into a different perceptual matrix—everything becomes new—is here mirrored by the nature of the alien sense. We ordinarily experience neurobiological time as a gradual darkening of novel surfaces. Sterling's alien sense literalizes and dramatizes this dynamic. The character sees the objects of the world standing in pools of time, masked beneath time's "hard fog." Time is externalized, pushed out of the brain. Time afflicts objects, not the permanently peeled senses of the Shattered.

The device produces unending novelty by placing a character's consciousness inside another nervous system. It accomplishes this transfer by using a combination of a drug called "PDKL," "adhesive eye-cups," and "microprongs" to stimulate the brain in radically new ways. When Proust, writing some sixty years before Sterling, imagines a technology for producing this effect, he calls it "music." For Marcel, Vinteuil's late music is a device for grafting the composer's sensorium onto the listener's brain, a procedure that endows the experience of the work with "permanent novelty" (III, 728).

Despite the originality of his description of the effects of Vinteuil's septet, which I take up in detail below, Proust's choice of music as his ideal art form is hardly idiosyncratic. Carl Dahlhaus has written of music's special status in the late nineteenth and early twentieth centuries. Music is an "untimely art" in this period, "neo-Romantic" in a modernist context. Dahlhaus shows how intellectuals saw post-Wagnerian instrumental works as offering "the prototype of an alternative world" (7).[2] He reads Nietzsche's writing about Wagner as the fullest formulation of a "comprehensive concept of absolute music which reveals the latent unity of musical aesthetics in the nineteenth century" (39).

In his early essay "On Music and Words," Nietzsche, while still under Wagner's spell, nevertheless resists the master's belief that the finale of Beethoven's ninth symphony had exposed the limits of absolute music and revealed the necessity of joining words and music in a new "total" artwork. For Nietzsche, this gets things exactly wrong. Music represents a pure transmission that is only polluted by words; music communicates a state that resists translation into our familiar semantic categories. By 1887, after completely breaking with Wagner, Nietzsche could write: "Compared with music all communication by words is shameless . . . words make the uncommon common" (*Will to Power*, 428).

Marcel Proust and John Keats approach the hard problem of Romantic aesthetics—the vulnerability of the work to neurobiological time—by creating imaginary musics. I begin with Proust, showing how he radicalizes Nietzsche's belief in music's communicative power to imagine a way of permanently translating the common world into the uncommon. I then examine the ekphrasis of music in several of Keats's key works, showing how he experiments with different kinds of imaginary sound and different kinds of imaginary listeners in order to overcome the paradox of "Bright Star," and to robustly imagine a way to "feel for ever." My discussions of Proust and Keats are linked by a section in which I argue that the concept of duration in Kant's *Critique of Judgment* provides us with a model for understanding the achievement of virtual aesthetics in making the unimaginable imaginable.

※

In Swann's encounter with the "little phrase" of Vinteuil's sonata, Proust describes the trajectory of aesthetic experience from an initial intense renewal of the feeling of life, to growing familiarity with and knowledge of the work's form, to recognition of an object that belongs to the understanding but no longer to the senses. By the end of the process, the life force that the work stimulated has ebbed, and the little phrase has become powerless to renew it. Even the most bewitching music suffers the same fate Proust ascribes to furniture. A striking new object arrives, you get used to it, and then you hardly even see it. We require new music to set the furniture on fire. Each given work comes with an experiential expiration date, so we need a constant supply of new works, new styles, new forms.

But later in Proust's vast novel, Marcel suggests that even new objects of experience might be insufficient to keep his senses young.

> A pair of wings, a different respiratory system, which enabled us to travel through space, would in no way help us, for if we visited Mars or Venus while keeping the same senses, they would clothe everything we could see in the same aspect as the things of Earth. (III, 732)

Here Marcel detects a flaw in what I have called the reasonable solution to art's hard problem. Critics ranging from Viktor Shklovksy to Michael Fried see the historical evolution of technique as ameliorating the limited ability of individual works to make time swell and stop. But Proust suggests that this constant tinkering with objects and techniques is deluded: the problem is in our heads, not in objects. Time's poison attacks our senses; switching styles is just switching deck chairs on the *Titanic*.

Of course, our best critics of innovation are hardly advocating the difference without a difference of consumerist novelty, the cynical alterations in packaging characteristic of the false, tranquilizing newness that Horkheimer and Adorno denounce in popular culture. Shklovsky and Fried consider artworks to be special objects, specially designed techniques for countering the slow death of perception, and for overcoming our inevitable adjustment to the last route to presentness.

But, Marcel worries, isn't there a limit to our susceptibility to these techniques? *In Search of Lost Time* understands habit to be a protean force, a powerful enemy. One can get used to anything. After enough time, couldn't one get used even to the experience of genuinely new works? Alternately, couldn't thirty or forty years of slowly congealing habit render us utterly immune to the shock that would crack the crust of neurobiological time and give us a glimpse of the world? Perhaps, Marcel speculates, the code of habituated perception eventually becomes too hard for the artistic code-breakers. He adapts the metaphor of travel to point to the all-too-familiar truth he suspects may apply to the artistic realm: wherever I go, there I am.

Earlier Marcel had compared art's ceaseless innovation to science. Now this innovation seems empty to him. While artistic change might provide ample scope for a pedantic history of styles, for Marcel it has lost its vital function as minister to a basic human need. The reasonable solution to the hard problem has come to seem to him like a cheap subterfuge designed to make us accept the slow work of time by tricking us with worthless remedies.

But he does not despair. The passage above comes after he has concluded that Vinteuil's sonata can no longer speak to him. But he has discovered a new work, a late Vinteuil septet, which has opened his eyes to the possibility of a radical solution to the hard problem. Here is how the passage continues:

> If we visited Mars or Venus while keeping the same senses, they would clothe everything we could see in the same aspect as the things of earth. The only true voyage, the only bath in the Fountain of Youth, would be not to visit strange lands but to possess other eyes, to see the universe through the eyes of another, of a hundred others, to see the hundred universes that each of them sees ... and this we can do ... with a Vinteuil. (732)

Like Swann, Marcel experiences music as a "fountain of youth." But the episode from which I excerpt this passage marks a complete reversal of the logic that drove Swann's rapture. For Swann, intensity of perception is coincident with the initial fuzziness of the work's form. When he got to know it, when the form resolved into clarity, the magic fled. As Germaine Bree writes, "In the last analysis, music has made him live more intensely—but only for a moment" (194).

When Marcel hears the late septet, the new work "made me feel as keen a joy as the sonata would have given me if I had not already known it" (725). The effect—arresting neurobiological time, defeating habit, experiencing full life in perception—is the same for him as for Swann. But the means are utterly different. Now, knowledge of the work does not militate against its experiential effectiveness. Only Marcel's deciphering of the intricacies of this late music enables it to perform its work of renewal. And, above all, the late work is distinguished with respect to the earlier by its complexity. The sonata's power was concentrated in a single phrase. It is the septet as a whole that fascinates Marcel. This imaginary septet seems to be partially based on Beethoven's late quartets—renowned for their difficulty—and the addition of three extra parts seems intended to multiply the complexity.[3] Swann's phrase is a duration of modulated sound; it gives him a sonic impression, and is perhaps modeled on the impressionism of early Debussy or Ravel.[4] But the septet is a communication, and its complexity is dictated by the sheer magnitude of the information it is designed to convey.[5]

Like Nietzsche, of whom he was a devoted reader, Proust here understands music to be a fantastically efficient mode of communication. Music enables, through its direct transcendence of language's imbrication with familiar concepts, transmission of the composer's very perceptual organization.[6] In mastering the musical structure's dense web of relations, Marcel pieces together the sensory organization of another being. Music gives Marcel a glimpse of the world through the composer's eyes.

Vinteuil's works have the "apparently paradoxical and indeed deceptive quality of permanent novelty." Because the unique individuality of the composer's perceptual being permeates the work, "Vinteuil, although he had appeared at his appointed hour and had his appointed place in the evolution of music, would always leave that place to stand in the forefront whenever any of his compositions was performed" (728). Vinteuil's formal vocabulary is historical; anyone knowledgeable about music can tell he comes after Wagner, and before Stravinsky. But if his vocabulary renders him commensurable with other composers of his era and locates him in historical time, the particular use he makes of that vocabulary in his late works expresses the absolute singularity of an individual's perceptual experience, and removes him from every time scale.

Like Sterling's "Shatter," the Vinteuil septet recalibrates the listener's perceptual apparatus, tuning it to another key. Once deciphered and internalized, the work is not an object of experience; it is a subject of experience. Marcel feels as Vinteuil felt, he hears as the dead composer heard. Proust presents this aesthetic virtually, as a description of a character's encounter with an imaginary piece of music. But others have seen it as a reasonable description of how actual art works. Georges Poulet, for example, develops Marcel's reflections on Vinteuil into an influential critical perspective. In "Phenomenology of Reading" Poulet examines "this strange displacement of myself by the work" (59).

> When I read Baudelaire or Racine, it is really Baudelaire or Racine who thinks, feels, allows himself to be read within me. Thus a book is not only a book, it is the means by which an author actually preserves his ideas, his feelings, his modes of dreaming and living.... Indeed every word of literature is impregnated with the mind of the one who wrote it. (58)

The rise of poststructuralism, with its twin commitments to the death of the author and the indeterminacy of the text, led to an eclipse of Poulet's analysis of reading as the recovery of another's form of life. For critics influenced by deconstruction, the figural and rhetorical properties of texts block the transmission of an extra-textual reality such as the author's perceptual experience. But the recent proliferation of cognitive criticism has led to a partial resurrection of concerns roughly similar to Poulet's. These critics replace the deconstructive focus on the theoretical difficulty of aligning textual artifacts and mental states with wonder at the mental capacity that enables millions of readers to slip inside the minds of fictional characters every day. This capacity, which Alvin Goldman's influential study calls "mindreading," enables humans to impute subjectivity to certain kinds of objects—human faces and hands, but also poems, pictures, animals, and dolls. Blakey Vermule's *Why Do We Care About Literary Characters?* is among the most accomplished cognitively inflected studies of the ways that works invite us to imaginatively occupy another person's thoughts, feelings, and sensations.

While Marcel's encounter with the septet seems to share certain features with both Poulet's phenomenology of reading and the new cognitive work on empathetic identification, Proust offers a rather different account of the value of seeing through another's eyes. For Vermule, for example, we identify with characters because we are naturally (genetically) inclined to be interested in what other people are thinking and feeling. Our interest in mind-reading is an interest in the particular contents of those minds. We are drawn to certain kinds of characters, curious about what they think, "what makes them tick." Other kinds of characters might leave us cold.

But for Marcel, the value of getting under another person's skin has practically nothing to do with the particular qualities of that person. One enters another's mind in order to counter the habit that dulls our perceptions with time. The ability to imaginatively occupy another point of view, to see the world through another perceptual matrix, to taste and hear through a different set of associations, is for Marcel the one true "fountain of youth." The tools of the new cognitive criticism, while potentially illuminating Marcel's mechanisms of identification, are inadequate to his motive. Vermule speculates that we take pleasure in reading other people's minds because the "Machiavellian" capacity to figure out other people's plans confers an evolutionary advantage. Perhaps this way of tying our ability to read another person's subjectivity to a particular evolutionary function has merit. But even if this is so, Proust's motive is not the natural motive. In a move we shall observe again in Nabokov, Proust exploits a natural capacity to achieve an unnatural end: "permanent novelty."

To see through another's eyes is to see the world freshly. When absorbed in the webs of the septet, Marcel becomes Vinteuil in every way but one. Just as the character translated by the Shatter into the insect's sensorium is astonished by the way the world looks to an insect, so Marcel is amazed by Vinteuil's habitual ways of seeing the world. If the septet were actually to make Marcel feel exactly as Vinteuil felt, it would be nothing special. Vinteuil "is the native of an unknown country, which he himself has forgotten" (731). And in this sense he is like all of us. Our own ways of perceiving the world are invisible to us. We each contain "that ineffable something which differentiates qualitatively what each of us has felt and what he is obliged to leave behind at the threshold of the phrases in which he can communicate with others only by limiting himself to externals." But "the art of a Vinteuil . . . exteriorizes in the colours of the spectrum the intimate composition of those worlds which we call individuals and which, but for art, we should never know" (732).

Proust suggests that the difference between a great artist and an ordinary person has nothing to do with personality, but is entirely due to the artist's preternatural ability to "exteriorize" his perceptual organization such that another can see through his eyes. And seeing through his eyes, we see the world made new. It is as if the septet can convey the way habitual patterns and associations structure Vinteuil's sensations without also conveying the deadening effect those habitual patterns have on Vinteuil's experience of the world. The artist lives in forgetfulness in his homeland; we enter it in wonder, discovering a state of "permanent novelty." The fountain of youth gushes in other people's skulls; art opens those skulls to us. Unlike Vermule's description of the natural desires that animate readers, Proust's mode of art appreciation is not human but vampiric. Through the long straw of the work, Marcel sucks new life from the artist.

Of course, long use might eventually make Vinteuil's perceptual habits Marcel's own. He might eventually grow as forgetful of Vinteuil's native land as the composer. But there is no shortage of other composers forgetfully occupying new lands. And this move from one individual's world to the next is quite immune to the problems that beset the succession of styles and techniques. For in imaginatively inhabiting another person's nervous system, we are not switching objects, we are switching subjects. Instead of dragging our own tired eyes to Venus, we are seeing earth with someone else's eyes. Our innate ability to imagine the internal life of others is a slumbering power that will enable us to defeat time. This is the conclusion of Proust's experiments with virtual music.

❖

Proust's research strategy is founded on a low estimation of the effectiveness of art's perceptible form to counter time. Marcel's vampiric aesthetic—imbibing another's life through the work—emerges from the ruin of Swann's aesthetic. Swann discovers new life as a result of the immediate perception of the object. For Swann, the intense experience of the sonic shape of the phrase is an end in itself. When this intensity proves evanescent, Marcel, a more ambitious and tireless warrior against time, abandons the sensible qualities of the work, and instead endeavors to listen *through* musical form to grasp the code of the artist's sensibility. Access to this sensibility, and not the experience of form itself, renews life.

Other writers, however, refuse to give up on the time-defeating potential of form as an object of perception. Keats, as we shall see, values music not as a super-efficient means of transmitting the contents of a composer's perceptual matrix, but, in more familiar Romantic terms, as the absence of the distinction between form and content. Wordless music is pure form for Keats. His virtual musics investigate the possibility of an experience of form resistant to the habituation that kills off the little phrase.

But Keats shares with Proust an acceptance of the tragic limits of the artifact to counter experiential time. To understand the scope of his ambition we must distinguish between the celebrated music of the Keatsian line, and those *images* of virtual music at the heart of such major poems as "Ode to a Nightingale," "Ode on a Grecian Urn," and "Hyperion." Robert Mitchell's recent essay on "suspended animation" in Keats and Shelley offers a useful contrast with my approach. Mitchell describes early experiments with cryogenic suspension as a fascinating context for what he calls "Romantic-era techniques of poetic suspension" (116). Keats and Shelley "developed techniques for introducing forms of suspension into the experience of reading literature, treating literature as a technology for creating 'altered states'" (112). Keats's "To Autumn" thus "enacts a slowing of forward movement," while Shelley's "Mont Blanc" "seeks to produce a similar state of tense suspension in its auditors and readers through its peculiar use of rhyme" (114). Shelley's irregular rhyme makes the poem "a technology for producing trances in readers" (113).

Mitchell believes that Keats and Shelley intend to project a certain kind of experience—in this case, a "trance"—and craft poetic forms to create this experience in their audience. This is an empirical claim, and as such it asks to be judged by the experience of actual readers. I am such a reader. I have read "Mont Blanc" and can testify that if it put me in a trance, it was of an exceptionally weak variety. At most I experienced a mild sleepiness in the middle. As a technology for producing trances, Shelley's poetry seems far less effective than flashing lights and droning music. It is possible that your experience may vary; you may be literally hypnotized by the irregular rhyme scheme of "Mont Blanc." But I doubt it.

It is more likely that the effect Mitchell imagines, if real, is extremely subtle. To adapt the old saw about the talking dog, it is not the power of this poetic suspension that fascinates the critic; it is the idea that a poem has any somatic effect at all. But Keats's vision for transforming the body through art is anything but subtle. And even if one could find a reader who found her heartbeat appreciably slowed when reading "To Autumn," her experience would still be vulnerable to the tendency minutely analyzed by Proust: it would wear off after a few readings.

Mitchell's procedure in this passage of his otherwise excellent essay illustrates a tendency that Oren Izenberg refers to as the "fetishism" of form: our compulsion to trace everything valuable about poetry to the effects of particular formal features (*Being Numerous*, 12). The problem becomes especially acute in a poet like Keats. The scale of his ambition—the desire to fuse vital intensity with inorganic stasis, expressed so forcefully in "Bright Star"—compels him to the ekphrastic mode. Irregular rhyme cannot answer the desire to "live for ever." But the nightingale's song and Apollo's music do. These are forms designed not to produce an empirical effect on readers, but to enable the writer to probe the mechanisms of experiential time with a view to their eventual overcoming. We have nuanced and flexible accounts of actual poetic form from the new criticism of Wimsatt and Beardsley to the sophisticated historicisms of Mitchell and Marjorie Levinson. But these methods are of no help here, and we need to look elsewhere.

In his description of Rimbaud's *Illuminations*, Leo Bersani articulates a dynamic similar to that which interests me in Keats. For Bersani, Rimbaud's prose poems are animated by a desire that cannot be satisfied by artistic form (233). On this basis, Bersani draws a crucial distinction between Rimbaud's prose poem and Mallarme's. Whereas Mallarme's prose poems constitute the formal achievement of "an equivalence between the semantic dimension of words and their status as objects," Rimbaud's "advertise a mocking indifference to *all* possibilities of verbal sequence" (248).

In the *Illuminations*, "written poetry is reduced almost to the status of stage directions in the textual version of a play" (253). Unlike Mallarme's, Rimbaud's language knows that it is not where the action lies. It points out beyond itself; it indicates that the action will take place elsewhere. Between his abandonment of verse and his abandonment of writing, Rimbaud writes prose poems. And in them, he jettisons the achieved forms of art in favor of virtual forms, images of form. One remembers Rimbaud's famous criticism of Baudelaire: "Unluckily he lived in too artistic a circle . . ." (16). Rimbaud's ideal form is not a poem but an imaginary science—mathematics, engineering: "Chemistry without virtue and impossible melodies" (280).

Allen Grossman, in an essay on Hart Crane's "intense poetics," provides another account of virtual poetry. "Crane's one subject," he writes, "is the deep desire to free the poem and the life from demands inconsistent with their inevitable common destiny in the actual world" (86). Given the limits of the transformative potential of actual poems read by real readers, Crane projects imaginary forms adequate to the ambition that animates his writing. "In the absence of the invention of new structures, Crane's poetry tends to hallucinate or thematize structures (building, bridge, tower)" (89). Proust's and Keats's musics are examples of such hallucinated structures.

The virtuality I develop here should be distinguished from another sense of the term that has recently enjoyed wide currency in the humanities. In *Parables for the Virtual*, Brian Massumi writes, "The body is as immediately virtual as it is actual" (30). By *virtual* he refers to those embodied, affective states that cannot be captured by language or registered by consciousness. Massumi has interpreted studies of audience response to art as providing evidence for how artworks activate this virtual dimension.

Ruth Leys, in her careful survey of this work, argues that Massumi "willfully misreads the data" in his interpretation of scientific experiments (467). I will return to one of these experiments in my next chapter, but for now I want to point out a curious feature of this concept of the virtual which writers like Massumi develop from Deleuze's reading of Bergson. In her recent study, Suzanne Guerlac argues that Deleuze's understanding of the virtual departs from Bergson's, and grows out of the former's anti-Freudian vision of the unconscious as a "desiring machine" (189–90). This "Deleuzian sympathy for the machine" underlies the curious effort on the part of his followers to bracket the role of conscious experience (191). Katherine Hayles analyzes this tendency in terms relevant for our study in her diagnosis of the equation of nonconscious informational processes with the human. "If we can become the information we have constructed, we can achieve effective immortality" (13). Thus the Deleuzian concept of the virtual would seem to belong to the history of classical immortality, as opposed to the Romantic effort to extend life.

The excitement with which Massumi greets the prospect of Deleuzian virtuality is puzzling. He seems convinced that the study of nonconscious states offers a more mysterious and surprising field for humanities scholarship than the study of conscious states, and one that offers greater opportunities for meaningful collaboration between the humanities and the sciences. This may, as Leys argues, stem from a misguided belief that neuroscience offers a new way of pursuing the traditional poststructuralist and psychoanalytic suspicion of intentionality. Regardless, the sense of mystery and excitement Massumi finds in the study of the nonconscious, and his belief that it gives scholars a chance to "stir up" neuroscientific research, must seem perverse to anyone who has attended to this research. Consciousness is the great destabilizing factor in our intellectual world. As John Searle points out in his review of a major new work, consciousness is the focus of a "sizable number of important research efforts," efforts which "do not appear to be making much progress" (48). As we shall see in our survey of addiction research, it is the very profundity of the problems that surround consciousness that drives researchers back onto the relatively safe ground of nonconscious mechanisms.

While virtuality for writers like Massumi means the search for the nonconscious effects of artworks, I use *virtual* to refer to the tendency of artworks to project blueprints for a kind of conscious experience that we can't yet actualize. Immanuel Kant's theory of pure form—which, I will argue, is also virtual form—remains the richest philosophical treatment of this dynamic. This theory provides us with a vocabulary for investigating Keats's virtual musics. Nineteenth-century English literature was saturated with Kantian and quasi-Kantian ideas. But whether or not the philosopher exerted a direct influence on Keats, his *Critique of Judgment* constitutes a basic resource for conceptualizing the Romantic effort to defeat time.[7]

⁕

Given the long association of Kant's aesthetics with the formalist study of actual artistic structures, my suggestion that the *Critique of Judgment* furnishes a model for the analysis of virtual structures may seem strange. In addition, while everyone is familiar with *The Critique of Pure Reason*'s description of time—along with space—as an a priori category for organizing experience, few will associate Kant with a concern for that feature of neurobiological time that interests us here: the deadening effects of habit on perceptual vivacity. A fullscale reading of Kant's aesthetics lies beyond the scope of this work. But by drawing on key findings of recent scholarship on the *Critique of Judgment*, I want to show both the scope and the value of Kant's thinking for our subject.

For Kant, aesthetic judgment refers to a subject's disinterested feeling of pleasure or displeasure in an object. He argues that the nature of this disinterested pleasure provides the ground by which an entirely subjective verdict claims a universal scope (53–54). Much of the secondary literature has focused on the nature and plausibility of Kantian "disinterest," and on the related question of the meaning of subjective universality. But for our purposes, the first question is: what does he mean by *pleasure*?

Henry Allison takes up this issue in his authoritative recent study of the *Critique of Judgment*. His account challenges certain traditional assumptions in part by tracing the development of Kant's concepts through his voluminous lecture notes.[8] Allison points out that pleasure is a recurrent theme in these lectures. There Kant consistently refers "to pleasure as the feeling of the promotion of life and displeasure as the feeling of the hindrance of life" (69). After comparing the use of "pleasure" in the *Critique* with his usage throughout his career, Allison concludes that "Kant understands by pleasure and displeasure something like a sense of the increase or diminution of one's level of activity, particularly one's activity as a thinking being" (69). This reading accords with such earlier accounts as Gadamer's, who similarly argues that for Kant aesthetic pleasure is an intensification of the feeling of life through perception (52).

For Kant, the experience of pleasure is accompanied by a desire to make it last, to keep it from fading. At several points, Kant refers explicitly to pleasures that lose their luster through habituation (Allison, 55).[9] But his concern with experiential time transcends the explicit language of habit. At crucial moments throughout the *Critique*, Kant describes pleasure not simply as an intensified feeling of life, but as the effort to preserve this vital state. Desire gives aesthetic pleasure a prospective dimension. As we shall see, the language of the *Critique* in fact suggests something stronger. Kant argues that we take pleasure in the prospect of an indefinitely extended vitality. This addition of desire to the feeling of pleasure gives the latter a virtual dimension.

Here is Kant's definition of pleasure. "Consciousness of a representation's causality directed at the subject's state so as to *keep* him in that state, may here designate generally what we call pleasure" (cited in Allison, 121). The subject of aesthetic attention takes pleasure in an image that seems designed to preserve in him a state of perceptual intensity. I will unpack this dense and, to some, counterintuitive definition of pleasure by exploring the understanding of desire, subjectivity, and perception that underlies it.

First I want to address objections that might arise when I speak of Kantian aesthetic pleasure as a form of desire. This may seem to create a tension with another basic component of Kant's theory: his claim that aesthetic pleasure is disinterested. Doesn't becoming disinterested mean refining away my desire for that image or for what it represents?

For Allison this is a false problem, based on a misunderstanding of Kantian disinterest as signifying "without desire." Allison argues that by "disinterested" pleasure Kant means the intense aliveness one feels when simply *perceiving* the image, as opposed to the pleasure one takes in possessing or consuming it. This latter state counts as "interested" pleasure in that one wants to procure the object, rather than dwell on how it looks, sounds, feels (53). For the disinterested listener to wordless music—a form Kant, like Keats and Proust, places at the top of his hierarchy of arts—a "state of increased vitality is precisely what the subject endeavors to preserve" by listening (122). It is because we desire this state that "we linger in our contemplation of the beautiful" (131). Therefore disinterest has nothing to do with a lack of desire or a distance from corporeality. It refers to the life one feels in perception.

To understand this is to reveal the limits of Bourdieu's influential reading of Kant. For Bourdieu, the drive to acquire social distinction underlies Kantian disinterested aesthetic attention. This analysis is based on the intuition that the desire for prestige is more real than whatever ethereal pleasure the aesthete pretends to acquire by listening to Debussy or staring at Picasso. This intuition has been supported by a weak reading of what Kant means by pleasure. But the experience of having one's senses come alive is something everyone knows. A desire for such perceptual intensity is at least as basic as the pursuit of recognition. Indeed, one might speculate that the eclipse of the classical model of immortality—in which one pursues the social recognition of one's name and deeds after one is no longer conscious—and its displacement by the Romantic model signifies a cultural shift in favor of the intuitive, even biological, appeal of Kantian disinterest.

Kant's emphasis on the feeling of life in perception is also the key to understanding the subjectivism of his aesthetics. This subjectivism goes far beyond the claim that one's capacity for judging art, unlike one's capacity for judging whether there are two or three chairs in the room, is subjective. Rather, as Allison writes, "what is *discriminated* is a state of the subject . . . of which one can become aware only through feeling" (129). Like Swann praising the sonata, what the Kantian subject praises in the work is his own feeling of renewed vitality.

But what is this vitality, and how do images trigger it? Kant says that pleasure-giving images "occasion an enhancement or diminution of one's cognitive faculties," an enhancement experienced as an enhancement of life itself. We have seen how Proust associates Swann's initial pleasure in the sonata with his drive to grasp its form, and how Baudelaire's rapture on first hearing Wagner is accompanied by an insatiable desire to "turn pleasure into knowledge." Similarly, for Kant the sensation of perceptual vitality is simply what it feels like when one's cognitive faculties are fully engaged.

While admitting that the *Critique* is opaque on the precise dynamics of this cognitive engagement by the image, Allison writes, "the basic idea is presumably that the imagination in its free play stimulates the understanding by occasioning it to entertain fresh conceptual possibilities, while, conversely, the imagination, under the general direction of the understanding, strives to conceive new patterns of order" (171). The image consists of parts related to each other and to the whole in a way that challenges us. Like Swann, who works to discern "new patterns of order" within the formless dynamism of the sonata, our wrestling with the new work feels like learning a new language.

Cognitive engagement amounts to a striving to understand, to grasp the form of the work, a striving we have also seen in Proust, Baudelaire, Winckelmann, and Noe, and one that seems to attend the encounter with a genuinely new object of perception. What Kant adds to these writers is a fuller description of the nature of this cognitive striving. He distinguishes it from simple sensation on the one hand, and on the other, from the kind of cognitive effort involved in actually trying to learn a new language or work out a difficult math problem. What one attends to in the aesthetic object for Kant is its form. The attention to form is "indeterminate," in that one recognizes that it cannot be understood through a concept. Music without words is a particularly rich example for Kant of "free beauty." One puzzles out the relations of the piece's parts without recourse to semantic categories, an effort Kant refers to as the "free play" of the faculties (139).[10] As Allison remarks, the details of Kant's exposition are obscure, and perhaps the best explanation of some of his ideas, such as the notorious "purposiveness without purpose," is that they are designed to address the requirements of other aspects of Kant's total philosophical system. But the *Critique*'s description of the process of aesthetic attention is clear enough in its general outline. The aesthetic encounter with the image engages cognitive faculties, and the response of those faculties to the image's structure mimics the dynamics of understanding.

But this also suggests that the Kantian aesthetic object is vulnerable to the same erosive force as Proust's. If the cognitive effort to grasp the form produces a feeling of life, then, as we saw with Winckelmann, Proust, and Baudelaire, the consequence of cognitive mastery appears to be a lapse back into dullness. Paul Guyer argues that in his analysis of aesthetic pleasure, "Kant describes what is clearly a unified but also a temporally extended psychological state" (83). But how long can the vitalizing striving to grasp the form be maintained? Guyer writes that this pleasure does not admit of "indefinite extension" (84). Because when the coherence of a given form "comes to be expected, even if it is not traced to a determinate concept, the pleasure of aesthetic response must fade" (84). Kant describes how the object to which one has become habituated, more than simply fading, passes from being a source of aesthetic pleasure to becoming a "tedious constraint on the imagination" (84). Guyer points out that one might continue to relish one's cognitive mastery over the form as "an accomplishment, like a discovery," but this kind of pleasure is clearly distinct from the striving that yields the discovery itself, and offers poor compensation for the lapse into perceptual tedium (85).[11]

Thus Kant's account of the temporality of aesthetic pleasure in an object's form closely resembles Proust's. Swann may not have understood the sonata in the same way as one understands a problem in long division, but there is no doubt that the pattern became clear to him, that it ceased to require the cognitive intensity it initially inspired, and that it ceased to make him feel vividly alive. This did not of course, preclude him from discovering or associating new *meanings* in the sonata.[12] It did, however, mean the end of pleasure in the Kantian sense, the end of the feeling of life in the perception of the image.[13]

Swann's case does not appear to be isolated. In fact, some people tend to incorporate an awareness of the mortality of any individual work into their aesthetic practice as listeners. I have a friend who, when hearing a new song, will predict how many listenings it will take until the song has been "used up" for him, and rendered fit only to provide nostalgia or the dull comfort of the utterly familiar. He tells me he feels a more intense pleasure if the first listening is accompanied by an intuition that the particular mixture of conventional and novel promises an extended life for the song. Whether this tendency is widely shared, the feeling my friend expresses is familiar enough. It is like the pleasure one takes on the first day of a vacation. The Tibetan philosopher Chogyam Trungpa expresses something similar when he writes that the heart's desire is to exist forever in the "glowing promise" of the moment before dawn (9). For my friend and Trungpa, the anticipation of continued intensity seems to constitute part of what it means to fully enjoy an intense experience. Their testimony, along with that of Proust and Baudelaire, may make us sensitive to those moments when the mortality of the image becomes a problem for Kant. They may help us to appreciate the significance of Kant's curious definition of pleasure as "consciousness of a representation's causality directed at the subject's state so as to *keep* him in that state."

This definition has been hard for Kant's readers to take. The philosopher, Allison writes, "appears to make pleasure consist in the *awareness* of the causal power of a representation to preserve a (presumably harmonious) mental state, rather than in the mental state itself" (122). Allison's excavation of Kant's usage of pleasure enables us to presume that Kant's use of the term here involves reference to a state of heightened life in perception. But I cannot follow Allison when he argues that we must interpret this passage so that it does not "commit Kant to the highly counterintuitive view that pleasure consists in the awareness of the causal power of a representation to keep one in a mental state" (123). As I hope will be obvious, this awareness is not counterintuitive from the perspective of the Romantic effort to defeat time. In fact, attunement to "the causal power of a representation to keep one in a mental state" is a good description of one of the most ambitious aesthetic programs of the past two centuries. Placing Kant between Proust and Keats provides us with a powerful model for understanding their search for an object of perception that will *keep* one in a state of vital intensity. On the other hand, this juxtaposition enables us to take seriously a neglected aspect of the philosopher's work.

The Kantian aesthetic object is not simply that which produces an immediate sense of perceptual vitality in me. It is also that object which I sense as having the capacity to *extend* this vitality. Recognition of the role time plays in aesthetic attention has deep implications for our understanding of Kant's view of the subject of aesthetic experience. If one takes it seriously one cannot endorse the radical subjectivism of Genette's influential interpretation of the *Critique of Judgment*. For Genette, the beautiful aesthetic object is simply that which happens to please me. Beauty is utterly in the eye of the beholder, and his theory does not admit the possibility that art could have a transformative effect on the subject. Determination is entirely one way, from subject to object.

Charles Altieri is closer to the reading I advance here when he writes that Kant creates a model of the "virtuality of the audience" (106). In trying to grasp the interrelation of the work's parts, "I myself become someone different"

(106). With the benefit of Allison's and Guyer's excavation of the centrality of psychological time to Kant's theory, we can specify the nature of that transformation. The aesthetic object awakens me to vivid perceptual life, and, through its structure, defeats the tendency of that vividness to fade. As Allison argues, when I praise an image as beautiful, I praise the feeling that contemplation of the image gives me. But this feeling is a very strange thing. Unlike happiness or sadness, aesthetic pleasure is not a state that I simply detect in myself. Aesthetic pleasure extends into the future, beyond my present capacity to feel. But in the object, I perceive a guarantee of that extension. What I greet in the aesthetic object is my life, rescued from time.

But surely Kant had no such dramatic effect in mind. An image that remains *forever* vivid is an imaginary image, and the philosopher, after all, does not seem to be describing imaginary music. While Proust and Keats present images of imaginary aesthetic experiences, Kant seems to offer an account of actual aesthetic encounters. Therefore, while Kant's description of the temporal dimension of aesthetic pleasure may well admit a virtual element into aesthetic experience, he hardly suggests that the effective aesthetic object must be an imaginary aesthetic object.

I recognize that Kant, in describing the ways we take pleasure in an image that promises to keep us in a state of enhanced life, does not say that we expect that it will keep us there *forever*. This is a nontrivial distinction between his description of aesthetic objects and the description of ideal artworks by the writers I consider. On the other hand, I don't see evidence that Kant believes our *desire* to maintain the feeling of life in perception is intrinsically limited by an acknowledgement of some absolute temporal limit, however much experience might demonstrate the intractability of such limits.[14] Rather, I think it is simply the case that Kant did not pursue this line of thought. Much of his concern in the *Critique* as a whole is not with overcoming the temporal limitations of the feeling of life, but with overcoming the barrier between subjective feeling and universal communicability.

But, with this caveat, is Kant's description of music without words really that different from Proust's and Keats's? Isn't there, after all, something virtual in the very form of his discussion of music? He doesn't actually give us any concrete example of music. The *Critique* is famously light on examples. There are no scores, no references to actual compositions. Kant describes forms instead of creating examples of them. Perhaps this is just to say that he is a philosopher, not an artist. But if this is so, then Proust's and Keats's ekphrastic practice is also a kind of philosophy. In fact, in its basic structure, it is the same kind of philosophy as Kant's. Our overview of the *Critique* highlights five features of this philosophy:

1) To value an aesthetic object is to value the intense feeling of life it produces in me.
2) I evaluate the aesthetic object in terms of its capacity to preserve this vital state, not simply in terms of its capacity to produce it.
3) The intense feeling of life produced by the aesthetic object is a result of my effort to understand it.
4) This effort does not rely on concepts. The aesthetic object's ideal form is wordless music.
5) Its actual form is words about music.

❂

Keats's words about music represent his most sustained effort to imagine a form capable of fusing stasis and the rhythm of life, and thus to make the impossible desire voiced in "Bright Star" poetry's animating principle, rather than its despair. I want to explore this effort by juxtaposing the description of Clymene's encounter with Apollo's music in "Hyperion" with the representation of "unheard" music in "Ode on a Grecian Urn."

> There came enchantment with the shifting wind
> That did both drown and keep alive my ears.
> I threw my shell away upon the sand,
> And a wave fill'd it, as my sense was fill'd
> With that new blissful golden melody.
> A living death was in each gush of sounds,
> Each family of rapturous hurried notes,
> That fell, one after one, yet all at once. ("Hyperion," 490)

> Heard melodies are sweet, but those unheard
> Are sweeter; therefore, ye soft pipes, play on:
> Not to the sensual ear, but, more endear'd,
> Pipe to the spirit ditties of no tone. ("Ode on a Grecian Urn," 461)

In each passage, music transforms time and fuses life and death, though the poems pursue this transformation by different, and as we shall see, incompatible strategies. This difference turns on the poems' different response to the basic question of ekphrasis. What happens when one art form represents another? I will argue that in "Ode on a Grecian Urn," the poem's description of music figures an aspect of poetry's own capacity. Poetic music is driven by language's temporal powers, and circumscribed by language's temporal limits. In "Hyperion," by contrast, the experience of imaginary music becomes a way of testing the possible conditions of an ideal art form, a project that closely resembles Kant's, even as it outstrips it in its ambition. In Keats's last, fragmentary epic, a wordlessness made of words pictures final liberation from the limit of time itself.

We will begin with Keats's unheard melodies. "Ode on a Grecian Urn" stops time by spatializing music. The poem attributes to a visual image of music powers that the ineluctably temporal form of heard music lacks. The poem's particular mode of visuality does not represent a simple surrender to stasis, but a method for fusing movement and stillness. Murray Krieger, who develops earlier arguments by Cleanth Brooks into what is perhaps the postwar era's most influential discussion of ekphrasis, investigates this fusion. In an extended reading of the poem's first line ("Thou still unravish'd bride of quietness") Krieger distinguishes between "still" as the "stilling of movement," and "still moving as a forever-now movement, always in process, unending" (109). The circularity of the urn furnishes Keats with an emblem of a form containing motion. But for Krieger, ekphrasis here is not an image of what poems would like to do and cannot. The urn is a symbol of the poem's actual achievement. Because poems pen the flow of language in delimited and iterable wholes, all poetry, he writes, manifests "the identity of recurrence together with the unceasing change of movement" (124).

Krieger's reading inspires two kinds of dissent. Helen Vendler represents the first when she complains that by focusing just on the first stanza's confidence in the urn's time-defeating capacity, one misses how the later stanzas dramatize "the strain of maintaining timelessness in the vocabulary of time" (129). In the second stanza, for example, Keats describes the figures on the urn in a way that brings out the fatal contradictions of the prospect of frozen life.

> Bold lover, never, never canst thou kiss,
> Though winning near the goal—yet, do not grieve;
> She cannot fade, though thou hast not thy bliss,
> For ever wilt thou love, and she be fair! (462)

Vendler notes that the desirability of unfading beauty is here quite eclipsed by the eternal torture of the marble youth's Tantalus-like condition.[15] She reads this moment as indicative of Keats's abandonment of the impossible project of arresting life and prolonging intensity through art. Keen appreciation of the contradictions involved in even an imaginary realization of this aim sets him on the road to the poem's—and the poet's—final embrace of eternal truth as literature's high and achievable goal. And of course the poem famously concludes not with the urn's stilled music, but with its speech: "Beauty is truth, truth beauty." Krieger dismisses such emphasis on the final line by arguing that from the perspective of such a reading, "poetry is hardened into static, Platonic discourse that has lost touch with—indeed that disdains to touch—our existential motions" (127). He thinks that Keats's claim on our attention derives not from his production of stasis, but from his ability to contain vital motion in poetic form.

If Vendler wants to free the poetic artifact from the trap of human time, another kind of critic argues that poetry's true function is to perform a total immersion in lived time equally incompatible with Krieger's strong description of the achievement of form. "Writers on time in the vitalistic tradition of Bergson," Krieger writes, "have commonly claimed that . . . language tends to give death to the dynamism of experience by spatializing it and thus freezing its undemarcated ceaseless flow of unrepeatable and indefinable, un-entitled units" (127).

For such critics, and he counts Poulet chief among them, the reader of poetry attempts to look through the form for traces of its author's experience. Such a reader must constantly work against form's spatializing tendencies to glimpse the reality of lived duration, to recover the life of frozen bodies. Kreiger counters Poulet by arguing that artistic structure can translate time into space without destroying the quality of lived experience. By imitating the circular shape of the urn, Keats's poetic artifact preserves the onward flow of duration and makes the unrepeatable repeat.[16]

While Krieger's reading develops important insights into Keats's ambition to arrest lived time, he doesn't register the full force of the Bergsonian complaint. His essay dates from 1965, and for several decades afterwards the primary objection to formalism was not that it failed to register the impossibility of stopping time, but that its description of form as a unified whole occluded the structural instabilities revealed by deconstruction. But things have changed, and today's critical scene witnesses a renewal of the 1965 debate. Critics have again taken up Bergson's thinking as a challenge to a resurgent formalism. This thought—and especially Bergson's conviction that language violates the experience of time—illuminates both the limitations of the spatialized music in the "Urn" and the possibilities opened by the image of music in "Hyperion."

We can approach the Bergsonian perspective by way of a commonsense objection to Krieger. It seems obvious that a representation of an experience is not the same thing as an experience. This is just a fact about reference. A picture of an urn is not an urn. But this is exactly what Krieger denies by arguing that Keats's poem not only represents the urn, it *is* a kind of urn, and it does what the urn does. For Krieger, ekphrasis closes the gap between representation and represented. "Ode on a Grecian Urn" is not about the stilling/still moving of lived time, it embodies that stillness.

As for John Dewey, art for Krieger is shaped experience. Helen Vendler might reply that art is not the transmission of experience but the communication of meaning, a communication thematized by the poem's final lines. Giving voice to truth is not only what poetry can do, it is the most valuable thing poetry should do. The Bergsonian critic will not assent to Vendler's values. For Bergsonian critics, nothing is more important than the transmission, expression, recovery, preservation, and analysis of the author's experience of lived time. But such critics agree with Vendler's conclusion about the limit of poetic language. For Bergson, it is not simply that language cannot embody the experience of lived time. He describes a fundamental antagonism between linguistic meaning and temporal experience. This tension not only places enormous burdens on our ability to conceptualize that experience but it also erodes our capacity to have such experiences at all.

In *Thinking in Time*, Suzanne Guerlac summarizes Bergson's philosophy of time with the statement: "We never feel the same thing twice" (64). The experience of duration is of a changing of felt qualities. These qualities present as a "confused multiplicity" in which sensations are fused rather than distinct (83). "States . . . succeed one another without distinguishing themselves from one another" (97). Bergson uses the figure of melody to represent duration, the modulation of tones in time (66).[17] But as soon as we try to express our experience of duration in words, we misrepresent its reality. Language turns time into space, replaces the chaotic modulations of feeling with delimited objects. Language's spatializing tendency does not simply create a problem for the accurate conceptualization of the experience of duration. The infiltration of our experience by language pollutes that experience. So by *duration* Bergson does not refer to a state that we naturally inhabit in our everyday life, but to a rare experience. It is difficult to experience duration (158).

To return to Bergson's use of melody as a figure for the experience of time, it should be clear that we cannot describe every encounter with music as the experience of undifferentiated and confused modulation. But this does seem like a good description of the first time one hears a piece of music. And in fact Proust, who was deeply influenced by Bergson, provides just such a description when he evokes Swann's first encounter with the Vinteuil sonata as "a sort of liquid rippling of sound, multiform but indivisible, smooth yet restless, like the deep blue tumult of the sea."[18] And in Swann's attempt to grasp the form, we can see Bergson's spatializing tendencies at work, a process that culminates in Swann's appropriation of the sonata as a symbol of his love for Odette. The music takes on the deathly stillness of linguistic reference. The understanding of a meaning replaces the experience of duration.

Now we can see why Krieger's account of "Ode on a Grecian Urn" underestimates the challenge of preserving duration. The poem presents a succession of distinct images. This is a problem even if we grant Krieger his redescription of the iterable poetic text as the urn-poem's capacity to make an *experience* repeatable. The forever panting youth, the "green altar," the "heifer lowing at the skies," the marble pipes: these clearly delimited images lack the "multiform indivisibility" Proust associates with vivid experience, the "confused multiplicity" Bergson associates with duration, and the "indeterminacy" Kant sees as necessary for the vital cognitive effort of aesthetic pleasure. All three describe vivid perceptual experience in such a way as to make its achievement incompatible with representational art, and thus wordless music occupies a privileged exemplary role for each.[19] Whatever truths it might express, from the perspective that values the eliciting of vivid perception in art, "Ode on a Grecian Urn" resembles an old German clock, with its eternal round of deathly figures emerging on the hour. Keats's "sylvan historian" keeps dead time, not living time.

Yet if we seek a form that will not simply elicit a vivid response but will "keep us" in that state, actual nonrepresentational art won't do. The problem is to keep nonrepresentational art from becoming representational art, to keep music from becoming words. Proust, Kant, and Bergson associate the deathliness of habituation with the achievement of cognitive mastery. Actual music can offer no defense to this habituation. The demon recognition waits in the wings of every premiere. We will not find a music immune to experiential time in a concert hall. But we do find it in "Hyperion."

Keats enshrines his ideal music in a poem obsessed by the paradoxes of immortality. "Hyperion" tells the story of the Titans after their overthrow by the new Olympian gods. Consider the description of the goddess Thea:

> One hand she press'd upon that aching spot
> Where beats the human heart, as if just there,
> Though an immortal, she felt cruel pain. (477)

Thea might be the speaker of "Bright Star," who has suffered the ironic granting of her wish to "feel forever." The intense awareness of the contradictions of the wish for immortality in "Hyperion" has been a central part of the influence of this poem. For example, Dan Simmons's celebrated science fiction novel *Hyperion* imagines a race made immortal by a cruciform parasite that degrades the flesh it preserves. The critic Maureen McLane argues that "Keats ceaselessly interrogates immortality—of the soul, of the song—from the perspective of mortality, usually figured as deep embodiment or sheer corporeality" (201).

As we have seen, in "Ode on a Grecian Urn" the paradox of prolonged life motivates the ideal artwork to abandon the effort to stop experiential time and to turn to the very different timelessness of propositional truth. But in "Hyperion" the pressures of that paradox form the crucible in which Keats's most ambitious imaginary music is forged. The poem grants us access to Apollo's music through Clymene's report of her experience of it. The music's "enchantment," she affirms, "did both drown and keep alive my ears." Here we have the strong claim of the accomplished fusion of stasis and life, a happy fusion that contrasts with the many images of immortal bodies wracked by unending pain that litter the poem. In the contexts both of this poem and of Keats's poetry as a whole, this claim should arouse intense suspicion. But immediately afterwards Keats provides a formal description of the music that I will suggest works to mitigate this suspicion.

> A living death was in each gush of sounds,
> Each family of rapturous hurried notes,
> That fell, one after one, yet all at once. (490)

The strategies actual composers use to defeat habituation will enable us to understand how Keats radicalizes these strategies in his description of Apollo's virtual music. Since Leonard Meyer's groundbreaking work in the 1950s, musicologists have explored the extent to which the pleasure of music "arises through the composer's choreographing of expectation" (Huron, 2). In a way analogous to Kant's description of aesthetic pleasure as the interplay between recognition and indeterminacy, musicologists describe the interplay between audience expectations—both conventional and those set up by the individual work through repetition—and the tactical violation of those expectations. The music of Keats's poetry—as the rhythms of the lines of poetry quoted above demonstrate—manifests this principle by distributing stresses around the expectations set by iambic pentameter. Were those stresses to coincide absolutely with the standard supplied by the meter, the poetry would succumb to the tedium of the metronome.[20]

One does not need to denigrate the power of Keats's actual poetic music to acknowledge that metrical variance will not secure for him the triumph Clymene attributes to Apollo's music. But this very brief musicological observation enables me to formulate a preliminary characterization of the virtual music in "Hyperion." *Keats turns the oscillation between anticipation and violation—characteristic of actual music's pleasurable organization of subjective time—into an oscillation between one after another and all at once.* Through this phantasmatic technique, Apollo's "rapturous hurried notes" fuse the stasis of death with the rhythm of life.

"Notes / that fell, one after another yet all at once." What are we being asked to imagine in these lines? Features of the ordinary experience of music will be of only limited assistance here. But features of pathological listening can help to solidify the contours of Apollo's imaginary melody. Oliver Sacks tells the story of Clive Wearing, an accomplished musician suddenly struck with severe amnesia that destroyed his consciousness of everything beyond the few seconds of short term memory. "It's like being dead," Wearing reported (203). And yet when he is playing or listening to music, he becomes "wholly alive" (228).

Sacks suggests that Wearing's case shows that our experience of music is of a vital present tense that contains the notes past and notes to come while binding them in an instant. "Hearing a melody is hearing, having heard, and being about to hear, all at once" (228). Sacks quotes Victor Zuckerkandl, who writes that "it is even a condition of hearing melody that the tone present at the moment should fill consciousness entirely, that nothing should be remembered, nothing except it or beside it be present in consciousness" (228). This resonates with a feature that Kant singles out in his description of music. A melody, he writes, consists of "changing impressions" that one is able to "grasp . . . all in one" (Guyer, 82).

But these descriptions surely disqualify many, and perhaps most, actual experiences of melody. Certainly they disqualify familiar music. In *Music and*

*Memory*, Bob Snyder demonstrates the extent to which ordinary musical perception depends on a constant comparison of the present sensation of melody with one's memory of other melodies. It is the disjunction between sensation and the expectations derived from memory that produces the intense absorption in the present and causes melody to "fill consciousness entirely." But habituation diminishes this absorption, until finally "memory and perception become indistinguishable" (24). Memory eventually swallows perception, obliterates the intense contact with the present. In listening to a habituated melody, there is death, but no life. Therefore Wearing's amnesia would not seem to highlight an extraordinary aspect of everyday musical experience. Rather, his condition illuminates the *possibility* of experiencing melody as both succession of notes and a simultaneity. Keats's representation of Apollo's music as living death is anchored on this possibility.

But something else is required to bind life and death together as tightly as they are in the music of "Hyperion," to prevent the "new tuneful wonder" from fading. Another strategy is needed to ensure that life does not seep out of the moment's arrest and leak away. To discern this strategy, we need to distinguish between two kinds of memory. One kind enables the vital experience of the notes as both successive and simultaneous. The other kind substitutes for immediate experience the recognition of a previously experienced form. To use the terms of the psychology of music, the problem is to *keep* the melody in short-term memory, and to *prevent* it from moving into long-term memory, where it becomes available to the mechanisms of habituation. Psychologists have found that the short-term memory that composes the experiential present can hold five to seven elements at once, or up to twenty-five elements bound into five groupings. A musical "phrase" is defined as a segment of a composition that can be held at once in the present of short-term memory (Snyder, 14). Through "rehearsal"—repeated exposure—a phrase then passes into long-term memory, and then into habituation.

Proust's acuity as a phenomenologist of musical perception will again aid us in illustrating this dynamic. As we have seen, Swann's "phrase" first appears as a liquid, indeterminate whole, and then, upon repeated listenings, resolves into a distinct form, in the process becoming "disenchanted." I want now to point out a different feature of Swann's experience, one that distinguishes it from Clymene's, and that therefore holds a key to what allows Apollo's music to escape the sonata's fate. Lacking a recording of Vinteuil's, each of Swann's encounters with the phrase involves a different performance. But Swann tends to focus on what the performances have in common, rather than what differentiates them. In other words, Swann attends to the *composer*'s phrase, seeking to dislodge its form from the contingencies of any given performance.

In "Hyperion," however, Clymene—and, later, Mnemosyne—witness Apollo's performance without any sense of a form "behind" the heard music. This representation of performance is significant, and suggests a second way musicology's insights might amplify our ability to imagine Apollonian music. A *nuance* in music refers to the variance each given performance manifests in relation to musical form. This is different from the composer's violation of expectations at the level of form discussed above because the nuanced performance, unlike a formal surprise, appears intrinsically resistant to habituation. John Sloboda, discussing Diana Raffman's hypothesis of "nuance ineffability," writes that nuance ineffability "comes about because we do not have categorizations or schemas as fine-grained as the stimuli we can discriminate" (159).

Snyder draws on a distinction in the psychology of perception to explain this ineffability. Our brains process sensations at several different levels in creating perceptions out of raw sensory data. At the first level, "perceptual categorization," sounds are recognized in terms of pitch. At the second level, "conceptual categorization," strings of pitched sounds are recognized in terms of previously heard melodies, or in terms of genre, style, composer, or era. We have a more difficult time making distinctions within categories than between categories. It is easy to tell a bear from a lion, but hard to distinguish between two bears. A nuance is an example of an especially subtle variation within a category, in this case, a variation on a melody. Nuance ineffability applies even to performances that lack the standardized differentiation between score and interpretation characteristic of classical music. One can hum the tune of one's favorite pop song in such a way as to make it recognizable to someone else who knows it. But this is a very different thing from being able to reproduce the tonal variations of the singer's delivery of that tune. Thus, Snyder writes, "nuances may be present at the beginning of perceptual categorization, but are absent at the level of conceptual categorization. They can be noticed, however, because they may be brought directly into perceptual awareness, bypassing the category structure of long-term memory" (86).

This tension between perception and conceptualization will immediately recall the terms of Kant's analysis of aesthetic pleasure as dependent upon conceptual indeterminacy. It will also be obvious that the oscillation of Apollo's musical performance between succession and simultaneity projects the possibility of persistent indeterminacy foreclosed by the urn's lucid, delimited spatial images. Thus it appears that Keats plausibly invests musical performance with the capacity that Krieger implausibly attributes to both the imagined urn and the actual "Ode." Snyder unconsciously echoes Kant's description of a form that will "keep us" in a state of vital attention when he writes that nuance "is probably the major reason why recordings, which freeze the details of particular musical performances, can be listened to many times and continue to seem vital and interesting" (88).

But there is a limit to the vitality even of recordings, a limit which Sloboda intimates when he argues that nuance, even if it resists conceptualization, does not absolutely preclude habituation. Some people, after all, are able to exactly reproduce the singer's delivery of a favorite song. And in fact many kinds of music instruction seek to develop this facility. Sloboda points to the role that *example* plays in music pedagogy. A student of the violin learns to recognize the pattern of a Heifetz performance's nuances, even if she might not be able to describe this pattern.

The limited nature of performed music's resistance to habituation in turn points to the limits of using studies of actual music to explore virtual music. Such studies are useful only in that they suggest the extent to which Keats draws on deep insights into musical phenomenology to identify features he will then radicalize. To summarize, these features are:

a) The typical division of melody into phrases fitted to the capacity of short-term memory, with the result that one experiences the phrase as both simultaneous and successive.

b) The structure of performed nuance, which enables melody to adhere to short-term memory. Performance accomplishes this by adding fine-grained features to the melody that cause it to slip through the categorical understanding through which habituation operates, with the effect of prolonging the work's freshness.

I think Keats's radicalization of these features gives Apollo's music a shape and a texture that rescues this vision of stasis fused with motion from the incoherence of "Bright Star." But we must not be misled by the way the impossible ambition of "Bright Star" becomes an *imaginable* image in "Hyperion" to think we are here presented with an *actualizable* image. We are not likely to hear Apollonian music soon. In the Romantic spirit I will, however, risk an immoderate further point. If we ever do discover habit-resistant music, it seems likely that it will involve the further development of the strategies by which Keats builds his imaginary melody.

⁕

Clymene's experience of Apollo's music as a "living death" provides the template for Keats's description of the god's assumption of immortality.

> Soon wild commotions shook him, and made flush
> All the immortal fairness of his limbs;
> Most like the struggle at the gate of death;
> Or liker still to one who should take leave
> Of pale immortal death, and with a pang
> As hot as death's is chill, with fierce convulse
> Die into life (495)

This final line has received significant attention in recent criticism, which reads Apollo as a figure for Keats, and the description of the god's apotheosis as a commentary on Keats's own poetry. Denise Gigante reads this commentary in the context of the problem of "organic form," a concept that conceals a fundamental tension between "life" and "formal containment" (48). For the Romantics, she argues, form is ultimately a kind of stasis. "Stasis was the ultimate form of death, and morphological prolificacy . . . provided a model for the fluid organization manifest as, and in, poetry" (48). In her ingenious account, Keats's actual poems achieve his aim of creating an artistic channel through which the life force might flow. This channeling becomes manifest in the restless generation of images in Keats's poems, and culminates in the creation of "monstrous" imagery, forms disfigured by the pressure of life trying to escape. Apollo's dying into life thus depicts the shattering of the static form of the beautiful that will allow life's energy to rush into the monstrous figures of "Lamia," which Gigante reads as a continuation of the "Hyperion" fragment.

Andrew Bennett, by contrast, reads "die into life" in terms of the sacrificial death necessary to secure the immortality of the text. "Hyperion figures death as a pre-condition for inspiration, it is a poem crucially concerned with the notion of dying into poetic creation, a mortal creativity" (*Keats, Narrative and Audience*, 151). This reading also has a great deal to recommend it. As evidence for Keats's commitment to what I have been calling the classical mode of literary immortality, Bennett draws on Keats's known preoccupation with his imminent death as well as on other poems in the oeuvre, such as "This Living

Hand," with its intimation that the posthumous life of the poet depends on those who survive him.[21]

But both Bennett's and Gigante's readings depend on occluding one basic fact about this poem. Keats cannot be figuring his own poetry in Apollo. Everything he writes about Apollo and his music emphasizes the gap between Keats's actual verse and the virtual music which that verse represents. As we have seen, Apollo's imaginary music—at once simultaneous and temporally extended—achieves the aim of fusing stasis and life through a process unavailable to language. Nor is this virtuality restricted to Apollo. "Hyperion" is a poem obsessed with pointing out the difference between its language and the forms it describes. Here is Keats's description of the goddess Thea early in the poem:

> Some words she spake
> In solemn tenour and deep organ tone:
> Some mourning words, which in our feeble tongue
> Would come in these like accents; O how frail
> To that large utterance of the early Gods! (477–78)

Later, the Titans' feelings are said to be "too huge for mortal tongue or pen of scribe" (480). And still later, Saturn's voice "load[s] his tongue with the full weight of utterless thought, with thunder, and with music" (487). Thus we should beware of closing the gap between Keats's lines and the music of his gods. Such a reading inevitably diminishes the scale of Keats's ambition by fitting it to our sense of what the poem's actual language can achieve.

To say that Keats does not represent his art in Apollo's is not, however, to say "Hyperion" has nothing to say about "mortal tongue or pen of scribe." Keats sets Apollo's phantasmatic melody in a narrative in which it is opposed by a different, less effective music. In her speech to Saturn, Clymene recounts how she

> Took a mouthed shell
> And murmur'd into it, and made melody—
> O melody no more! for while I sang
> And with poor skill let pass into the breeze
> The dull shell's echo, from a bowery strand
> Just opposite, an island of the sea,
> There came enchantment with the shifting wind
> That did both drown and keep alive my ears.
> I threw my shell away upon the sand. (490)

She then describes her experience of the Apollonian music's supernatural formal qualities, qualities guaranteed to make her "feel forever." And yet Clymene doesn't feel it forever. As she continues her speech, we learn that her enjoyment of the music is in fact shockingly short-lived. The virtual music fails to keep her joyously suspended between life and death. Instead, her rapture turns to grief.

> Grief overcame
> And I was stopping up my frantic ears,
> When, past all hindrance of my trembling hands,
> A voice came sweeter, sweeter than all tune,
> And still it cried "Apollo! young Apollo!
> The morning-bright Apollo! young Apollo!"
> I fled, it follow'd me, and cried "Apollo!" (490)

The failure of the music's rapture is not due to any aesthetic defect in the music, but to Clymene's belief that the artwork also puts her in a non-aesthetic relation. Her fellow Titan Oceanus gives this other relation a name when he declares that the impossible beauty of the new gods, "a power more strong in beauty," spells the Titans' doom. From this perspective, to feel the beauty of Apollo's music is also to suffer his domination. Beauty is power, power beauty. If "Ode on a Grecian Urn" acknowledges the failure of art to sustain life by equating beauty with truth, "Hyperion" accomplishes that failure by equating beauty with power.

Because Clymene is a listener *and* a singer, her rapture at Apollo's song is the sign of her own song's poverty. Thus the triumph of imaginary music—to keep the listener in a state of intense vitality—ensures its failure in the one act of listening the poem records. The music's sweetness turns to poison in Clymene's ear. Instead of the one-after-another/all-at-once notes, she begins to hear instead the taunting name: "Apollo! Young Apollo!"

Beauty is power, power beauty. And this proposition itself is not innocent. It plays a strategic role in the war between Titans and Olympians. Clymene is convinced that Apollo's beauty represents domination over her. And that conviction itself, by corrupting the beauty, enables her to avoid domination's full force. In the Titans' paranoid logic, to call beauty beauty is to suffer tyranny. To insist that the beauty of Apollo's music is political, just another move in the struggle between opposed groups, is to diminish both his beauty and his power.

But this critical strategy cuts both ways. The demystification of Apollo's beauty exacts a terrible price from the Titans. Keats depicts them in chains, in stasis. Apollo's music, as we have seen, promises to transform that stasis by fusing it with life. But the Titans refuse this gift. Clymene denies herself the joy of Apollo's perfect music as the sacrifice necessary to break that music's perfection. Her ear turns "rapturous hurried notes" into the words of a despotic enemy incessantly repeating his own name.

The emergence in this poem of the idea that beauty is power marks a victory for what will come to be known as disenchantment. Thus the critical perspective that will expose aesthetic pleasure as an insidious form of social power does not need to be added to the poem.[22] It is the Titans' own perspective. And the poem we have—Keats's poem—is the Titans' poem, Clymene's poem. It is not Apollo's poem. Apollo's brief, interrupted speech at the end of "Hyperion" reveals a mind utterly unaware of the power struggle the Titans think he is waging. Apollo is filled with simple wonder at his own immortality. There is a hint, as he "dies into life," that he is becoming his own ideal listener, the listener that Clymene refuses to be. But the poem breaks off after little more than a hundred lines of Apollo's speech.[23] Beauty is power. This is the message of the actual poem, closing like a fist around the ghost of the virtual.

# 2   THE ADDICTIVE IMAGE

TWO GENERAL APPROACHES to the relation of literature and science can be discerned in the criticism of the past decade. The first approach, canvassed briefly in my introduction, takes the reading, writing, and interpretation of literature to be the objects of scientific study. In their different ways, critics like Elaine Scarry, Lisa Zunshine, and Blakey Vermule use scientific models of cognition and perception to describe literature and literary experience. While this pioneering work has succeeded in placing the question of the relation of the humanities and science at the forefront of current debates, the particular form that relation tends to take in this work renders it of limited value going forward. Wendy Jones's recent *ELH* article exemplifies the problem when the author argues that Austen's *Emma* is "a text that demonstrates, through its representation of thoughts, feelings, and relationships, what neuroscience tells us about how the brain works" (317). In the aftermath of the Sokal hoax, this critical modesty perhaps has something to recommend it.[1] But humanists can be forgiven for failing to greet the prospect of so reductive a deferral to science with much enthusiasm.

The second recent approach to the relation of literature and science argues that literature shows us a gap in scientific knowledge, and an opening for a kind of knowledge peculiar to literary studies. Again, in its broadest form this idea is nothing new, and is at least as old as Keats's complaint that Newton unwove the rainbow. What's different is the nature of recent attempts to move past a traditional sense that literature and science are simply different and incompatible enterprises. Recent books by Barbara Maria Stafford and Steven Meyer seek to open a special place for literature and art in scientific discourse by pointing to a particular caesura in the scientific study of human life.

This gap is experience. What cognitive, biological, and neuroscientific descriptions of human thought and behavior leave out, according to these critics, is what it feels like to think and act. The quality of first-person experience, the special feeling of seeing a blue sky or tasting an apple or thinking of a friend, this is what is missing from scientific descriptions that could as easily apply to robots or zombies entirely devoid of the rich phenomenal world of living humans.[2] Literature, Meyers and Stafford suggest, potentially provides just the kind of rich description of experience that science has not (21–30, 198–203). If literary studies were to make good on this claim, then scientists would need to engage with knowledge originating in literature departments.

This approach is tantalizing. But problems quickly emerge. The question of whether and how science has missed some aspect of experience has bedeviled philosophy of mind for over three decades, yet good answers—and even the right questions—remain as elusive as ever. The basic reason for this confusion is not hard to see. If science can give an adequate functional account of human thought and behavior without any reference to what it feels like to think and act, then at what point does phenomenal experience actually affect thought and behavior? For some, like David Chalmers, the answer is never. For others, like Daniel Dennett or Alva Noe (though in rather different ways), the idea that phenomenal experience presents a unique challenge to philosophy and science is simply incoherent.

What Chalmers has famously called the "hard problem" of phenomenal experience immediately confronts any literary study claiming that literature grasps something about experience that science can't. Of course, there are many things literary studies can concern itself with that science does not—various kinds of cultural history for example—without anyone's thinking that science is missing anything. But at least part of what drives the current interest in the relation between literature and science is the perception of a "crisis" in the humanities, and the sense that it would be a good thing to establish the interdisciplinary value of the knowledge produced by literary scholars. Therefore it's important for critics like Meyers and Stafford to show that science should be interested in what literature contains. But the problem with arguing that science misses some aspect of ordinary experience is that once you've defined experience in such a way as to make it look as if science can't analyze it, you've also made it look as if it doesn't have any effects in the world. On literature, for example.[3]

And yet the idea that literature's special relation to experience can produce valid and scientifically relevant new knowledge has an intuitive appeal. The neglected insights of the tradition I have been exploring in this book may help us to make good on this intuition. Stafford and Meyer suggest that there is a rich world of experience going on all the time inside of us that science misses when it treats us like automatons, as if we think, act, and perceive automatically. But is science so wrong here? As we have seen, writers from Augustine to Shklovsky offer a rather different perspective. Most of the time, Shklovsky writes, we act, think, and perceive habitually. "If we examine the general laws of perception, we see that as it becomes habitual, it also becomes automatic. . . . Gradually, under the influence of this generalizing perception, the object fades away . . . life fades into nothingness. Automatization eats away at things, at clothes, at furniture" (4–5). Literature, for Shklovsky, doesn't show us a world of rich subjective experience that science misses. Most of the time we don't have this rich experience. By defeating the habit that turns us into machines, by defamiliarizing, literature creates a vivid phenomenal experience where none exists. Writing's operation is fundamentally transformative, not descriptive.

From this perspective, it is not that empiricism fails to account for vivid subjective experience and therefore ends up treating us as if we were machines. Empiricism is right, and the failure is not in science but in life. Most of the time we are indeed functioning more or less automatically. What needs to be corrected is not the scientific method but the human nervous system. And literature does this. Or at least it tries to. Through some miracle of art, the ideal work counters habituation. It's always new. In its vicinity, experience remains alive. Time doesn't touch it. The reader's nervous system remains suspended at the very first time, in all the "hard, gem-like" (Pater) richness and rarity of a real human experience.

This real human experience is not natural but—in Coleridge's word— "supernatural" (313). Defamiliarized perception is supernatural not in the sense of revealing another world, but in the sense of genuinely experiencing this world. This is the celebrated experience that, as recent critics and philosophers remind us, science leaves out when it produces descriptions of humans as bundles of automatic processes. It is in literature's supernaturalism—and not in the way it supposedly illustrates or describes the natural—that I propose to discover the most practical relation between literature and science.

Let's think a little longer about the ideal art object of the Romantic tradition we've been examining, this object that successfully counters habituation, that never gets old. Were we to find such a supernatural object, we might want to spend some time with it. Maybe even all our time. In *Dune*, Frank Herbert invents an imaginary "addictive" substance called "spice" (258). "Can you remember your first taste of spice?" one character asks another. "'It tasted like cinnamon.... But never twice the same,' he said. '... it presents a different face each time you take it'" (64).

Here the addictive substance is always new; no matter how many times it's encountered, it remains somehow always the first time. Herbert's description of spice is an instance of a way of representing addictive objects in literature that extends back at least to the early nineteenth-century interest in the supernatural qualities of the perception of novelty. Sometimes the arresting of subjective time occurs as an effect of ingesting the addictive object. Poe, in "A Tale of Ragged Mountains," writes that "morphine had its customary effect—that of enduing all the external world with an intensity of interest" (Quoted in Marcus Boon, 43). Rimbaud discovers a renewed vision by the "disordering of all the senses" wrought by alcohol or opium (6). And Proust describes the experience of being drunk as a suspension in the present (II).

The literary interest in the description of the striking effects of addictive substances is familiar. Less often noted is the curious divergence of these descriptions from empirical studies of the experiences of addicts, for whom a dulling and deadening of perception is a characteristic effect of narcotic and alcohol addiction on the sensorium.[4] Indeed, it is the addict's sense of the progressive failure of the addictive substance over time to deliver the desired effect that in part authorizes the description of addiction as a disease. If you spend all your money on a Ferrari, you have simply made what many will consider a bad choice. If you spend all your money on a series of Toyotas, always thinking that the next Toyota will drive like a Ferrari, then people may begin to think of you as having some kind of disease.

In any case, and for reasons that will shortly become clear, I think that texts concerned with the effects of consuming the addictive object mystify and displace the root of its fascination for literature. I think the logic of the literary interest in the addictive object is most clearly and fully expressed by that subset of works which attributes the time-transforming operation not to the effects of the ingested drug, but to the appearance of the drug itself. Thomas De Quincey's *Confessions of an English Opium Eater* is the urtext of this ekphrastic tradition. The perceived shape and color of the addictive object exerts a gravitational pull on De Quincey's prose, which compulsively returns to the image of the bottle of laudanum or the lump of opium. The source of this fascination with the image of the drug is the first time he encountered opium. "I feel a mystic importance attached to the minutest circumstances connected with the place and the time, and the man (if man he was) that first laid open to me the Paradise of Opium Eaters" (42–43). The druggist who sold him laudanum for the first time "has ever since existed in my mind as the beatific vision of an immortal druggist" (43).[5]

The circumstances and images associated with the first ingestion of the drug are for De Quincey supernatural in Coleridge's sense: they never get old. "It is so long since I first took opium, that if it had been a trifling incident in my life, I might have forgotten its date: but cardinal events are not to be forgotten" (42). The first perception of opium is "not forgotten," but neither is it quite remembered. Indeed, that first time is always present to De Quincey in the shape of the decanter of "ruby-colored laudanum" that he keeps always before him (68). The sensible surface of the addictive object is like a screen onto which the first time—in all its rich novelty—is continually projected.[6]

For De Quincey, the first encounter with the addictive object is "immortal" and inescapable. To encounter the addictive object is thus always to encounter it for the first time. The logic of addiction De Quincey discovers resonates through the many works inspired by his account. For example, in his 2008 work *Night of the Gun* David Carr writes that "Every addict is formed in the crucible of the memory of that first hit. Even as the available endorphins attenuate, the memory is *right there*" (19). The drug makes the "memory" "present" "for years on end." Here again the addictive object performs an operation for which the term *memory*—with which we typically describe the subjective experience of past time—isn't quite adequate. The religious terms De Quincey applies to the strange persistence of the first time—*beatific vision, mystic importance*—have greater phenomenological accuracy.

In an extraordinary passage, De Quincey uses the supernatural mechanism of the addictive object as a pattern for his description of art. Consider his representation of the experience of attending the opera: "A chorus . . . of elaborate harmony, displayed before me, as in a piece of arras work, the whole of my past life—not, as if recalled by an act of memory, but as if present and incarnated in the music" (51). Here De Quincey adapts the language he used in his description of laudanum to describe an artistic form that makes the past new.[7]

In the juxtaposition of De Quincey's description of art with his description of opium, two dimensions of addiction—addiction as disease and addiction as literary topic—come into contact. On the one hand, De Quincey's modeling of the experience of artistic form on the experience of addictive form shows how the addictive object comes to serve as the image of an ideal art. Laudanum remains always new to the addict; the object manifests the capacity to suspend time, to counter the automatism of habit, and to trigger an intense and enduring perceptual experience. If, as Shelley writes, "poetry makes familiar objects be as if they were not familiar," then poetry would do well to study the addictive object.[8]

De Quincey's text—in the context of the Romantic aesthetics which he studied and espoused—thus suggests that an aesthetic desire is at least part of what motivates literature's intense engagement with addiction over the past two centuries. But the *Confessions* show us something else. By modeling aesthetic experience on addicted experience, De Quincey also intimates that an aesthetic problem lies at the heart of addiction as a disease. Part of what makes De Quincey so susceptible to the "spell" of opium is the way that the image itself remains always somehow suspended at the "immortal" first encounter. Literature wants to become like an addictive object; this impossible desire in turns reveals something about addiction.

In what follows I will take the structure of obsession in Nabokov's *Lolita* as my central example in arguing that in the relation between these two features of addiction lies the model for a new relation between literature and science. After describing the picture projected by Nabokov's efforts, I will engage in depth with what many literary and cultural critics have seen as a more obvious interdisciplinary context for understanding addiction: the theory of the capitalist commodity. The result of this engagement will be to present the terms of my own interdisciplinarity, and to prepare the way for *Lolita*'s illumination of one of addiction's key philosophical and neuroscientific problems.

Literature—from *The Confessions* through *Dune*—takes a particular perspective on addiction. This perspective, as I've begun to argue, is shaped by the desire for the truly effective work of art—the work that will destroy habit and arrest experiential time. But what that perspective reveals, in terms of the specific features of addiction that literature's desire picks out, also has a potential extra-literary interest. In taking the addictive object as a model for its own ideal form, literature produces scientifically valuable knowledge. It produces this knowledge in a way inassimilable to the claims and methods of the two critical positions surveyed above. Those positions are based on a conception of what literature does. Seen from Zunshine's position, literature exercises the faculties for perceiving complex relations that cognitive science has revealed in the brain. Seen from Stafford's, literature captures the rich everyday experiences that science has completely missed. In the following I will argue that literature produces its most valuable knowledge not by what it does, but as a by-product of its failure to do what is impossible.

※

For Humbert Humbert, the sight of nymphets never becomes automatic. As for most people, for Humbert the encounters with most categories of objects in the world—cars, plates, houses, men, women—fail to rouse any intense experience. They are drearily familiar. The nymphet, however, is immune to this indifference. The nymphet is a category of objects in the world—the bodies of certain girls between nine and fourteen—with which Humbert is obsessed, or, in his word, by whom he is "bewitched" (16).

The source of the perceptual intensity that radiates from the image of the nymphet is the first nymphet he ever encountered, Annabel, with whom he fell in love as a child on the Riviera. In a striking image, Humbert compares his first love for Annabel to a "wound," and declares that something about that early encounter left a "poison in the wound" so that "the wound remained ever open" (18). The sensations aroused by that first encounter remain exposed, on the surface. For Humbert, to see a nymphet is always somehow the first time he ever sees a nymphet. Therefore, as he writes of the nymphet he first encounters in middle age, "in a certain magic and fateful way Lolita began with Annabel" (14).

Here is Humbert's first encounter with Lolita:

> I was still walking behind Mrs. Haze through the dining room when, beyond it, there came a sudden burst of greenery—"the piazza," sang out my leader, and then, without the least warning, a blue sea-wave swelled under my heart and, from a mat in a pool of sun, half-naked, kneeling, turning about on her knees, there was my Riviera love peering at me over dark glasses.
>
> It was the same child—the same frail, honey-hued shoulders, the same silky supple bare back, the same chestnut head of hair. A polka dotted black kerchief tied around her chest hid from my aging ape eyes, but not from the gaze of young memory, the juvenile breasts I had fondled one immortal day. (39)

The day of his first sexual encounter with Annabel is an "immortal day" in the same sense that De Quincey's first experience of opium is "immortal." The very first time Humbert perceives a nymphet is literally present—in all its vividness and intensity—in the tenth, the twentieth, the ten-thousandth time he perceives a nymphet. The literal presence of the first time in his middle-aged encounter is "magical." This adjective is not isolated. Humbert continually refers to Lolita, and to nymphets in general, as "demons," as "immortal," as "fairies."

Humbert's problem is not psychological, but magical. He rejects the psychoanalytic explanations of his disease that his description of his first love as an open wound might otherwise seem to solicit. "Psychoanalysts wooed me with pseudoliberations of pseudolibidoes," he writes (18). What is the content of this distinction between psychology and magic? "The idea of time plays ... a magic part in the matter" (17). The magic involves the experience of temporal suspension that characterizes his experience of nymphets.[9]

We might contrast the suspension of time in Humbert's experience of a magic wound with the psychoanalytic theory of trauma. Trauma, as Cathy Caruth defines it in her celebrated study, is a wound that is "experienced too soon, too unexpectedly, to be fully known and is therefore not available to consciousness until it imposes itself again, repeatedly, in the nightmares and repetitive actions of the survivor" (4). Caruth's understanding of the persistence of a past experience in time—in keeping with the source of that understanding in Freud's *Beyond the Pleasure Principle*—relies on the concept of the unconscious. "The space of unconsciousness is, paradoxically, precisely what preserves the event in its literality" (17–18). The centrality of the unconscious to psychoanalytic accounts of trauma has also been important to scholarship on the interest of modernist art in shock effects, from Benjamin's "On Some Motifs in Baudelaire" (*Illuminations*) to Brigid Doherty's exploration of Dada's mimicking of "the automatic movements of shock reactions" (114).

Humbert's open wound is not the unconscious "impact" of an event that manifests in "automatic" repetition behaviors. This is why he mocks the psychoanalytic proposal to "release [him] from the 'subconscious' obsession" by consciously replaying the initial train of events with Lolita (167). He does replay the initial scene of wounding, and it does not release him. The unconscious plays no role in Humbert's condition. His problem is not a hiccup in the blind processes underlying experience and behavior. What is preserved by Humbert's disease is an intensely conscious experience, an experience immune to the automatizing effects of habit.

Humbert presents the unusual conscious intensity of his perception of nymphets as a cause of his repetitive nymphet-seeking behaviors. This is crucially different from psychoanalytic accounts of obsession and compulsion and, as we shall see, from all accounts of addiction that rely primarily on automatic processes.[10] The perceptual intensity of the nymphet for Humbert—brought about by the supernatural persistence of the first encounter in all subsequent encounters—is not the effect of an unconscious or automatic attraction to nymphets.

Indeed, the perceptual intensity of the nymphet's image is—to a degree—independent of the sexual satisfaction that the image represents. Humbert desires nymphets, and he has sex with nymphets. But what strikes him first on seeing Lolita—and what constitutes the "magical" element of that perception—is that Lolita is the first nymphet he ever sees. He knows she is not. And yet he looks at her, and she is. The magic of the image itself—of the first-time perceptual freshness that is supernaturally preserved in it—constitutes an allure, a source of fascination, conceptually and experientially distinct from the fascination that accrues to the image qua object of sexual desire.

We can go farther. For all the pleasure that Humbert takes in his sexual relations with nymphets, there is at least as much guilt, shame, risk, and regret. The feature that makes his involvement with nymphets an obsession and an addiction—and causes him to speak of himself as diseased and bewitched—lies in the repeated resumption of predatory sexual behavior towards underage girls despite his knowledge of the cost to his self-esteem, and the risk that lies in violating ethical and legal standards. In the long passage quoted above we see the description of the perception that precipitates one such resumption. In it, his eyes do not light upon a body he recognizes as an object of sexual desire but knows he shouldn't touch. In such a case, we might imagine, it would be possible to quickly shift his gaze away, or to continue staring. The recognition of Lolita as a desirable body would present this kind of choice, and he would emerge from it either as having resisted that desire or as a victim of what Donald Davidson calls "weakness of the will."[11] But the spectacle of Lolita's half-naked body does not immediately confront him with this choice. Instead of recognizing Lolita as a sexual object, something quite magical happens. He suddenly finds himself gazing fascinated at the body of an attractive girl for the first time.

Humbert is attracted to the bodies of underage girls. No doubt in every form of sexual attraction a wide variety of memories, associations, biological drives, or social pressures are compounded. But something out of the ordinary is at work here. Exactly how much this extra element accounts for in Humbert's behavior, and whether or how much it qualifies his responsibility for his actions, are not questions that can be pursued any great distance when confining ourselves to the text of the novel. For example, we may think that the magic that endows the girl's body with this extra fascination might, by postponing his recognition of her as the object of his dangerous desire until he has already given himself over to staring at her for several seconds, weaken his resistance to indulging that desire. Imagine that you are on a diet, and suddenly a cookie catches your eye. Your resolve to resist is strong. But before you can look away something magical happens to the cookie that causes you to take a much closer look at it. Then, as you awaken to your situation and find yourself staring at the cookie, your desire for cookies and your resolution against indulging that desire again rises to the surface of your consciousness. Is your resolve now weaker?

Maybe, but maybe not. We might think that this perceptual anomaly wouldn't change the basic situation in its fundamentals. We might also feel that Humbert simply has a very weak resolve against indulging his desires, and that the basic human and social requirement of the subject of such a desire is total resistance. These are interesting questions, but the novel gives us no good grounds for deciding them. What *Lolita* does make clear is that the magic perceptual anomaly that attaches to certain young girls is something extra added to Humbert's sexual desires, however strong or perverse. There is a difference between seeing a desirable body and seeing the very first body one ever desired.

What difference does this difference make? What kind of animal is Humbert? Is he primarily a man who desires girls between nine and fourteen, or primarily a man who literally sees the first girl he ever loved in certain girls between nine and fourteen? The facts of Humbert's case allow us to take either feature as taxonomically primary. But the primary literary interest—and, as I will suggest, the primary scientific interest—attaches to the latter feature of his condition. The image that bewitches Humbert has a quality that no other image has for him. Thus at the heart of Humbert's disorder is the experience of an image.

In other words, his disease is aesthetic. Furthermore, it is aesthetic in the Kantian sense explored in the last chapter. The novel's distinction between the attraction of the nymphet's image as an instance of never-fading novelty and the attraction of that image as a symbol of sexual fulfillment exactly replicates the Kantian distinction between disinterested and interested attention. Humbert's book would very much like to catch his aesthetic disease. In its final sentences Humbert—who, like Proust's narrator, is a character in the book of which he is also the author—writes of his reason for wanting to remain alive long enough to finish his memoir.[12] "One wanted H. H. to exist at least a couple of months longer, so as to have him make you live in the minds of later generations. I am thinking of aurochs and angels, the secret of durable pigments, prophetic sonnets, the refuge of art. And this is the only immortality you and I may share, my Lolita" (309).

Critics have long recognized the relation of the aesthetic to Humbert's obsession with nymphets. Sharon Cameron writes of how Humbert's "words coax the objects of his descriptions—much as he coaxes the little girl—out of the dull plane of ordinary temporality and into the immutable radiance, the soul-time of that impossible love" (21). In some of the most interesting recent criticism, this has been discussed in an ethical register, as the process of aestheticization that transforms the person Lolita into the timeless image. Thus Susan Mooney discovers a "self-serving solipsism" in the process by which Humbert sees only his own past in the other's body (121). Leland Durantaye argues that Humbert's failure to encounter Lolita as an other should be understood and condemned in ethical terms. He writes, "We are led astray because we are offered the wrong optic through which to see *Lolita—the optic of art—* and we are too eager to be worthy of it to suggest that it should not here apply" (321). Humbert's success in creating artistically successful images of Lolita threatens to blind us to the fact that "the artist cannot live in the world as he lives in the world of words" (325).

All of these critics think that Humbert's artistic skill gives Lolita's body a power that it either cannot or should not have in real life.[13] Thus the ethical denunciation of Humbert is similar to Benjamin's denunciation of fascism in "The Work of Art in the Age of Mechanical Reproduction" (*Illuminations*): Humbert, like Goebbels, has illicitly transformed life with the power of art, and has applied artistic standards to real situations. I want to suggest that exactly the opposite occurs here. The artist—whether Humbert or Nabokov—cannot do in the world of words what the image of a nymphet does to Humbert. Under cover of a cautionary tale about the evils of mixing art and life, the novel conceals its own inability to attain the status of art as it defines it. Art here is held to a standard drawn from life and found wanting. Compared with what Humbert's disease does with the image of Lolita for him, his own descriptions of her for us must appear very weak indeed.

The evocations of Lolita are at the stylistic center of the book, and are presented in some of the most elaborately and richly figured sentences of the career of perhaps the most celebrated postwar prose stylist. "Lolita, light of my life, fire of my loins. My sin, my soul" (9). "Her honey-brown body, with the white negative image of a rudimentary swimsuit patterned against her tan, presented to me its pale breastbuds" (125). "She crept into my waiting arms, radiant, relaxed, caressing me with her tender, mysterious, impure, indifferent, twilight eyes—for all the world like the cheapest of cheap cuties. For that is what nymphets imitate—while we moan and die" (120).

These sentences are parasitic on Humbert's disorder in two ways. First, the descriptions are always cast as Humbert's attempt to make us see what he sees, to reproduce for the reader the magical effect Lolita's image has for him. Second, what Humbert sees is described as the effect of a disorder that renders certain images immune from the effects of time. And at key moments, instead of attempting to *show* us Lolita as Humbert sees her, the prose is forced to *tell* us that for Humbert, to encounter this image is always to encounter it for the first time. "You have to be an artist and a madman . . . in order to discern at once, by ineffable signs . . . the little deadly demon among the wholesome children" (17). Here, in the distance between how Humbert says Lolita's image works for him, and how the image of Lolita on the page works for us, we can measure the distance of Humbert's—and Nabokov's—art from its goal.

The relation of Nabokov to his most famous character is a vexed critical question.[14] But I think we have grounds for believing their views of art to be identical. In an interview, Nabokov leaves no doubt that Humbert's desire for art to achieve immortality in the sense of preserving an experience without time is also his own. Here is Nabokov's hierarchy of being: "Time without consciousness—lower animal world; time with consciousness—man; consciousness without time—some still higher state" (cited in Alexandrov, 25). The achievement and dissemination of this "higher state" is the goal of art, and Nabokov aims at creating "consciousness without time" in his work. But the idea that he actually achieves this as a reliable effect of his prose cannot withstand a moment's scrutiny. Vladimir Alexandrov's otherwise admirable study verges on the ridiculous when attempting to describe Nabokov's artistic success. Because the novels are so complexly patterned, Alexandrov writes, they "confront the reader with having to pay attention to the text as closely as Nabokov indicates is necessary in order to achieve the level of consciousness that underlies timelessness" (40).

This is not to deny that the novel succeeds under some definitions of artistic success. It is simply to deny that it succeeds under Nabokov's definition.

In the object of Humbert's addiction—the image that never grows old, that is immune to the automation of habit—Nabokov sets up an impossible goal for writing. Literature's power to renew our perception of the world, often in life-changing ways, is well-documented, and is surely familiar to many readers from personal experience.[15] But it is not difficult to see how even the most powerful of such reading experiences fail to reach Nabokov's goal. The transformative reading experience—the experience from which the reader looks up from the book at a new world—may often be initially accompanied by the perceptual intensity that attaches to novelty. At a minimum, the images and sentences of the interesting new work itself are new. In the best cases, those images act as an interface with the material world that gives it a new, defamiliarized vividness.

But as writers from Kant to Proust have seen, almost at once that sensation is changing. It quickly ceases to be a matter of perceptual vividness and intensity. After reading the transformative work, one thinks about the world in different ways. One writes differently. One considers the relations between things in a different light. The reading experience as transformative event becomes embedded in various social, literary, historical, economic, psychological, and sexual processes that come to determine the nature of that transformation.[16] This embedding is productive. As an event becomes embedded and entangled in ongoing discourses, one can say something about it, insert it in history. Nabokov's importance to an individual reader, like his importance in various literary historical accounts, comes to rely less on a moment of perceptual intensity than on the relation between his text and various other texts or discourses. Thus, in saying that a text is rich and that we return to it many times, we are like Swann returning to the sonata after it has lost its magic. Richness now refers to semantic richness, to the fact that in it we find new meanings, and new relations between old meanings. If, like Swann, we discover traces of our first impressions, they are likely to be in the form of a pale, distant, and weak nostalgia which seems unable to support any attribution of great value.

On the other hand, what Nabokov aims at when he reaches for "consciousness without time" is the indefinite extension of the novelty of the image. Michael Wood, one of Nabokov's best readers, captures something crucial about Nabokov's practice when he describes the moments when time appears to stop in *Speak, Memory* as the "fulfillment of a wish in dreamland" (89).[17] Some measure of the supernatural quality of this state is provided in Augustine's *Confessions*, when he imagines heaven as a world immune from habit-formation. Secular critics who, like Shklovsky, think it possible for art to create such a heaven don't imagine that immortal novelty could be achieved by a single work, but consider it rather the work of the unfolding history of art, as it moves from one new form to another.

Speaking from my own experience as a reader, I can testify that the first time I read *Lolita* was a vivid and intense experience. As I have returned to the text several times over a decade or so, the complexity and semantic richness of the images provide new matter for thought. As I read more books, my sense of the relation of those images to images in other texts has expanded. In addition, a certain distant glory shines from some of what I take to be the more powerful images, a kind of aftershock of their intense initial freshness. So the book endures in my life as both an object of intellectual interest and of a kind of nostalgia. Seen from a broader, cultural perspective, *Lolita* does seem likely to achieve a genuine immortality of the kind classically exemplified by Shakespeare's sonnets. The sonnets are still being read. Shakespeare's art is a successful technology for making people want to preserve his texts. It seems plausible that Nabokov's art will be met with some degree of the same success. If *Lolita* is immortal, it is immortal in the natural sense of a preserved object, not in the supernatural sense of a preserved life. But for Nabokov, the measure of art's immortality is its success as a technology for countering experiential time by enabling the repetition of a vivid impression across chronological time. For myself, I can confidently say that if his novel were a successful example of such a technology, I would have read it several thousand times more than I have.

·

The addictive object—De Quincey's laudanum, Nabokov's nymphet—constitutes a special kind of referent for writing. This referent opens a hole in the practice and reception of literature, a hole through which we see writing as a bottomless desire to defeat time. This hole might seem as if it is the least likely place to ground a claim for literature's special institutional authority. What is the value of wanting the impossible?

We can begin by rehearsing the special structure the writers examined above attribute to the perception of the addictive object. 1) For the addict, the addictive object has a special perceptual intensity. 2) This intensity is of a particular kind: the intensity of a novel object. No matter how many times it is seen, the object always looks new. 3) The writers describe this effect as the persistence of the way the object appeared the first time it was ever encountered. 4) The sexual or physiological pleasure the image of the object represents is conceptually and experientially distinct from the curiously persistent novelty of that image. Proceeding from these four points we can, I think, add a fifth that seems implied by them. 5) This curious perceptual feature of the addictive object may constitute a distinct cause of addiction. It may to some degree account for the persistent return to the addictive object after it has been renounced.

As I have argued, the features of the addictive object enumerated above are particularly salient for writers because they are also features of the ideal work of art. Of all the many facets of addiction, the artistic ambitions of Nabokov and De Quincey cause them to pick out and to dwell on *these* particular features. In doing so, as I will now show, they discover something that is useful for the scientific effort to understand addiction. This is something that scientists have not yet seen, but that is supported by scientific evidence.

Before proceeding to present this evidence, I need first to clarify the principles of my interdisciplinary engagement. Fortunately, the critical tradition of writing about addiction offers an especially vivid contrast to my approach, and a consideration of this tradition's key moves will enable me to more clearly present my own. For examples of this approach, we need look no farther than some of De Quincey's most distinguished recent readers. Jerome Christensen, Margaret Russett, Alina Clej, and Sanjay Krishnan interpret De Quincey's addiction in such a way as to render it homologous with economic phenomena. In this criticism, as in literary and cultural studies as a whole, there is a strong and a weak claim for the relation of addiction and capitalism. The weak claim is that the context of consumer capitalism broadly shapes the discourses surrounding addiction. Perhaps the best version of this approach is Eve Sedgwick's essay "Epidemics of the Will." Sedgwick compellingly argues that the tendency—notable in 1990s popular culture—to call an increasingly wide range of activities "addictions," is caused by paradoxes inherent in the discourses surrounding free choice. If I am continually told that I am free, then I may tend to react to evidence that my choices are constrained by pathologizing the constraint, rather than viewing it more rationally as a normal consequence of a social situation in which individual choice is always circumscribed by a wide variety of factors.

Part of the persuasiveness of Sedgwick's argument about the tendency to expand the label "addiction" is her unwillingness to take the further step of suggesting that addiction is an artifact of capitalism. But critics like Marc Redfield do take this additional step, and from noticing that the way writers represent addictive objects in some respects resembles the way literary critics have traditionally represented commodities, imply or explicitly state that addiction is a mode of commodity fetishism. It is worth analyzing this move at some length. I believe it to be representative of a mode of interdisciplinarity central to the criticism of the past three decades, the untenability of which motivates my own approach to Nabokov and De Quincey's ekphrasis of the addictive object. In describing in some detail the nature of these critics' specific engagement with economic questions, I will therefore be concerned with raising general questions about the relation between literary studies and other disciplines.

The plausibility of critics' treatment of addiction in terms of commodity fetishism stems from the ubiquity that commodity theory enjoys in the discipline.[18] This theory, which enters literary studies through Lukacs and Adorno and is then refined and circulated by Jameson's influential work, purports to show that the commodity's appeal is not a matter of subjective choice but an objective social phenomenon. According to the marxist economics on which these critics draw, the commodity derives its value from the alienated labor that composes it. People come to believe the commodity's value inheres in its properties, but this value is in fact nothing but their own objectified work. This mistake is systematically generated by a system of productive relations that severs the living connection between worker and product.

Thus according to this theory, consumer choice is "objective" in a much stronger sense than that we intend when we speak of a subject shaped and constrained by various social, cultural, and economic forces. For commodity theory, consumer choice is, as Horkheimer and Adorno put it, produced in the same way and through the same process as the objects of that choice (114–18). It is important to distinguish this strong sense of commodity fetishism—as an allure produced by the structure of productive relations—from the various analyses of the ways commodity design, social norms, or advertising solicit the consumer's desire. What I say below applies only to the strong view of the commodity's pull as a compulsion irresistible to subjects because ultimately nonsubjective in nature. If one believes the strong version of commodity theory, it makes perfect sense to think of the irresistible lure of the addictive object as a species of the commodity form.

But why should anyone believe this? Commodity theory as practiced by writers from Adorno and Lukacs to Jameson and David Harvey is unintelligible without reference to the classical labor theory of value, which describes a commodity's value in terms of the labor that goes into it.[19] It is only by believing that labor is the source of value that one can describe the commodity's allure as the objective social consequence of alienated or reified labor, as opposed to the complex result of constrained choice. But the consensus about the labor theory of value among social scientists is that it is unworkable, and this consensus is nearly a century old. The labor theory is controversial in exactly the sense that evolution is controversial: the controversy is almost entirely restricted to those without an understanding of the discipline or its history.[20] But in fact this analogy is inexact, because while proponents of "intelligent design" are often eager to debate the findings of academic biologists, in those departments in which artifacts of the labor theory still enjoy plausibility—mostly literature departments—its proponents rarely attempt to defend it or to acknowledge its explanatory flaws. There is thus no real controversy surrounding the labor theory or the commodity theory that it supports. In fact, the last serious attempt to debate it was carried out by the "analytical marxism" movement of the eighties. Jon Elster, G. A. Cohen, and Erik Olin Wright—among others—sought to rehabilitate marxism as social science. They did this by debating the labor theory of value and distinguishing those aspects of marxism intelligible without it—like the theory of exploitation and the critique of imperialism—from those aspects that are not—like the theory of the commodity fetish.

To get a sense of the debate, consider just one technical example. A common hedge against one of the labor theory's more obvious explanatory weaknesses is the concept of "abstract" or "socially necessary" labor. This is meant to explain how a television I spend a year making in my basement will be worth much less than a television Sony makes in a fraction of the work-hours. By arguing that the relevant measure of value is not actual labor but "socially necessary" labor—the labor performed by skilled workers on adequate equipment—some writers sought to show that despite appearances, value is still ultimately rooted in labor. John Roemer, as part of his influential attempt to rescue a marxist sense of exploitation as a useful social scientific concept, points out that the only way to calculate the "socially necessary labor" in capitalist production is through recourse to the price system, a fact which undermines the claim that labor determines price (99).[21]

This debate made relatively little impact in academia, for the simple reason that the labor theory had long ceased to be something anyone wished to defend. Those literary critics who made commodity theory a key part of their intellectual repertoire, and who could be expected to take up their fellow-marxists' challenge, took little notice. This fact highlights a crucial feature of the mode of interdisciplinarity that reigns in the field. To understand this feature, I will borrow a key concept from Fredric Jameson. In essays first published in the early 1980s, and later expanded in his seminal *Postmodernism* a decade later, Jameson adapts Kevin Lynch's idea of cognitive mapping to describe the way that capitalism prevents people from understanding their position in the global economy. And the idea of a failed cognitive map turns out to be a good way to describe his book.

Jameson wants to map the value and status of his descriptions of capitalism with respect to the variety of competing knowledges produced by the modern research university. A single example from the chapter of *Postmodernism* titled "Economy" will serve to illustrate how he goes about it. Here he wants to attack the sunny view of the marketplace of neoclassical economics, which sees economic activity in terms of the utility maximizing choices of self-transparent individuals. What Jameson wants to do is to bring the insights of one discipline, literary and cultural criticism, to bear on the conventional wisdom of another discipline, economics. Developments at the time of Jameson's writing provide a good example of how this can work. At that time, insights drawn from the field of experimental psychology were being successfully used to demolish the foundations of neoclassical economics. Milton Friedman, godfather of conservative free market economics, had famously declared that neoclassicism's description of human choice didn't need to be empirically proven. By empirically *dis*proving these claims, Daniel Kahneman and others persuaded many people of the weakness of the conceptual supports of neoclassical microeconomics. Analogous dynamics are visible today, in the way that the market disasters of recent years have provided evidence that left economists and political scientists are now attempting to use to radically revise mainstream macroeconomics.

Let's see how Jameson's attack on neoclassical economics compares with the program sketched above. After briefly quoting Gary Becker's description of the production of commodities, Jameson exclaims: "What immediately leaps to the eye, therefore, is the paradox—of the greatest symptomatic significance for the Marxian theoretical tourist—that this most scandalous of all market models is in reality a production model!" (267) In referring to a production model, Jameson refers to the idea that the value of things derives from the labor that goes into their production. To produce a plausible defense of the labor theory would be an accomplishment on the level of that which gained Kahneman a Nobel Prize. But Jameson is more modest. He doesn't defend the labor theory. Instead, he claims that his opponent is secretly committed to it. In effect, Jameson goes on the attack by attributing his own low-prestige theory to his opponent.[22]

As a model of the interdisciplinary value of literary criticism's understanding of capitalism, this underwhelms. First, no one familiar with neoclassicism could take seriously the idea that it harbors some covert commitment to the labor theory of value. But second, and more importantly, despite the power and brilliance of many of Jameson's readings of artworks, his understanding of capitalism here is not in fact drawn from literature or art. Throughout his discussion, economic theory is introduced at key moments in order to interpret literature. This economic theory is, to be sure, quite different from the kind of left economic theory found in most social science departments. But dropping literature into a context defined by this low-prestige theory has not served to produce more robust, defensible, or plausible versions of the theory.

And yet, while literature is not essential to the *content* of the understanding of capitalism here, it does turn out to be central to the *status* of this understanding. It as if the imaginative, virtual, and creative dimensions of literature are repressed at one level only to return at another. Literature is understood to reflect its historical situation, but this situation is described using models that the critic either cannot or will not defend in an interdisciplinary context. Thus the critic finds himself hard-pressed to convince anyone outside the literature department that he has produced valuable descriptions of actual capitalism. So Jameson and his successors produce virtual capitalisms after all. This virtuality has a powerful allure, in the autonomy it affords criticism with respect to other disciplines.[23] But unlike Nabokov's or De Quincey's virtual images, this kind of virtuality fails to produce valuable new knowledge.

This situation, I believe, is part of what motivates the turn to science surveyed at the outset of this chapter. Stung by the low prestige of literary scholarship produced on the Jamesonian model, increasing numbers of critics have undertaken a reversal of the stance I've been exploring, and seek to apply what they take to be scientific disciplines' authoritative models of cognition and behavior to literary texts. A study of addiction in literature consonant with the approach manifest in works like Zunshine's or Vermule's would begin by selecting one of the competing scientific descriptions of addiction and then showing how a writer like De Quincey reflects that description. But while these definitions emerge from an epistemology rather stronger than Jameson's, this approach has perhaps even more dangerous flaws.

First, it would be wrong to oppose the critical reliance on an indefensible commodity theory to the iron-clad solidity of a scientific definition of addiction. Scientists disagree on the salient features of addiction, as well as on such basic questions as whether it is a single disease or a group of related disorders, or the degree to which it has social or environmental causes as opposed to genetic causes. The scientific study of addiction is still in the early stages. Cognitive science-based approaches to literature have been criticized for taking often controversial scientific claims at face value, in their zeal to begin applying science to writing. In addition, as I argued at the outset of this chapter, slavish devotion to scientific models forecloses the possibility that literary studies might generate new knowledge of its own.

I think we can fashion a meaningful engagement with scientific research on addiction while avoiding the pitfalls associated with much of the current scientifically inflected criticism. Obsessed with art, De Quincey and Nabokov discover an aesthetic problem at the heart of addiction. Without cutting literary study off from other disciplines or simply applying an extradisciplinary model, I propose to bring literature into relation with the scientific study of addiction by testing this discovery.

※

Where is the scientific study of addiction in 2011, and where has it been? The earliest research programs assumed that addiction is driven by the pleasure given by the consumption of the addictive object. But as D. H Lende writes:

> More recently, a new neurological approach to the role of brain systems in drug abuse has emphasized not the rewards that drugs produce, but how drugs affect the motivations and incentives that individuals experience vis-à-vis drugs.... In other words, these theories have emphasized drug seeking over drug taking, proposing that wanting and drug seeking are central components of addictive behavior. ("Wanting and Drug Use," 102)[24]

Addiction cannot, scientists feel, be adequately explained with reference to the pleasurable effects of the consumed object. Indeed, habitual cigarette smokers or heroin users frequently report no pleasure in using, but simply the absence of the pain of withdrawal. In addition, what has seemed to many to be the key feature of addiction—the persistent return to the addictive object after giving it up—could not be well explained by the early models. By assuming that the pleasurable effects of the object explain the addict's obsession with it, research had explained away what is now felt to be the central feature of addiction. What does the addict see in the addictive object? The perception of the object before it is ingested has increasingly displaced the effects of the object after it is ingested as the focus of study. Over the past fifteen years, much research has been focused on the role of "cues" associated with the addictive object in attracting and holding the attention of the addict.

Upon entering a room, a smoker, even one who has been abstinent for some time, will tend to fixate on cigarettes, cigarette packs, and lighters. This over-attention to drug cues has often been characterized in terms of classical conditioning. The drug cue is a conditioned stimulus that becomes paired with drug use and consequently acquires physiological and behavioral relevance as a precursor to drug ingestion.[25] On this model, the smoker's attention is drawn to the cigarette because he associates it with the anticipated pleasure of smoking.

But in many cases, the addict's interest in drug cues reflects an intrinsic fascination with the circumstances of the drug use itself. A simple example will illustrate this point. Smokers attempting to quit often find themselves staring at packages of cigarettes. They will sometimes express an urge merely to hold or look at a cigarette. When reminded of their resolve to quit by a friend, these smokers might say, "But I don't want to smoke a cigarette, I just want to hold one." At this point the friend will probably laugh, judging that what the smoker really wants to do is to smoke the cigarette, not to look at it. And indeed, if given the cigarette to hold and look at closely, much of the time the erstwhile ex-smoker will relapse.

But Nabokov's and De Quincey's explorations of the perceptual features of the addictive object suggest we may want to take the smoker who just wants to look at the cigarette at her word. Perhaps the smoker really does find something compelling about the way the cigarette looks, independent of its status as a representation of the pleasure of smoking. While this phenomenon remains understudied, accounts of drug use and addiction in humans and animals reveal similar episodes of intense interest in drug cues, often without corresponding expectations of drug rewards. In these circumstances, drug-addicted individuals experience a persistent absorption in environments or cues associated with past drug use. One study describes compulsive crack cocaine foraging behavior ("chasing" or "geeking") in addicts who have no expectation of finding lost fragments of the drug.[26] A study of drug use rituals similarly suggests that drug cues and paraphernalia take on added significance for drug users even in instances where those rituals delay the impact of taking the drug itself.[27] Nabokov and De Quincey suggest a model in which the addictive object has an attraction for addicts that is in important respects independent from both a desire to use and from what A. David Redish, Steve Jensen, and Adam Johnson's comprehensive recent survey of research on addiction calls a "robotic," automatic, habitual response to cues (424).

I certainly do not wish to deny the role of such purely habitual responses in addiction, a role which is supported by numerous studies. It seems clear that much addictive behavior can be adequately explained as the effect of unconscious processes, automatic actions triggered by the perception of cues. But I think there are compelling reasons for thinking that this is not the whole story, and for exploring the features picked out by the literary representation of addiction further. Humbert's or De Quincey's fascination with the look of the addictive object corresponds to neurophysiological studies that pair drug cues with increased levels of dopamine in the mesocortical limbic system. In the early 1990s, Terry Robinson and Kent Berridge developed the theory of "incentive salience" to describe the behavioral effects of the process by which drug cues become "marked" with dopamine in the brain. They suggest that the association between drug cues and drug use is caused not merely by the cues' relation to hedonic response, in which cues become associated with the pleasure derived from the drug itself, but rather by their independent influence on the perception of the addictive object ("The Neural Basis of Drug Craving" and "Parsing Reward"). Berridge and Robinson draw a distinction between "liking" a drug and "wanting" a drug, and argue that drug cues, not drug effects, make the object "wanted" by the addict. While accounts of motivation have typically paired liking with wanting, Berridge and Robinson suggest that these processes correspond to distinct neural substrates and are, in fact, dissociable in the laboratory ("Incentive Sensitization").

While the theory of incentive salience has been enormously influential, exactly what feature of addicts' experience is referred to by *wanting* has been unclear. Robinson and Berridge have attempted to clarify wanting in terms that are useful for my present purposes:

> [T]he process of incentive salience attribution . . . transforms the sensory features of ordinary stimuli or, more accurately, the neural and psychological representations of stimuli, so that they become *especially salient stimuli, stimuli that "grab the attention."* ("Incentive Sensitization," 352, emphasis added)

Drug cues "grab the attention" because they release dopamine. Indeed, one study reports that, for cocaine addicts, "cocaine cues *by themselves* increase dopamine release" (Kotler et al., 251, emphasis added). Nabokov and De Quincey suggest, however, that another well-documented feature of dopamine release offers insight into the psychological processes that underlie addicts' experience of drug cues. I refer to dopamine's association with the experience of novelty.[28] A study of paranoid schizophrenic patients by Shitij Kapur, Romina Mizrahi, and Ming Li notes that "the dopamine system which under normal conditions is a mediator of context-driven novelty/salience in the psychotic state becomes a creator of aberrant novelty and salience" (59–61). This inappropriate marking results in patients reporting a subjective state characterized by fascination.

This link between dopamine and novelty suggests that the experience of the drug cue for the addict is a very particular kind of experience: the fascination of a novel object. If this is true, then the addict is someone for whom a certain class of objects in the world—objects associated with drug cues—never becomes familiar, never becomes dull, never loses the fascination that accrues to what is new. The association between dopamine release and drug cues is well established, as is the association between dopamine release and novelty. The literary image of addiction simply suggests that we put these pieces together. I suggest that doing so will bring out some important implications of Berridge and Robinson's work on drug cues. It may well offer a new way to characterize susceptibility to drug use as well as new avenues for drug treatment.

There are good scientific reasons to consider the addict's fascination with the always-novel way the addictive object looks as an important feature of addiction, and to design and implement studies that test this hypothesis. Indeed, from the perspective of the experiments undertaken by Berridge and Robinson, it seems as if this kind of study would constitute just a small, easy step. The peculiar obsessions of the literature of addiction may suggest promising new ways of making connections and drawing implications from existing scientific studies, but in fact the literary contribution is relatively modest. Although this kind of modesty is just the way things go in science and in those humanities fields—like philosophy—closest to science, literary intellectuals—like the writers they study—are far less comfortable with it. We like things to be a little more dramatic, even if at the risk of not having our claims about subjectivity, economics, politics, or science taken very seriously elsewhere. The argument advanced above—while having the benefit of being taken seriously by scientists—seems to do so at the cost of proposing only a small advance in the study of addiction.

But things are not as they seem. In fact, to take this additional step of studying the fascination that characterizes the perception of the addictive object would be to make a dramatic break with the scientific study of human behavior. Fascination is an experience. And if this particular perception of the cue is to have an effect on behavior, it will be as a result of its effect on experience. This is not the case with the existing scientific studies of addiction cues. In those studies, cues function *automatically*. All the thousands of subjects of Berridge's experiments have been rats. As I argued above, I take his work to imply that humans have a fascinating experience. But such an experience cannot be pursued in a framework where statements are restricted to what can be experimentally verified with rats. In a response to an earlier version of my argument, Redish, Jensen, and Johnson wrote that I "suggest that dopamine can drive increased attention, and that attention can drive motivational control. We note that temporal difference algorithms imply a shift in dopamine to cues predicting reward. These shifts occur in Pavlovian, instrumental, and habit systems" (464–65).

Redish and his collaborators think that the addict's brain identifies the dopamine released by perceiving the cue as predicting (with ultimately tragic consequences) a greater than usual reward. This form of novelty is quite different from the novelty associated with dopamine in the studies of schizophrenia noted above. From Redish's perspective, the benefit of thinking about the novelty of the cue in terms of its signaling greater than expected reward is that such a cue exerts an influence on behavior entirely automatically. The organism senses that there is to be a great reward from that object, and is automatically drawn to it. In this model, there is an automatic link between attention and "motivational control" that eviscerates the experiential feel of attention. There is no room here for the role possibly played by the intensely fascinating experience of novelty in the non-novel object.

The neuroeconomist Don Ross supplies another example of the way that scientific investigations of the role of novelty in addiction neglect experience. Ross argues that surprise and novelty are so important that "the intrinsic chemical properties of drugs are . . . distractions from the elementary nature of addiction" (143). For Ross, pathological gambling, with its simple expectation of surprise when the slot machine handle is pulled, is the purest form of addiction. But when Ross discusses how this surprise and novelty work, he makes it clear he has in mind an automatic process, not a conscious experience. The brain's reward system, he writes, "flag[s] novelty and provide[s] the 'go signal' to pursue it" (30). Apparently this go signal is something the addict isn't aware of. "We should not look for the surprises they [the drug cues] induce at the level of the person, but at the level of the reward system" (142). The addict's neurons get that fresh, first-time feeling. Not the addict. As Lende writes, what the science of addiction leaves out is "subjective experience" ("Addiction," 454).

What science misses, and what literature supplies, is a way of understanding the special role of experience. Science constructs a black-and-white picture of automatic processes, and literature colors experience back into the picture. This, of course, is a familiar kind of claim for the value of literature, and one of the recent critical approaches to the relation between literature and science surveyed at the outset of this chapter relies on it. But we must ask: just when is subjective experience relevant? Clearly—as Augustine, Coleridge, Shklovsky, and Nabokov see—not all the time. There are plenty of features of addiction, and of all other areas of human activity, where subjective experience is not necessary to explain behavior. Much of the time—perhaps even most of the time—we function more or less automatically. So it seems rather unfair to say that science has willfully ignored something—consciousness—that has a huge impact on things. Indeed, as I noted earlier, neuroscience and philosophy of mind have been hard put to identify a single area of human functioning where phenomenal consciousness makes a difference.

It will be useful to rehearse the broad outlines of this impasse. Over the past three decades, a large amount of work in philosophy of mind, neuroscience, and cognitive science has been devoted to the "hard problem" of phenomenal consciousness.[29] Thinkers have identified an aspect of human experience called qualia, referring to what it feels like to see, hear, taste, and touch. Philosophers like David Chalmers or Ned Block argue that what it feels like for an individual to see red, to take an often-used example, is distinct from the various behavioral, psychological, and social processes in which that perception is embedded. We can learn much about the experience of seeing red by learning about the psychological association of red with aggression, the cultural association of red with danger, or the way certain frequencies of light are processed in the eye, the optic nerve, and the brain. A description of these processes may even be one day sufficient to explain and predict the behavior and reactions of someone who sees red. But none of this will get us any closer to what it feels like to see red.

The mysterious first-person quality of the perception thus seems to float above scientific third-person descriptions. This way of framing the question of consciousness has made it appear as if consciousness is epiphenomenal, with no connections to other dimensions of human behavior or biology. Few have been happy with this state of affairs, or with the mind/matter dualism that it seems to imply. As I discussed above, some literary critics seem to see an opening for literature here, and argue that literature is able to provide descriptions of experience that science cannot. Of course, if the first person is the only way to access consciousness, then a poem will seem able to do what a brain-scanner cannot. But a bland statement like "I see red" will have exactly the same status in this regard as one of Keats's odes.

If we want to make a claim for the status of literary descriptions as *knowledge* of consciousness—as opposed to *expression* of consciousness—we face the same problem philosophy has faced for decades, a problem literary criticism has not yet fully come to terms with. How is consciousness related to the world, to behavior, to function? Thus far, attempts to identify a function for consciousness, to link it to some area of human behavior or function, have fallen short. The best attempts move forward by reframing the problem and giving up the mysteries of "what it feels like."[30]

Yet perhaps Nabokov suggests a way of making consciousness part of the story about addiction. It's not just that Humbert's awareness of Lolita is *different* from his awareness of Charlotte Haze, the house furnishings, or the suburban street: he is *more* aware of Lolita than of these other things. Part of the fascination he feels staring at Lolita is the feeling of awareness, of consciousness itself.[31] The scientist Bernard Baars has described consciousness as a "spotlight" of attention surrounded by a "fringe." This "spotlight" shines on the novel aspects of a given situation. Baars notices that the vast majority of the processes going on every instant in the human brain are unconscious, including much of the data streaming in from our senses. Why, he asks, is there this great discrepancy between what we're conscious of and what we're unconscious of? Given that 99 percent of what we do goes perfectly well without our being aware of it, why are we conscious of anything at all?

The answer, Baars suggests, lies in the fact that much of the brain's activity is carried out by bundles of neurons working in isolation from each other. We become conscious of something when all the different parts of the brain need access to the same bit of information. A new or unexpected situation, for example, for which the brain lacks an automated response, calls for consciousness in a way that a familiar one does not. When the spotlight of attention falls on that unfamiliar action, event, or perception, the information becomes available for all the brain's capacities, which Baars compares to an audience sitting in a darkened theater. The various brain capacities that may be needed to deal with the situation thus get access to the necessary information, and go to work on it.

When I get out of the shower and walk to my dresser to get a pair of socks, I'm not aware of the process of walking, or of the path I automatically take between the bed and the mirror-stand. But if I sprain my ankle, I suddenly become acutely aware of the way I lift my foot and set it down, of how the pressure is distributed along my foot, ankle, and leg, as I experiment with new ways of walking that protect the injured ankle. Or if there's a box lying in my accustomed path to the dresser, my walking quickly ceases to be automatic as I stare at the box and decide whether to jump over it or pick it up. These cases call for something other than the largely unconscious responses that typically govern my dressing routine. Baars argues that consciousness, by giving all the different parts of my brain access to the situation, enables it to determine which part or parts are needed to deal with the sprained ankle or the irritating box.

In these cases, novelty doesn't mean the difference between a thrill and boredom, but the difference between consciousness and unconsciousness. For Baars, the answer to the problem of consciousness lies in the brain activities that determine where the spotlight of attention gets pointed. The healthy brain automatically determines what features of an individual's perceptual field are new, and shines the light of attention on them. I believe there's reason to think that the addicted brain's novelty detection system is corrupted. For an addict, the "incentive salience" phenomenon discovered by Berridge and Robinson causes the brain to persistently misidentify visual cues associated with the drug as novel. If the addict's problem has traditionally been understood as one of too little consciousness, perhaps in some respect the addict suffers from *too much* consciousness. Perhaps addiction is, in part, a pathology of consciousness.

To show how this perspective goes against the received wisdom, consider addiction's unexpected appearance in one of Baars' papers, when he suddenly turns his attention to antismoking advertising. "By persuading smokers that the act of lighting a cigarette is life-threatening over the long term," Baars writes, "public health agencies aim to increase smokers' conscious involvement with smoking, intending thereby to create more opportunities for change in a largely automatic habit" (302). Shine the spotlight of attention long and hard on the smoker's habit, Baars thinks, and that smoker might stop smoking.

Here he relies on an old assumption of Western thought: more consciousness equals more rationality, more freedom. The more conscious you are, the more in control you are. Most of the time, this assumption is justified. But is it justified here? Does the smoker suffer from too little consciousness? Sometimes, yes. Smokers will describe suddenly realizing they have a cigarette in their mouth without being aware how it got there. Reports like these clearly illustrate the role of robotic, automatic habits in addiction. But is the smoker's problem *always* too little awareness? Imagine a smoker who has quit. Days, weeks, months later, she finds that everywhere she goes, the spotlight of attention falls on cigarette packs, lighters, and ashtrays. Could De Quincey have been freed of his addiction by becoming more conscious of his immortal bottle of laudanum?

But from the perspective of much current research, the question of whether addiction is caused or cured by conscious means may be less interesting than the shared presupposition that consciousness causes any behavior at all. An experiment conducted by Benjamin Libet in 1983 has played a central role in casting doubt on the behavioral role of consciousness, even in literary and cultural studies, where it has been disseminated by the work of Brian Massumi and others.[32] Libet asked his subjects to move one of their fingers, and to tell him exactly when they decided to do so. Other scientists had isolated the brain activity associated with simple finger movements, and Libet made recordings of his subjects' brains during the experiment. What he discovered was that the subjects' conscious decision to move their finger came *after* the brain activity associated with finger movement had begun. So the decision couldn't have caused the behavior.

Later, Daniel Wegner conducted a series of similar experiments. In one of them, subjects were instructed to use a computer to move a cursor around a monitor which showed various objects, and to stop it over an object every thirty seconds or so. Half the time the subjects were actually controlling the cursor, half the time it was controlled by Wegner or his assistants. Strikingly, when asked if they had caused the cursor to stop, the people who had not been in control of the cursor were just as likely to say yes as those who had been.

Many people interpreted these results as showing that consciousness is epiphenomenal, that is, that consciousness has no impact on human behavior. Wegner theorized that both human action and conscious experience are caused—at roughly the same time—by the same unconscious brain processes. Because we become aware of wanting to make a movement just before the movement happens, we assume that our conscious decision caused that movement. But this assumption is false. If we put the influence of experiments like these together with the fact that much of our knowledge about addiction is obtained through animal studies, and add the further fact that addiction just seems like a state where consciousness is *especially* ineffective, we will understand why addiction researchers tend to think the addict's conscious experience is irrelevant.

But not everyone accepts the view that consciousness is epiphenomenal. Bernard Baars, as we've seen, is one thinker who believes that consciousness plays an important role. The philosopher Shaun Gallagher is another. Gallagher argues that experiments like Libet's don't necessarily prove our conscious intentions don't matter. Just because so small-scale an action as a finger movement is automatic doesn't mean that we don't have some control of the bigger picture. Our various small-scale behaviors—moving one foot in front of the other, blinking, wiping sweat from our brow—often occur in the context of some larger plan.

To show this, Gallagher uses the example of a man standing in his backyard when he's frightened by a sudden movement in the grass (117–21). The man jumps. Then he looks, and notices the movement was caused by a harmless lizard. Since he collects lizards, he decides to catch it so he can add it to his collection. Now some of the actions involved in this sequence—his instant reaction to movement in the grass, the various minor adjustments of posture and muscle as he leans down to capture the lizard—are automatic. But the automatic micromovements involved in catching the lizard are set into motion by the man's reflection that such a lizard would look good under the glass of his lizard case. So even though many of the individual small-scale behaviors he goes through as he chases the lizard down might—like Libet's finger movements—have unconscious causes, they are in a larger sense caused by conscious awareness and reflection.

Now let's imagine a different situation. Take a man who has recently quit smoking. Something moves to his left and he jumps. He looks over, and sees it's a cigarette pack, which has just fallen from the mantel where he'd left it last week. He stares at it, fascinated. He picks it up. He turns it over. Then he opens it, takes out a cigarette, sticks it in his mouth, and runs off to light it on the stove.

Is this scenario like Gallagher's? Does consciousness play a role here, or not? Some neuroscientists, like Redish, will say no. They will say that the reward system marks the sight of a cigarette pack in such a way as to draw the addict to it. The addict reacts robotically. But what if, as I've suggested, that unconscious dopamine marking causes not robotic action, but a particularly intense conscious state? What if the unconscious processes function to intensify consciousness? If they do, then this state—this fascinated awareness—affects behavior in the same way as the lizard-collector's conscious awareness that he wants the object in the grass for his collection.

And yet, there's a crucial difference between the lizard collector and the addict. The lizard collector's jump at the movement in the grass is pure reflex. When he's catching the lizard, however, he's in control of his actions. But for the addict staring at the cigarette pack, consciousness works to *reduce* his self-control. The addict's fascination with the pack tends to keep him in the orbit of the drug, and every moment spent in that orbit increases the chance that he'll fall prey to the unconscious habits, the cravings, the genuinely robotic behaviors that soon cause him to pick up the pack, tear out a cigarette, and run wildly looking for a light.

There's another, even more basic, difference between the two examples. This has to do with the kind of consciousness involved. In Gallagher's example, consciousness means cognition. It refers to the man's recognition that the motion was caused by a lizard, his reflection that the lizard would look good in his collection, and his decision to capture it. Thinking, deciding, calculating: this is the kind of consciousness Gallagher has in mind.

But in my example, consciousness means something else. The addict staring at the pack is simply fascinated by the way it looks, fascinated by a special quality of awareness. And while many researchers agree with Gallagher that conscious thought and decision making might cause behavior, very few will agree that this second kind of consciousness is anything but epiphenomenal.

Yet I think a promising way to link phenomenal consciousness in its strong form to behavior can now be proposed. If the model presented above is right, the subjective experience of fascination upon perceiving the forever-new addictive object plays a role in addiction. How big is this role? For the modest payoff of my argument—advancing the study of addiction—the answer to this question matters.[33] For the ambitious payoff of my argument—the Romantic payoff—whether the behavioral effect of fascination is large or small is unimportant. I propose the following Romantic formula: Addiction lends salience to consciousness. Addiction makes experience matter. And it is literature—forever wanting to attain the status of the addictive object and forever failing—that informs us of it.

# 3  BIG BROTHER STOPS TIME

MOST READERS of George Orwell's *1984*—arguably the most popular and influential postwar English-language novel—agree that its importance has little to do with art. Critics have taken this absence of artistic qualities to mean that its status as a supremely important novel comes with an expiration date. Raymond Williams, for example, writes that Orwell's work is concerned with a "general argument" related to the "mood" of his own time. "It is not that he was a great artist, whose experience we have slowly to receive and value" (9). Richard Rorty, who finds much to value in the novel, admits that it is a "good example of what Nabokov described as 'topical trash,'" and predicts that it "will be widely read only as long as we describe the politics of the twentieth century as Orwell did" (169). Harold Bloom tells us that after we have digested the voluminous criticism on Orwell, "we are driven back to what makes *1984* a good bad book: relevance" (4). Richard Epstein fears that the relevance that made it a "good bad book" vanished with the end of the cold war, and suggests that the time has now come to assign it to a different genre. "*1984* will continue to be read, but, over time, read more and more as a period piece" (69).

Certainly *1984* continues to be "read more and more," if Amazon sales rankings and college and high school reading lists are any indication. But doubt about its "relevance" might go well beyond Epstein's belief that it no longer describes our current political situation. Exactly what political situation did it describe? When, and for how long, did we "describe the politics of the twentieth century as Orwell did?" Consider the politics Orwell describes. The monolithic regime that controls Oceania is constituted by a single, basic prohibition: "The Party told you to reject the evidence of your eyes and ears. It was their final, most essential command" (81). Political life in *1984* is defined by a prohibition against perceiving the external world. This prohibition elicits the protagonist's revolutionary politics: "Truisms are true," Winston declares, "hold on to that! Stones are hard, water is wet, objects unsupported fall towards the earth's center" (81).

*1984* describes a prohibition against the obvious, against perceiving the surface of the world, a prohibition resisted by the passionate affirmation of the hardness of stones and the wetness of water. When did we describe politics this way? When was the defense of truisms the key political issue? "Freedom is the freedom to say that two plus two make four," Winston writes. "If that is granted, all else follows" (81). Rorty tells us that the point of this sentence is to defend freedom of speech, to champion a value, not a truism. "It does not matter whether 'two plus two is four' is true, much less whether this truth is 'subjective' or 'corresponds to external reality.' All that matters is that if you do believe it, you can say so without getting hurt" (176).

Freedom of speech certainly is a recognizable political issue. And if free speech is what Winston's driving at with his talk of the hardness of rocks, then the "relevance" of *1984* becomes less of a mystery. But, as James Conant points out, it doesn't seem very likely that free speech is the point here. Conant notes the obvious: some kind of commitment to "external reality" plays a role in the statements quoted above. And Conant finds a different political relevance in this commitment. He argues that "stones are hard, water is wet" refers to an epistemology that would enable the verification of facts in the face of social disapproval. "The more totalitarian the scenario one inhabits, the greater the number of beliefs one will have that are likely to be both warranted and unacceptable to one's peers" (102). Therefore, Orwell's book is relevant as a description of the epistemology that underlies successful resistance to the kinds of "totalitarian scenarios" that proliferated, as facts and as threats, in the political life of the past century.

But how far does the wetness of water really get you in a totalitarian scenario? Hannah Arendt, in her *Origins of Totalitarianism*, published three years after *1984*, agrees that "the truism that 2 plus 2 equals four cannot be perverted.... It is the only reliable 'truth' human beings can fall back upon" once totalitarianism destroys the space of civil society (quoted in Ingle, 125). "But," she continues, "this 'truth' is empty or rather no truth at all because it does not reveal anything" (125). Contra Conant, Arendt argues that you can't ground political resistance—

or anything else—on the wetness of water. No values, no political position, no meaningful autonomy follows from truisms. "Truisms are true," Winston cries, "Hold on to that!" But the truth of truisms is precisely what does not need to be held onto. The hardness of rocks requires as little passionate defense now as it did under Stalin. Pointing out the obvious acquires the supreme value and power it has for Winston only in the book *1984*. Experiencing the hardness of rocks becomes an endlessly fascinating and interesting activity only in a world constituted by a prohibition against the obvious. And despite those critics who point to Orwell's relevance, that is not and has never been our world.

Of course, no one really thinks it is. The critics don't think Winston is really talking about the wetness of water. Rorty and Conant both read Winston's passionate affirmation that "stones are hard, water is wet," as a metaphor. Rorty thinks this sentence symbolizes Winston's commitment to free speech. Conant thinks this sentence symbolizes Winston's commitment to the scientific method.

In these writers' hands, "stones are hard" is a metaphor with a certain cognitive content, which they specify in different ways. The tendency to read Orwell's descriptive sentences as if they are metaphors has had the effect of reinforcing the conviction that Orwell is a writer who is not concerned with the aesthetic. To say that he is not concerned with the aesthetic is another way of saying that he is not concerned with the surface. The hardness of stones becomes soft and transparent in the critics' hands; stones lose the opacity on which Winston insists. *1984* appears as a book that is not exclusively and obsessively concerned with the surface of the world, with the obvious. Its surfaces become windows through which the critics look to discover its relevance. In the following, I will try to read Orwell's descriptive sentences literally. My premise is that the function of Orwell's writing is not to endow his descriptive sentences with another meaning. His writing has a different function: not to make the surface transparent, but to make it tangible.

"Stones are hard," Winston triumphantly declares, "water is wet." "In order to make us feel objects," declares Viktor Shklovsky, "to make a stone feel stony, man has been given the tool of art" (6). Shklovsky writes that habit, the operation of time in the human sensorium, tends irresistibly to destroy the surface of the world. "If we examine the general laws of perception," he writes, "we see that as it becomes habitual, it also becomes automatic" (4–5). For Shklovsky, as for writers from Shelley to Pater, the first time we see something, its surface is fresh and vivid. And then it begins to disappear. "Gradually, under the influence of this generalizing perception, the object fades away. . . . Life fades into nothingness. Automatization eats away at things, at clothes, at furniture" (5).

Like Proust, Keats, and Nabokov, Orwell invented a fictional device to stop the effect of time on human perception. He invented a fictional world in which the stoniness of stones is immune to what Arendt calls the "emptiness" that afflicts the obvious in our world. Oceania's totalitarian regime imposes a rigorous and unenforceable prohibition against perceiving the surface of the world. As I will show, the effect of this prohibition is to preserve the novelty of the world's surface. In *1984*, the hardness of rocks never dulls, never softens; the wetness of water never ceases to fascinate. The citizen of Oceania sees everything as if for the first time, day after day, forever. Time is excluded from the neurobiology of perception.

Orwell's invention arises out of a political condition in which the artistic plays a special role. Walter Benjamin famously defined totalitarianism as a mixing of the political and the artistic (241).[1] In *1984* the artistic is not a distinct sphere of life or form of cultural capital, but, as in the title of Shklovsky's essay, a "device." The artistic technology counters the tendency of the surface of the world to disappear.

*1984* is not a transparent political statement. An attentive reading will show how the book's fictional political regime serves to render its surfaces opaque. From the historical experience of totalitarianism, Orwell has extracted the principle of the total artwork. If Keats seeks to make the unimaginable arrest of subjective time imaginable through music, and if De Quincey seeks to make it imaginable through the addictive object, then Orwell seeks to make it imaginable through the total state. But to identify the artistic function of the regime's techniques is not to suggest that Orwell secretly admires his fictional totalitarians. It is to prepare to understand what his obvious hostility means.

In each of the writers we have examined thus far, a degree of ambivalence surrounds the prospect of successfully stopping time. Keats registers this ambivalence through his identification with the figure of Clymene in "Hyperion," and his inability to sustain Apollo's speech. In Nabokov and De Quincey this ambivalence is more sharply foregrounded in the representation of the experience of an ideal image as a form of enslavement. These writers hedge their inability to realize a truly time-arresting artifact with dark suspicions about such artifacts, suspicions that make the weakness of their actual works look like an advantage. Focused primarily on the mechanics of virtual immortality, we have not dwelled much on this aspect, in part because of the way works like

"Hyperion" or *Lolita* themselves mute what are possibly resentful suspicions about the impossible object of their desire. By contrast, Orwell's sharp foregrounding of the sinister dimensions of literary immortality in *1984* provides us with our best opportunity to analyze this tendency.

❖

*1984* is characterized above all by the intensity and frequency of its descriptions of the world's surface. The novel's first page describes Winston rushing into a building on "a bright cold day in April." He moves quickly through the doors, "though not quickly enough to prevent a swirl of gritty dust from entering along with him" (1). Inside, he looks out the window. "Down in the street little eddies of wind were whirling dust and torn paper into spirals" (2). Winston next notices "bombed sites where the plaster dust swirled in the air and the willow herb straggled over the heaps of rubble ... crazy garden walls sagging in all directions" (3). A third of the way through the novel, he is still noticing: "Winston noticed some tufts of loosestrife growing in the cracks of the cliff beneath them. One tuft was of two colors, magenta and brick red, apparently growing on the same root. He had never seen anything of the kind before" (134).

About halfway through the novel, Winston pauses while reading the secret book given to him by the Inner Party member O'Brian. "Winston stopped reading, chiefly in order to appreciate the fact that he *was* reading" (184). Instead of thinking about the book, he savors the feeling of reading. A few pages later, it happens again. "Winston stopped reading for a moment.... The blissful feeling of being alone with the forbidden book, in a room with no telescreen, had not worn off. Solitude and safety were physical sensations, mixed up somehow with the tiredness of his body, the softness of the chair, the touch of the faint breeze from the window that played upon his cheek" (199–200). Sensations have a curious way of not "wearing off" for Winston. On page five he experiences the taste of gin as a "shock." Five pages from the end of the novel, this shock has still not worn off: "The stuff grew not less but more horrible with every mouthful he drank" (293). Orwell's descriptive sentences are mimetic of the curious, never-fading intensity that characterizes Winston's perceptions.

Of course, a certain level of close description is characteristic of the genre to which *1984* belongs. One of the conventions that utopian/dystopian fiction shares with science fiction is the minute and painstaking description of particular features of the environment. These descriptions are made necessary by the fact that some of these features—teleporters, spaceships, telescreens—are unfamiliar to readers, and one of the chief pleasures of such novels is to see exactly what such strange objects look like. This convention, however, frequently comes into conflict with another convention: the attempt to present the future world as it appears to its inhabitants. The typical inhabitant of *Dune*, for example, would feel as little need to provide a minute description of a spaceship as the narrator of *Emma* feels when she refers to a chair by a single word. This tension often motivates the device, familiar in texts from *Gulliver's Travels*, to *Looking Back*, to *Brave New World*, of inserting a character in the story who comes from another time and world—our own, for example—and therefore needs all the new things explained to him.

Recalling the way description typically works in other novels belonging to the genre helps to clarify the strangeness of Orwell's procedure. In the first place, it is not just futuristic objects like the telescreen ("an oblong metal plaque like a dulled mirror") which get the full descriptive treatment here, but also things like the color of grass, the taste of gin, the feeling of reading, and the sensation of a breeze in a warm room (2). In the second place, as every reader will recall, the surface of the world described in *1984* is not at all some strange futuristic place. It is not what a reader in 1949 would expect of the future, not, in Winston's words, "something huge, terrible, and glittering—a world of steel and concrete, of monstrous machines and terrifying weapons" (74). It is instead the actual surface of the world in which the novel was composed, wartime and immediate postwar England: a world of "bombed sites" where "the willow herb straggled over the heaps of rubble" (3); a world of "decaying, dingy cities, where underfed people shuffled to and fro in leaky shoes, in patched-up nineteenth-century houses that smelt always of cabbage and bad lavatories" (74); a world of gin, laundry hung to dry on lines, people singing popular tunes in the street, cool breezes, cigarette rations, green grass, hard rocks.

Carl Freedman, one of the few critics to register the strangeness of description in *1984*, finds it difficult to reconcile the "naturalistic" description of "vivid particulars" with the "programmatic" description of the structure of the future society ("Antinomies of *1984*," 93). He discovers a tension between the vivid description of grass and gin and the presentation of the properly futuristic aspects of the world of the novel, such as the Ministry of Love, Big Brother, and the telescreens. Freedman describes this tension as a "generic contradiction," as if the book were a struggle between two different kinds of novel, naturalist and science fiction. For Freedman this struggle has a victor. "Naturalism in *1984* must finally yield to programmatic satire," the novel's true genre (93).

But to read the relation of the novel's vividly descriptive passages to its presentation of a fictional totalitarian state as contradictory seems to me mistaken. Rather, I would suggest, it is precisely the function of the totalitarian state Orwell invents to endow the surface of the world with its never-fading vividness. This regime—so poor at turning out decent boots or tobacco—generates the persistent vividness of its citizens' perceptions as its chief product. It does this in several mutually reinforcing ways. One of the most elemental, and most effective, is a simple framing procedure. Consider one of the novel's descriptions of gin.

> He took down from his shelf a bottle of colorless liquid with a plain white label marked VICTORY GIN. It gave off a sickly, oily smell, as of Chinese rice-spirit. Winston poured out nearly a teacupful, nerved himself for a shock, and gulped it down like a dose of medicine. Instantly his face turned scarlet and the water ran out of his eyes. The stuff was like nitric acid, and moreover, in swallowing it one had the sensation of being hit on the back of the head with a rubber club. (5)

The "bottle of colorless liquid" is labeled "gin" but smells like "Chinese rice-spirit" and tastes like "nitric acid." At another moment, he is surprised when he opens a packet labeled "chocolate" and finds a crumbly substance that tastes "like the smoke of a rubbish fire" (121). He is still more surprised when something presented to him as chocolate proves to taste like chocolate.

These simple examples show one method by which Oceania's regime frames perceptual experiences in such a way as to intensify them. Anyone who has picked up what they thought was a glass of coca-cola and discovered, while drinking, that the glass contains milk (or, worse yet, "nitric acid"), can testify to the intensity of the liquid's sensory qualities when compared with the way milk tastes in a glass one believes to contain milk. If this happens enough, as it does to Winston, one might be just as surprised when one finally does get milk when expecting milk.

The regime cultivates a background of expectations which are continually and dramatically frustrated. Nothing tastes, looks, or feels like it is supposed to. This departure from expectations surrounds each thing with the characteristic nimbus of perceptual detail which Orwell's prose reproduces. In Oceania, to use Heidegger's familiar example, every hammer you pick up is broken. Ordinarily, to a carpenter who reaches for a hammer to hammer in a nail, the various features of the hammer do not show up vividly. They remain in the background as the carpenter completes his habitual task. It is only when he discovers the hammer isn't working properly that he takes a real look at it. Then, Heidegger writes, the surface of the hammer explodes into "conspicuousness, obtrusiveness, and obstinacy" (quoted in Dreyfus, 70–71). What Heidegger, like Augustine, describes as the typical future-orientation of human life collapses. The present swells and expands, lifted out of the onrushing stream of subjective time, and the carpenter notices the broken hammer's every detail, every mark, every curve.

For Winston, the things of his world have just this "conspicuousness, obtrusiveness, and obstinacy." The framing that produces this effect works in large ways and small. Many of the things Winston tries to use—from boots to elevators—are in fact broken or defective in some way, and thus become "obtrusive." On a wider level, the regime cultivates the general expectation that the world of Ingsoc is "huge, terrible, and glittering—a world of steel and concrete, of monstrous machines and terrifying weapons" (*1984*, 74). And it is against this expectation—continually renewed by the telescreens, the newspapers one reads, the conversations one has—that the actual surface of "patched-up nineteenth-century houses" never ceases to shock and to amaze.

The prohibition against looking at the surface of the world constitutes another resource by which the Party prepares an intense and never-fading perceptual shock for its citizens. "The Party told you to reject the evidence of your eyes and ears. It was their final, most essential command" (81). Don't look at what's in front of you, don't smell what's around you, don't touch what you're touching. The effect of this prohibition is to endow the sensible surface of things with a fascination it cannot possess or retain in a world not structured by this prohibition.

The Party is well-aware of what Foucault has since taught us to recognize as the essentially creative effects of prohibition. "The command of the old despotisms was 'Thou shalt not,'" intones the Inner Party member O'Brian, "The command of the totalitarians was 'Thou shalt.' Our command is '*Thou art*'" (255). The Party makes extensive use of this effect in shaping sexual experience. "Its real, undeclared purpose was to remove all pleasure from the sexual act. Not love so much as eroticism was the enemy, inside marriage as well as outside it" (65). This prohibition serves as a constant incitement. "A narrow scarlet sash, emblem of the Junior Anti-Sex League, was wound several times around the waist of her overalls, just tightly enough to bring out the shapeliness of her hips" (10). By putting their mass-produced pornography in plain packets and circulating it surreptitiously, the Party ensures a ready stream of prole customers, excited by "the impression that they were buying something illegal" (130).

In a world where "a real love affair was an almost unthinkable event," sexual sensation achieves an incredible pitch of intensity (68). But the word "unthinkable" suggests special features of this particular repressive regime. The effect elicited by the repression analyzed by Foucault was expressed primarily in discourse—discourse internalized as thought or externalized as verbal and written confession. Here, what is elicited is an intensity of perception, an intensity procured not by embedding the sensation more deeply in layers of discourse, but by removing it from every possible discursive context. Sensation becomes "unthinkable." It is "astonishing." Or, in the key word Orwell uses to describe the sexual encounter, it inspires a feeling of "incredulity." When he finally beholds Julia before him in the secret place in the forest, Winston has "no feeling except sheer incredulity" (120). And again, "All he felt was incredulity" (120). Since the prohibition on the erotic is a species of a more general prohibition on the perception of the surface, the new perceptions enabled by the erotic encounter tend to drown out sexual desire itself. "He had no physical desire" (120). Here again we encounter Kantian disinterest in a most unexpected place. The temporal structure of desire for the object represented by the image falls apart. Just to look, to touch, to smell: the incredulous shock of present perception is the elemental experience elicited by Oceanic prohibition. And like Kantian music, the prohibition seems designed to "keep" Winston in this state.

Winston's "incredulity" at Julia's body, like his "astonishment" (124) at the sound of birds or his amazement at the color of grass (134), is a pure product of the "lunatic credulity" required by the Party (133). An absolute "lunatic credulity" in the Party when it tells you the bottle before you contains gin, the packet contains chocolate, the city is a futuristic paradise, the body you touch cannot be touched, prepares you for the "sheer incredulity" which greets the taste of gin, the sight of the city, the feel of the body.

Prepared by the intense activity of the Party, sensation in *1984* continually emerges into "sheer incredulity." Sensation is removed from its entanglement in beliefs, thoughts, and relations, its entanglement with the future and the past. What is most striking is how, instead of investing every aspect of experience with its discourse, the party creates a clean separation between its discursive categories and perception. Winston labors in the Ministry that produces the endless stream of discourse which the Party feeds its citizens. He notes of this product, "Most of the material you were dealing with had no connection with anything in the real world, not even the kind of connection that is contained in a direct lie" (41).

If one kind of propaganda aims to distort reality, to offer an interpretation of reality favorable to dominant interests, the Party sets up a vast discursive apparatus with *no* connection to reality at all. "Life, if you looked about you, bore no resemblance not only to the lies that streamed out of the telescreens, but even to the ideals that the party was trying to achieve" (74). "How easy it was, thought Winston, if you did not look about you, to believe that the physical type set up by the Party as an ideal—tall muscular youths and deep-bosomed maidens, blond-haired, vital, sunburnt, carefree—existed and even predominated" (60). But of course, Winston does look—with incredulity—at the "beetle-like" shapes of the actual human bodies around him.

It would have been possible, and more familiar, for Orwell to frame this gap between discourse and sensation as an epistemological question. But in all these examples one can see that the venerable question of the connection between language and the thing-in-itself of reality is irrelevant. If you are asked how well the word *chair* describes the reality of the object you are sitting in, you have an epistemological problem. If you are told that your office will have a chair, and when you open your office door you discover there is no chair, you have a different kind of problem: someone has played a trick on you. The success of the trick is registered in your surprise when you open your office door and look around. Of course, one might take this situation as an epistemological problem ("there is a chair here that I cannot see"), but in fact no one in *1984* does this. When Winston is told to expect a roomful of people with yellow hair and finds a roomful of people with brown hair, he doesn't imagine that he has been mistaken in his understanding of the color-sensation expressed by the word *blond*. He is simply surprised. He stares at the brown color of his colleagues' hair with incredulity.

The painstaking construction of a worldview with no connection to reality goes by the name *doublethink* in the book. The party doubles the sensible world with a "shadow-world" (41). A set of expectations and beliefs form a shadow reality which, at every perceptual instant, disperses like smoke over the unexpected surface of the world. The key fact here is that the false account of the world doesn't *replace* actual perception, but exists alongside it. Orwell does not imagine the kind of "implanted" perception found in science fiction from Phillip K. Dick to *The Matrix*. Rather, a set of false expectations of the world frames one's actual perception. The practice of doublethink exposes the citizen of Oceania to constant intense, unfamiliar, unexpected, and shocking sensations.

At every moment, one discovers that one's entire nexus of beliefs and expectations has *no* relation to what one is seeing. Thus every sensation resembles Orwell's description of Winston's childhood memories. "Nothing remained of his childhood except a series of bright-lit tableaux, occurring against no background and mostly unintelligible" (3). Orwell describes the memories of others in identical terms. "They remembered a million useless things, a quarrel with a workmate, a hunt for a lost bicycle pump, the expression on a long-dead sister's face, the swirls of dust on a windy morning seventy years ago; but all the relevant facts were outside the range of their vision. They were like the ant, which can see small objects but not large ones" (93).

The Party's thoroughgoing abolition of history is another way of making the surface of the world strange. This abolition means that ordinary people have trouble inserting the shapes collected in their memories into a coherent life narrative. Ordinarily, when one suddenly remembers some sharp detail from the past, the rest of the relevant facts do not remain outside the range of vision for long. Ordinarily the objects in a random personal memory can be dated and contextualized, inserted into a collective history, dropped back into the flow of time. One remembers what else was happening in the world, and this helps to place the remembered image that floats randomly into the mind. One proceeds from the sharp registering of a random detail—bright red hair, a lunch box—to a general picture of a certain time: "I remember the early eighties, I had a PAC-MAN lunch box"; "I was in third grade when *The Challenger* exploded. My teacher had red hair." The remembered shapes lose their uncanny timelessness as they take their place in a coherent narrative about the past.

But the shapes remembered by people in the book—"the swirl of dust on a windy morning," "a quarrel with a workmate"—exist outside of any intelligible pattern. The shapes retain their strangeness, their uncanniness, their unfamiliarity. The intensity with which the details of these shapes are registered is a function of their heterogeneity with respect to any context: they don't fit in any scheme; they are unassimilable into any recognizable time. The novel locates these remembered sensations not in history but outside of time. And again, the novel does not emphasize the epistemological problem here. The impossibility of placing these shapes in a pattern is consistently represented in terms of a characteristic perceptual effect, in terms of how this impossibility intensifies the way they are perceived, of how the subjective sense of onrushing time is interrupted.

The sense in which the pastness of things serves to prolong and intensify their perception is underlined in Winston's visit to the antique shop in the prole section of London. "Winston came across to examine the picture. It was a steel engraving of an oval building with rectangular windows, and a small tower in front. There was a railing running round the building, and at the rear end there was what appeared to be a statue" (97–98). Here, Winston is looking at an old picture of a church. He is seeing a church for the first time, and, as with any object seen for the first time, the features of the church's shape show up with an unusual perceptual vividness. But while Winston looks at this object as if he is seeing it for the first time, we quickly discover that he has in fact seen it many times. After a pause, he tells the shopkeeper, "I know that building. . . . It's in the middle of the street outside the Palace of Justice" (98).

The framing of the familiar building in terms of an unknown past renews its shape for Winston in the present. In the picture frame in the antique shop, the familiar shape loses its familiarity. I want to stress the formal identity of the novel's representation of Winston's perception of the taste of gin, his perception of Julia's naked body, and his perception of the shape of the church. The party's abolition of history, which causes objects from the past to show up "against no background," takes its place with the prohibition on sensual experience and the circulation of false expectations about the world as a third method of endowing a familiar thing with the quality of a first impression.

❖

Through these techniques, Oceania's regime causes its citizens always to experience everything as if for the first time. The Party directs its activity against the movement of time. The "secret book" Winston reads refers to the regime as a "huge, accurately planned effort to freeze history at a particular moment of time" (216). This effort to stop history doesn't have an obvious motive. "I understand HOW," Winston writes, "I do not understand WHY" (80). One doesn't want to "freeze history" just for the sake of freezing history. The desire to stop history requires to be explained in terms of some other desire, and the "secret book" circulated by the secret police suggests several: the desire to stop history is a desire to maintain power, it is a desire to freeze the class dialectic, it is a desire to prevent unpredictable technological advances. The book itself suggests that none of these explanations quite satisfy, and Winston's arrest prevents him from reading what promises to be a definitive answer. "'This motive really consists . . .' Winston became aware of silence" (217).

I want to approach the question of motive here by looking more closely at the novel's image of time. Most readers have seen history as the only relevant kind of time here, but the key passage actually points to two distinct temporal modes. It refers to an effort "to freeze history at a particular moment of time" (216). I want to think about this passage from collective "history" to subjective "time." Earlier in the novel, Winston suggests a causal relation between stopping history and stopping time. "History has stopped. Nothing exists except an endless present" (155). History stops, then he feels time stopping. I want to suggest that the motive for stopping historical time is to stop experiential time.

Unlike the desire to stop history, in this novel the desire to stop time is something that no adult human needs explained. "They were born, they grew up . . . they went to work at twelve, they passed through a brief blossoming period of beauty and sexual desire, they married at twenty, they were middle aged at thirty, they died, for the most part, at sixty" (71). "'You got your 'ealth and strength when you're young,'" the old proletarian man says. "'When you get to my time of life you ain't never well'" (92).

Unlike Party members like Winston, the proles, the lowest segment of the population and the only segment systematically deprived of the Party's perceptual prohibitions, are represented as abjectly vulnerable to the effects of time. For persons subject to time—like the proles inside the book and like everyone outside the book—the desire to stop time is obvious. Winston discovers it in the prole woman he sees washing clothes outside the window of the antique store. "One had the feeling that she would have been perfectly content if the June evening had been endless" (141–42). For those, like Winston, in the top fifth of Oceania's social structure, the Party's methods have achieved this endlessness: "Nothing exists but an endless present" (155). The regime creates this "endless present" in the sensorium of citizens who experience everything as if for the first time, always. Not chronological, but neurobiological time stops in the endless novelty of the world's surface.

A horror of neurobiological time is detectable in the anxiety that shadows George Orwell's own love for the surface of the earth. This love is well-documented. Orwell expresses his admiration for his favorite writer by saying of Shakespeare, "he loved the surface of the earth," and he attributes the same love to himself in the essay "Why I Write" (Gleason, 79). In an early novel, the narrator wonders, "Why don't people instead of the idiocies they do spend their time on, just walk around *looking* at things?" (cited in Sandison, 11). In an essay composed around the time he was finishing *1984*, Orwell wrote, "So long as I remain alive and well I shall continue to feel strongly about prose style, to love the surface of the earth, and to take pleasure in solid objects"

(Sandison, 10). But his confidence that he will "continue to feel strongly" about the things he loves sometimes falters. In a letter, he wrote, "I always feel uneasy when I get away from the ordinary world where grass is green, stones hard, etc." (10). Like James Conant, Alan Sandison, whose important early study collects these examples, interprets Orwell's lifelong "obsessive" "focus on the surface of the earth" as an epistemological commitment (14). In the midst of a terrible century, Orwell discovered that the individual's perception of physical reality is ultimately the only thing that can't be taken away. "The senses are inalienable," Sandison writes (10).

If this were true, we might wonder why Orwell's description of the surface of the earth betrays the fear that it might disappear. "I always feel uneasy when I get away from the ordinary world where grass is green" (Sandison, 10). We might wonder at Orwell's "unease," and ask how the fact that stones are hard can slip away from him. But perhaps, as Abbott Gleason suggests, "Orwell's commitment to the principle of 'objectivity' was not really an epistemological position at all" (85). Perhaps, instead of worrying about losing the *knowledge* that grass is green, Orwell is concerned about losing the *sensation* of the greenness of grass. And this worry is entirely reasonable. As the art and science we have been exploring in this book have shown us, the senses are profoundly alienable when it comes to something like the greenness of grass.

In Proust's *In Search of Lost Time*, Marcel writes that his life has been "erased by the india-rubber of habit" (III, 514). Proust understands habit as a force that removes sensations, and erases the perception of the world's surface. William James describes how habit causes perceptions to move irresistibly from freshness to dullness (*Pragmatism*, 175).[2] While in my introduction I presented recent neuroscientific evidence of this process, Shklovsky, like many of the writers we have examined, rests his argument that habit erases the world on a simple appeal to the reader's own experience: "If someone were to compare the sensation of holding a pen in his hand or speaking a foreign tongue for the very first time with the sensation of performing this same operation for the ten thousandth time, then he would no doubt agree with us" (5). Habit is the neurobiological form time takes. In the processes of perception, time is measured not in months and years, but in the distance between "the very first time" and "the ten thousandth time." Across that distance, the surface of the world grows faint and dull, and finally disappears. "Life fades into nothingness" (5).

Orwell's desire to prevent the "surface of the earth" from fading away locates him in the Romantic tradition shared by Proust and Shklovsky, and provides a clue to the motive of his fictional regime in creating an "endless present." When he writes, "I always feel uneasy when I get away from the ordinary world where grass is green, stones hard," he suggests that what good writing like Shakespeare's does is to preserve the surface of the world. As we have seen, Winston—"stones are hard, water is wet"—inhabits a world where the surface of things never dulls. Artistic mastery is the preserving agent for Orwell the writer and reader, while totalitarian control serves the same function for Winston the party member. What Orwell thinks good art does, and what Orwell thinks bad government does, thus turn out to be curiously identical.

So the hard interpretive problem here turns out not to be the one we were pursuing. It seemed that the question was why Oceania's regime would invest such vast amounts of labor into creating an artificial "endless present," a world where the hardness of rocks and the greenness of grass are always new, always interesting. If it were simply a matter of gaining control over a population, surely easier and more direct methods could have been used instead of the elaborate defamiliarizing techniques and prohibitions discussed above. But the mystery of the regime's motive—"I understand how, I do not understand why"—dissipates when we realize that Orwell shares this desire to stop time, and indeed that he shares it to the point of assuming that the reason one wants to stop the greenness of grass from fading is so obvious it doesn't need to be explained. Thus we don't need to search for some mysterious further end served by Oceania's attempt to freeze subjective time. Freezing time is an end in itself.

But the identity of the effects produced by good writing and bad politics solves one problem only to open a more difficult one. If Orwell describes the regime and art as aiming at the same effect, why then does he love art and hate the regime? One way of putting this problem is to say that while at one level the novel expresses a desire to erase the distinction between art and politics, at another level the novel wants to maintain this distinction. As we will see, the novel associates the separation of art and life with the separation of human and inhuman, male and female, the free and the slave. To understand why Orwell shrinks from the fusion of artistic and nonartistic, it will help to first understand why Shklovsky urges this fusion.

Shklovsky begins by asking us to think of the difference between the first time we do something, and the ten-thousandth time. He then imagines a technique that will turn back the clock to "the very first time." He calls this technique "art." Art is a means of "intensifying the impressions of the senses" (3). "The removal of the object from the sphere of automatized perception is accomplished in art by a variety of means" (6). The writer "describes [the object] as if it were perceived for the first time" (6). Shklovsky makes brutally apparent a feature of the tradition we have been exploring that is only implicit in earlier critics from Coleridge to Pater. At a single stroke, the Russian's early-twentieth-century formulas dispense with the sociological understanding of art. Here, the existence of artworks is not a consequence of the historical emergence of an artistic sphere and its differentiation from the economic or the religious. Artworks are no longer defined tautologically, as that class of objects that people recognize as art. Art-as-function stands opposed to art-as-culture. The artwork no longer requires the name and the status of art. *1984*, a fictional world in which art has ceased to exist because the state flawlessly executes its function, presents an extreme version of the opposition of art-as-culture to art-as-function. As we have seen, the novel's extraordinary wealth of vivid descriptive detail is not simply an artistic effect layered by Orwell over his political message. The very features that identify this work as artistic prose—its abundance of vivid perceptual details—are produced by the fictional political regime as its characteristic effect. The novel's artistic features are the effect of a function that in the world of the novel does not go by the name of art.

To collapse the border between art and life by identifying art with a function is familiar, as is the association of this collapse with totalitarian politics.[3] But the particular function Shklovsky and Orwell describe, and the kind of interpenetration of art and life they imagine, is as strange today as it was sixty or one hundred years ago. Here I want to rehearse the signature emphases of the twentieth-century critical response to Shklovsky's concept of art as defamiliarizing technology, with a view to identifying particular caesura. Critics have become familiar with the mixing of art and life, but not with the prospect of art's capacity to alter biological processes. We are familiar with how art distorts, refracts, or contains history, but not with the artistic ambition to cancel the effect of time. And yet Shklovsky could not be clearer: "The removal of [the] object from the sphere of automatized perception is accomplished in art" (6).

As I discussed at the opening of this book, Elaine Scarry is one of the few critics who have pursued this way of thinking about literature, but, as I have argued, her account suffers from a drastic underestimation of how difficult the operation Shklovsky describes would be to achieve consistently. Her brilliant descriptions of the techniques by which Proust mimics intense perception occlude Proust's bitter consciousness of the way habit erodes works of art just like everything else. Scarry's attempt to cordon off the question of experiential time from the question of perceptual vivacity succeeds only in making artistic vivacity itself virtual. After long familiarity, I might not actually experience the vivacity of Proust's description of his bedroom, but on Scarry's account the passage will retain its "vivacity."

This kind of argument tries to sever questions of vivacity from questions of subjective time by making vivacity a property of the object. Usually we conceal the subjective dimension of perception in speaking of properties like an object's color, and usually there is no problem. A red object will always appear red to most people in normal light. But a problem does arise with the kind of objects Scarry has in mind. As writers from Kant to Proust understand, vivacity is abjectly vulnerable to the erosive force of neurobiological time. With Keats and Nabokov, we have seen the difficulty of even imagining a work endowed with the power of countering subjective time. Yet only the possession of such a power could justify speaking of vivacity as a property of an object.

But if Scarry's attempt to understand literature's perception-renewing capacity founders on the problem of time, most of the critics who have taken up Shklovsky's theory as a description of the actual achievements of individual artworks have done so by replacing defamiliarization as a perceptual problem with defamiliarization as an epistemological problem. Just as critics from Alan Sandison to James Conant have insisted on reading Winston's insistence "water is wet, stones are hard" as the assertion of a realist epistemology, so critics have preferred to read Shklovskian defamiliarization as a procedure that intends a new understanding rather than a new sensing. Carlo Ginzburg, for example, finds two distinct ways of reading defamiliarization in Shklovsky. On one reading, art, by removing things from their familiar contexts "provide[s] a standpoint for a critical, detached, estranged approach to society" (15). Ginzburg distinguishes this idea of defamiliarization as an epistemological tool, a way of lifting the critic out of a familiar conceptual scheme and enabling "moral and political criticism," from defamiliarization as a vehicle of "impressionistic immediacy" (20). Ginzburg's interest lies exclusively in the former mode.[4]

Frederic Jameson addresses defamiliarization through a similar distinction between perception and meaning, although he presents it as a difference between Shklovsky and Brecht. The point of defamiliarization for Brecht, Jameson writes, is "to make you aware that objects and institutions you thought to be natural were really only historical" (cited in Vatulescu, 37).[5] Jameson separates this critically useful version of defamiliarization from Shklovsky's, which "suffers from ahistoricity and essentialism since it is based on the belief that objects exist in a 'unitary, atemporal way' prior to being made strange by the artist" (37). Unlike Ginzburg's splitting of defamiliarization, Jameson's splitting into "two forms, the metaphysical vision and the social critique," is less a split within a single cognitive process than a distinction between two different epistemologies (*The Prison House of Language*, 57). Yet Shklovsky's theory of perception does not, as Jameson thinks, conceal an epistemological commitment to the "unitary, atemporal" existence of particular objects. His vision is not "metaphysical," it is not concerned with the gap between my experience of an object and the object itself, but with the gap between the "very first time" I see something, and the "ten thousandth time" I see it.

The tendency to understand the artistic practice of removing a thing from its familiar context in epistemological terms was strengthened by the ways deconstruction handled the question of context. Critics like Marjorie Perloff understand poetic defamiliarization in terms of the "indeterminacy of meaning" which, on Derrida's account, proceeds from the iterability of linguistic elements.[6] If the meaning of an utterance can only be established in a context, the fact that any element of that utterance can appear in any other context subjects its meaning to a constant sliding. While for Derrida indeterminacy is the general condition of meaning, for Perloff and those influenced by her, this semantic sliding is an effect of artistic defamiliarization. And whether the critic adopts a post-deconstructive or a neo-sociological account of the epistemological value of literature, she is setting herself an achievable task. The history of the criticism of any major author—from Shakespeare through Orwell—proves the fertility of the work as a generator of new ideas.

The *unwritten* history of reading, however, is filled with gigantic, swollen moments, moments when the rush of experiential time stutters and stops. Shklovsky's original formulas present themselves as a criticism attuned to this history. "The purpose of the image is not to draw our understanding closer to that which this image stands for, but rather to allow us to perceive the object in a special way" (10). One writer who comes close to Shklovsky's alignment of artistic language with perception is Donald Davidson, who in his celebrated essay "What Metaphors Mean" writes "I deny that metaphor does its work by having a special meaning, a specific cognitive content." "We must give up the idea that a metaphor carries a message," Davidson continues, "that it has a content or meaning (except of course for its literal meaning)" (222). Instead of asking what artistic language means, we should ask what it "brings to our attention," what it "makes us notice...." And "what we notice or see is not, in general, propositional in character" (223). Consider again the sentence where Orwell describes Winston's gin as being "like nitric acid" (5). If Orwell had meant this simile to express the badness or the toxic qualities of the gin, he might, Davidson suggests, simply have said that. On Davidson's account, we should not take this phrase as expressing some particular meaning about the gin. Rather, we should pay attention to how the juxtaposition of gin and acid makes us notice certain features of gin.

While Davidson suggests that artistic language is primarily addressed to our "attention" rather than to our "understanding," he does not attempt to specify exactly how art affects our attention. The absence of specificity accounts to a large degree for the power of his argument. The juxtaposition of gin and nitric acid could cause people to notice a wide range of different things—the sharp taste of gin, its colorlessness, the burn it causes in the stomach, the burn it causes on an open wound—which they might then put forward as interpretations of the metaphor's meaning. Davidson accounts for the fact that some metaphors elicit a wide range of different interpretations, not by making a claim about the indeterminacy of meaning or by trying to rule some interpretations out by restricting the meaning to the one Orwell intended, but by arguing that metaphor isn't about meaning at all. For Davidson, metaphor is about attention, experience, noticing. The variety of interpretations metaphors generate are therefore to be taken as expressions of what interpreters notice about a thing in the world, not as claims about what the metaphor means. Interpreters of artistic language are not trying to "decipher an encoded content," but are rather "telling us something about the *effects* metaphors have on us" (222).

In seeing the artwork as the occasion for an experience that is not strictly determined by it, Davidson's account is broadly compatible with reader-response critical models. It also fits into the pattern of contemporary literary criticism in a way that Shklovsky's does not. Because although Shklovsky is also concerned with describing the activity elicited by art as "noticing" rather than "deciphering," he has a very particular kind of noticing in mind. Art "removes the object from the sphere of automatized perception." It makes us see the familiar thing "as if for the first time." Whereas Davidson refrains from attempting to characterize what artistic juxtaposition causes us to notice in any but the most general terms—the metaphor causes us to notice *something*—Shklovsky argues for the transformation and renewal of perception by art. The critical tendency to read defamiliarization as generating (Jameson) or exemplifying (Perloff) a certain kind of meaning is thus only part of the reason Shklovsky's essay still sounds so strange. This unfamiliarity is not just a consequence of

Shklovsky's emphasis on experience over meaning—an emphasis shared by writers like Davidson—but also of the special place his theory of perceptual experience makes for art.

That theory, the classic twentieth-century expression of Romantic immortality, is simple. The first time we see, touch, smell, or hear something, the sensation is vivid, intense. We are acutely aware of the thing's texture, the shape and contour of our sensation of it. As we continue to experience it, the vividness fades until we almost completely lose our sensation of it. We take our seat at our chair and begin to type away without being focally aware of the color of the desk, the shape of the chair, the little chips in the paint on the wall, or the feel of the keys' surface. It is the same way at home. We sit down on our couch without noticing it. We barely taste the spaghetti. Life has become dull. We don't feel as if we are alive. We look back with regret to a time before our sensations became weak and dull. We seek out ways of renewing our sense of the world. We buy a new couch. We travel. We try new spices. We read a novel where something shocking happens in an ordinary office like ours. When we return to our own office, we see it in a new way. For Shklovsky, time has a distinct effect on perceptions: it erases them. We experience time as a fading of perceptual detail. And because of this link between time and perception, we all know exactly how it would *feel* if time stopped: everything would continue to look the way it did the very first time we saw it. To continue to see things as if for the first time is to exist, in Orwell's phrase, in "an eternal present."

Michael Holquist and Ilya Kliger, in their recent study, rehearse the conventional suspicion of all this when they write that, "as is well known," Shklovsky based his work "on a rough and ready psychology of perception" (615).[7] From the perspective of the psychoanalytic models that have dominated literary criticism, Shklovsky's theory does indeed seem crude, even as the desire that animates it—the rescue of life from time—seems hubristic. Certainly he takes very little trouble to prove his claims. For evidence, he simply refers his readers to their own experience, stating that anyone who takes even a moment to examine their life "would no doubt agree with us" (5). The truth of his theory of perception is, he claims, utterly obvious. And once one has grasped the obvious fact that familiarity erases the world, then art's defamiliarizing function provides it with an obvious value.

And isn't he right? I doubt there are many readers who, when asked to compare the "very first time" they saw a given object to the "ten thousandth time" would describe their experience in ways that differ significantly from

Shklovsky's. I take it that the obviousness of this fact about experience is not at issue in the "well-known" problems with Shklovsky's psychological model. Rather, the problems concern the value of this obviousness. The Freudian and then Lacanian models favored by psychological criticism have—to say the least—not tended to ground their claims on what is obvious to everyone. I suggest that the very obviousness of Shklovsky's theory of perception has presented a powerful obstacle to its critical acceptance. Can one practice a criticism that is content to repeat the obvious?

We can try: All things being equal, we tend to feel the new *more*, we feel it *longer*, and we tend to experience it as affectively *better*. Holquist and Kliger's description of this kind of claim as psychologically "rough and ready" is abundantly refuted by the recent research surveyed in my introduction and second chapter. I think slightly better grounds for Holquist and Kliger's objection rest on a fear that Shklovsky's theory, by harping on the simple distinction between the first and ten-thousandth time, drowns out nuance and interpretive rigor. The entire range of emotional and intellectual values seems crudely compressed into a choice between a dead dullness and an Orwellian "incredulity." Why the great value on the incredulous, very-first-time feeling? Doesn't a commitment to evaluating art exclusively in terms of the old-new, familiar-unfamiliar binary exclude all the historical, emotional, sexual, and economic information which good criticism is committed to recovering?

I think this worry arises in part out of a mistaken assumption about the status of Shklovsky's claim. His distinction between the first time (intense) and the ten thousandth time (dull) can look like a value judgment, and he certainly makes such a judgment when he prefers the time-stopping experiential payoff of the new image to the new knowledge it produces. However, the intensified feeling of life Shklovsky attributes to "the very first time" is not a judgment, but a neutral description of the neurobiology of perception. It is possible that, with Winckelmann, one might prefer a "quiet mind;" one might find the heightened feeling of life to be a distracting prelude to what one takes as the superior state of achieved knowledge of the work's form. But when Shklovsky remarks that one feels more vividly alive before experiential time has reduced the perceptual qualities of the object, he is simply describing how life works. Thus the importance of the familiar-unfamiliar binary in Shklovsky's critical scheme should not be understood as a problematic privileging of one issue above others. This binary is situated not arbitrarily above traditional critical topoi but below them, as a feature of immediate perception.

And yet the critical neglect of the heart of Shklovsky's famous essay is not simply based on a mistake about the status of his claim about the first time. This neglect is a rational response to the radical program for art he builds upon this claim. Shklovsky's theory enables us to see art in terms of an intervention at an elemental biological level. Art makes the familiar new. Artistic technology, for Shklovsky, turns the affective clock back from "the ten thousandth time" to "the very first time," from vanished to present, from dull to live. We can describe the intervention performed by this technology with a formula adequate to Winston's existence in the "eternal present" of a state that has perfected the artistic function: Art stops neurobiological time. Time stops at the eye, the ear, and the fingertip of the organism shaped by art.

If human brain time oscillates between the familiar and the unfamiliar, the sensorium modified by the effective work of art is no longer the subject of a human experience. This modification, and this work, is effective only to the extent that it constantly changes. Both Shklovsky and Orwell think of this work in terms of a process, a strategy, an evolving "technique." Novelty and vivacity for them are not, as in Scarry's treatment, properties of particular artistic works, but the products of the art system. I have described this as the "reasonable" solution to the problem presented by the tendency of individual works to lose their time-altering capacities with repeated exposure. But now we can begin to see that academic critics, professional writers, curators, and almost everyone involved with the culture of art will find this reasonableness impossible to accept. To accept it is to believe that a work's transformative value quickly wears out, and that there is no reason to preserve once-effective works as anything but curiosities, or exhibits in the history of technique.

In Oceania, Orwell shows us what a world organized by Shklovsky's radical redefinition of art in terms of function might look like. Particular methods don't stop time for very long; the endless *work* of the regime keeps it stopped. This work makes the hardness of rocks and the wetness of water the kind of news that, in Oceania, stays news. This ceaseless activity accounts for the fact that Winston drinks the same gin every day for years and never gets used to it. Winston's bio-stasis is supported by an elaborate, ever-changing structure.

But if we can understand opposition to this work on the part of critics who fear the violence such a practice would do to artistic culture, it appears that this is not the source of Orwell's opposition. In his fictional world, a strong objection that arises in our world to Shklovsky's vision is neutralized. Even Shklovksy would have a hard time abandoning Tolstoy once the initial intensity fades, but who could possibly miss yesterday's message from Big Brother? The statements that issue from Oceania's telescreens are no more than tactical adjustments of a defamiliarizing meta-technique. It would be absurd to attribute to them some hidden semantic richness that emerges only with time. Thus Orwell's distaste for his artistic state does not stem from identifying a neglected dimension of the objects that are recruited to the artistic function. It must involve some more basic fear of this function itself. Ginzburg, Jameson, or Holquist do not manifest this fear; they might prefer other aspects of art, but they don't actually hate its ability to renew perception.

Now we are in a position to register the true scale of the interpretive problem posed by *1984*. The ceaseless, feverish activity Shklovsky finds in the history of art, and Winston finds in the self-consuming history that supports the anti-history of Oceania, amount to running to stand still. The ongoing functioning of art—the constant defamiliarizing of the world's surface—keeps the brain at the year one. The surface of the world is lit up and preserved in an unfading incredulity: "Stones are hard, water is wet!" Time stops in the sensorium's eternal present. Who wouldn't want this?

> Down in the yard the red-armed woman was still marching to and fro between the washtub and the line. . . . One had the feeling that she would have been perfectly content if the June evening had been endless. (141)

And yet in *1984* this desire is not just anyone's. This is where Shklovsky and Orwell part ways. Earlier, I noted the interpretive problem raised by the fact that Orwell's letters and essays praise art for stopping time while his novel condemns a regime for doing the same thing. But this tension, this pull between the desire for an eternal present and a horror of it, runs through the novel itself. To begin with the most obvious example, Winston, who feels himself to be living in the timelessness created by the regime's techniques, cannot embrace the desire that animates his condition. His obsessive attempts to get a sense of time, to verify a past and to anticipate a future, set him in opposition to the basic principle of the regime, which imprisons him to cure him of this tendency.[8] He is perhaps the only one in Oceania who misses what Big Brother said yesterday; a key sequence of the novel shows him discovering and desperately seeking to preserve a scrap of newsprint recording the pronouncement of an earlier day. Winston—before his imprisonment—hates the "endless present." He is not the one who wants it. He attributes the longing for the June evening to be "endless" to the anonymous "red-armed" proletarian woman he sees outside his window.

And yet, Winston writes: "If there is hope, it lies in the proles" (82). Hope is a desire attuned to futurity, to the kind of temporal unfolding that Oceania's regime has foreclosed for the top twenty percent of the social order. Winston believes the proles will create the future he is unable to grasp. But when he allows himself to imaginatively inhabit the desires of a prole, he finds only a hope for stasis, for "endlessness."

There is one more twist. Winston makes his observation about the prole's desire for endlessness immediately after he hears her singing a popular song "with deep feeling."

> They sye that time 'eals all things,
> They sye you can always forget;
> But the smiles an' the tears across the years
> They twist my 'eartstrings yet!

> Her voice floated upward with the sweet summer air, very tuneful, charged with a sort of happy melancholy. One had the feeling that she would have been perfectly content if the June evening had been endless. (141–42)

Her song

> was one of the countless similar songs published for the benefit of the proles by a subsection of the Music Department. The words of these songs were composed without any human intervention whatever on an instrument known as a versificator. But the woman sang so tunefully as to turn the dreadful rubbish into an almost pleasant sound. (138)

In Oceania, only the proles use artworks. They love art that invites them to imagine a state in which time does not heal all things, in which feeling doesn't fade with years. By performing these mechanically generated songs, the proles imbue them with "deep feeling." What do we make of the fact that the only authentic desire for endlessness in the novel is generated by an act of artistic reception?

The social category of art has been rendered obsolete among the upper levels of Oceanic society. Compare the total efficiency of the regime's defamiliarizing techniques with the modest effects of forms that still bear the label of art. If the regime's techniques produce "an endless present," the songs and novels distributed among the proles accomplish nothing so dramatic. They don't defamiliarize, they don't stop time. They merely present a weak and blurry image of a world where "smiles and tears" last "across the years." Art is humble. It doesn't produce an endless present; it merely gives a watery image of such a state, an image that raises a longing for endlessness.

As we have seen, the state in *1984* is broadly consistent with the idea that totalitarianism collapses art into politics, in that the regime takes over the artistic function of defamiliarization. But the novel also leaves room for the representation of art in more traditional terms, as a relatively autonomous sphere of activity. In Oceania, the difference between art that has been mixed with politics and art that retains the name of art is the difference between more and less effective techniques, or between virtual and actual modes of endlessness. The songs and novels paint imaginary pictures of stasis; the defamiliarizing regime actually achieves it.

So why does the novel prefer the proles' virtual mode of access to endlessness to the party members' actual experience of it? It is possible to deny that this is the novel's preference. Winston's hope lies in the proles, and the proles' hope lies in the state of endlessness Winston has achieved. Thus one could read this as a circle, as what Jameson has referred to as the absolute closure of the dystopian form, a symptom of a stasis from which there is no escape.[9] On this reading, the value Winston finds in the proles' desire for stasis would be no value at all, simply an image of how desire might be fully enclosed by a total system.

But I think a better way to read this is as the privileging of a prospective relation to endlessness over its achievement. Why can't Winston—for whom the hardness of rocks and the wetness of water is news that stays news—feel the desire that animates his condition? Why is this desire found only among the proles, who are left to stoke it with the weaker forms of art? This is simply to raise the question of the larger displacement that frames the entire novel. Why does Orwell, who often repeats his love for "the surface of the earth," portray the *effective* care of that surface as the work, not of the artist, but of the kind of regime he hates?

We can pose this as a question about Orwell's own artistic practice. Orwell prided himself on his vivid descriptive sentences, a technique he practiced and honed throughout his career. And yet, in *this* novel the Orwellian descriptive sentence has a dual status. It is a sign that the novel is a work of art (or at least that it has artistic pretensions). And it is mimetic of the kind of perception produced by the totalitarian regime. *1984*'s striking descriptive passages are mimetic of the way that Winston, in the grip of the Party's circulation of false expectations and prohibitions, always encounters the surface of the world as new and astonishing. Thus Orwell works to perfect a vivid descriptive style, but condemns a world in which that style has become the rule of perception.

Consider, for example, the sentence describing Winston's perception of "vistas of rotting nineteenth-century houses, their sides shored up with balks of timber, their windows patched with cardboard and their roofs with corrugated iron, their crazy garden walls sagging in all directions" (3). This sentence operates on two levels. On one level, it is an example of art, of Orwell's love of carefully crafted detail. A sentence like this exemplifies his aesthetic, which he describes as an attempt to preserve "the surface of the earth" by fixing the rich features of that surface in art. But on another level, this sentence represents the fictional Winston's experience as he is continually shocked into vivid awareness by the regime's manifold techniques. Here, the relevant technique is the expectation that Oceania should be a gleaming world of futuristic skyscrapers. This expectation is continually renewed only to be continually shattered as Winston stares at Oceania's actual surface, and every detail of each sagging house comes into sharp focus.

The sentence exemplifies two different methods of achieving perceptual vividness: the method of artistic prose and the method of total politics. These methods have a number of differences, but perhaps the central difference lies in their respective degrees of effectiveness. No matter how good one thinks Orwell's descriptive sentences are, I doubt anyone would argue that *1984* will produce anything like the same effect on its reader as the fictional regime achieves in peeling back Winston's nerves for each new sensation. As defamiliarizing technique, art is much weaker than the kind of politics the novel represents. Thus the two sides of the Orwellian descriptive sentence mirror the distinction between the proles' weak, prospective art and the regime's fatally effective politics.

We have seen similar dynamics in the relation between Clymene's song and Apollo's song, and between Humbert's descriptions of Lolita and his experiences of her. But the particular shape this dynamic takes in *1984* allows us to formulate the tradition's ambivalence about its virtual forms in a new way. Orwell suggests that it is acceptable for art to aim at timelessness only because we know art isn't strong enough to achieve it. The "eternal present" targeted by the proles' weak song looks beautiful to Winston, but he hates the eternal present he occupies. I have approached virtuality in this tradition as writers' acknowledgement of the temporal limits of actual artistic form and their expression of a desire to transcend those limits. But does *1984* show us instead that this is simply a case of preferring the virtual as such to the actual? Or does it intimate that the desire for effective art is the kind of wish that one regrets as soon as it is granted? Is defamiliarization best kept where it will be least effective and do least harm, best kept, that is, in the social category of art? Is the artistic the category where we expect to believe in effects we know will never work? To think about experiences we don't have? To turn experiences into meanings?

The ambivalence that characterizes Orwell's relation to the possibility of an eternal present generates these questions. I will conclude with one final feature of this ambivalence. Consider this conversation between Winston and Julia, near the center of the novel.

> "We are the dead," he said.
> "We're not dead yet," said Julia prosaically.
> "Not physically. Six months, a year—five years.... We shall put it off as long as we can. But it makes very little difference. So long as human beings stay human, death and life are the same thing."
> "Oh rubbish! Which would you sooner sleep with, me or a skeleton? Don't you enjoy being alive? Don't you like feeling: This is me, this is my hand, this is my leg, I'm real, I'm solid, I'm alive!"
> "Yes, I like that," he said. (136)

As I have been arguing, the fascination with sensation that Julia urges is the condition of a new mode of existence outside temporality. In *1984*, "death" and "life" are alternative descriptions of this state. Winston's description isn't prospective. He doesn't say: "Since we will die eventually, right now we are as good as dead." He says that, in his present condition, the question of "physical" life or death makes very little difference. "Life and death are the same thing."

In this novel Orwell presents the collapse of the border between art and life as the collapse of the border between life and death. When the state takes over the defamiliarizing function, defamiliarization becomes effective. It lifts the sensorium of its subjects out of time. It suspends temporality. Our most familiar model for such a suspension is death. Orwell's own proximity to the border between life and death while he wrote this book (he was dying when he wrote it and dead within a year of finishing it), perhaps accounts for the power of his portrayal of sensation at the instant it loses the familiar definition given by time.

But we may, nevertheless, want to distance ourselves from Orwell's identification of the defamiliarized sensorium with death. For Orwell, this identification, and the hostility it expresses, is generated by a third category: the human. "So long as human beings stay human," to arrest habit, to stop biotime, is to die. Orwell's original title for *1984* was *The Last Man in Europe*. Like the protagonist of the roughly contemporary near-future novel *I Am Legend*, Winston is surrounded by organisms who are no longer the subjects of human experience. What will we call this nonhuman, atemporal experience? Winston's—and Orwell's—description of it as "death" seems counterintuitive. The name the new organisms—like Julia—give to their condition seems like the obvious one: life.

# 4 THE CULTURED IMAGE

WE HAVE SEEN how writers have scoured the phenomenology of music, the structure of addictive perception, and the logic of the total state for means of imaging the arrest of neurobiological time. To this point, the virtual images that have arisen from this process operate by suspending the object of perception before the moment of its assimilation by habit. Another word for the habitual processes that prestructure perception by replacing intensely sensed color, sound, and shape with recognizable form is "culture." For the phenomenological tradition that takes its cue from Heidegger, the individual's assimilation into the world of a culture involves the replacement of the raw present-tense immediacy of perceptual contact with an awareness dispersed in time, organized according to conventional, future-directed projects, and mediated by the norms of a historical society. Given these associations, it is unsurprising that culture has not been an important term for the writing we have been exploring. Indeed, from this perspective, Orwell's Oceania is less a culture than an anticulture, less a tradition than a means of preventing anything like tradition from taking root in the individual's sensorium.

But in the last three decades of the twentieth century, a different kind of blueprint for the ideal image emerges. Compared with the strategies discussed in earlier chapters, the basic principle by which this virtual image operates is reversed. If earlier writing is committed to the value of turning the clock back on the known thing, certain strands of postwar science fiction and experimental poetry become interested in the value of making the unknown thing familiar. Taking

John Ashbery as my central example, I will argue that his poetic career consists of a rigorous and sustained effort to take something you have never seen before, and show you what it would look like if you had seen it every day of your life.

This reversal of methods records the discovery of a new means of achieving the aim of writing against time. I will show how a peculiar feature of the encounter with an alien thing as it appears in the context of an alien culture produces a shape with strange properties. Ashbery's familiarizing procedure results in the invention of a new kind of shape, and a new kind of value. In these examples of images that successfully counter time, we will find a new motive for the ubiquitous engagement of late twentieth and early twenty-first century writing with the forms of other cultures.

❂

In a 1977 essay on Raymond Roussel, Ashbery proposes a striking analogue for the kind of thing he wants to produce in his poetry. He writes that Roussel's images "are like the perfectly preserved temple of a cult that has disappeared without a trace, or a complicated set of tools whose use cannot be discovered."[1] The artifact from another world,[2] the tools of an unknown culture: these objects show up in Ashbery's poems in a variety of registers. Sometimes they come from the past, as in the 2001 poem which finds the speaker "caressing the knocker,/ a goblin's face, that drew us back a hundred years" (*Your Name Here*, 71). Or consider this thing from the title poem of 2002's *Chinese Whispers*: "Mute, the pancake describes you / it had tiny roman numerals embedded in its rim. / It was a pancake clock. They had 'em in those days" (31). *Girls on the Run*, a book-length narrative poem from 1999, inhabits the world of Henry Darger's paintings and drawings, uncovering "a thighbone guitar," a "pansy jamboree," and "ice-cream gnomes" (43, 4). The speaker of one recent Ashbery poem has a "money fish . . . strapped to my thigh" (*Whispers*, 37); another refers to "Zombie set-to's, that kind of thing" (*Can You Hear, Bird?*, 111).

Ashbery's poems are elaborately constructed theaters where alien and unfamiliar objects appear as they would to someone who is familiar with them. I will attempt to trace some of Ashbery's painstaking, cunning, and obsessive labors in attempting to *familiarize* the unfamiliar object.[3] Let's return to some of the things I listed above, to show how listing these things distorts them in a way Ashbery takes great pains to prevent. When I mentioned the "zombie set-to's," I should have noted that they appear in a conversation between two characters. The reference to "pancake clocks" in *Chinese Whispers* is accompanied by a reference to a foreign ritual: "I was a phantom for a day. My friends carried me around with them" (*Whispers*, 32). To take another example, the "sheaf of suggestive pix on greige" that appears in "Daffy Duck in Hollywood" is part of a list of things that a certain song reminds Daffy of (*Selected Poems*, 227). I'm not arguing that one shouldn't extract the things I've listed from their context in the poems. In fact, as I will show, the relevant context for a thing like the "money fish strapped to my thigh" is not the poem in which it appears. Rather, to attend to Ashbery's description of things is to note how the poems provide these things with a definite relation to an unknown context.

An Ashbery thing is an artifact of another culture. Furthermore, it is described in the poem just as it is described in that culture. This kind of description is deeply familiar. When Jane Austen tells us Elizabeth Bennet entered a "handsome modern house," the description condenses the norms, the customs, the world of nineteenth-century England (154). Elizabeth does not stop, wondering, before the house. She doesn't see the house like someone who has never seen a house like it before. She does not encounter a rectangular gray stone building thirty feet high with ivy on the walls and a large oak door ten feet wide flanked by square windows. I will argue that Ashbery deploys the descriptive conventions of novelistic realism to show us things that have the same kind of shape as Austen's "handsome modern house." As he puts it in "Self-Portrait in a Convex Mirror," his descriptions are examples of "unfamiliar stereotype[s]" (*Self-Portrait*, 73). He describes a knot, a tangle of cultural conventions rather than a solid, delimited object. Like the "temple of a vanished cult," his things are bound up with a context we know nothing of; they embody the norms of a different world.

For Ashbery, as for Austen, a certain abstraction, a certain leaving things out, is basic to the mimesis of things as they show up in a world. One must distinguish this version of novelistic description from the idea of the novel as a project of complete description, the novel Flaubert sometimes dreamed of, in which the writing renders a blade of grass in minute perceptual detail and a house as a gray stone rectangle. For Ashbery, in contrast, to describe a thing as it shows up for someone familiar with it involves leaving this kind of perceptual detail out. He is concerned with the *abstraction* of novelistic description from the outset of his career, writing in an early poem, "this leaving out business, on it hinges the very importance of what's novel" (*The Mooring of Starting Out*, 199). A poem from *Self-Portrait in a Convex Mirror* describes "a woman reading," and continues, "All that is unsaid about her pull[s] us back to her, with her / into the silence that night alone can't explain. Silence of the library, of the telephone with its pad / but we didn't have to reinvent these either: / they had gone away into the plot of a story / the 'art' part-knowing what important details to leave out . . . the background" (5).

Here Ashbery articulates his view of the "leaving out process" of novelistic description. The poem reads like a manual for describing things. The "art" of this kind of description is knowing what to leave out. In order to describe a woman reading alone at night in her library, the writer leaves out the "background," the things that surround the focal image, the "important details" like the "silence of the library," or "the telephone with its pad." There is no attempt at an exhaustive specification of what is there; the writer doesn't need to reinvent the background, because it is already present. Silence, books, a telephone, a telephone pad, vines on a house's exterior: these things are associated in a world; they are gathered around the focal image by the norms, customs, and history of a culture.

Again, this is a familiar principle of a certain kind of novelistic description. If Dashiell Hammett tells us that Sam Spade walked into a kitchen and sat down, we do not feel surprised if he later gets a beer out of a refrigerator, nor do we feel that Hammett should have told us there is a refrigerator in the kitchen (70–77). There are a vast number of aspects of the background he can safely leave out: that the refrigerator is not on top of the counter, that there is a sink and a stove, that there is a bottle opener in a drawer, and so on. This background is already present, and there is no need for Hammett to do any reinventing; he does not need to motivate the device of having a refrigerator in the kitchen. Hammett doesn't invent the logic associating refrigerator and kitchen, nor is this logic spelled out in the definition of the words. The relation between refrigerator and kitchen is not syntactic or semantic; one violates no linguistic law in speaking of a refrigerator in a dining room, or in the middle of a street. Rather, these relations manifest the background norms and associations of a cultural world. It is only to someone unfamiliar with this world that each thing in the background emerges as clear, distinct, strange, notable. If one wants to represent a thing as it appears to someone *familiar* with a world, one makes use of the background. And one makes use of the background by leaving it out.

When Ashbery writes of his reading woman that "all that is unsaid about her pulls us back to her, with her," he refers to the sense in which this figure arises in, and remains part of, a world. The form of the woman reading is not complete, is not entirely given in the description; something remains inexplicit, unsaid. The image is necessarily partial, and in recognizing this partiality we are pulled towards the world. This kind of description embodies a view from within a world. The thing is not cut off, autonomous, bounded, and complete, but condenses relations and associations, the whole background network of connections that organize a culture. As Ashbery writes in another poem, "We copy certain parts... they imply/complex relations with one another" (*Houseboat Days*, 35).

"What is unsaid" about the woman, the partiality or incompletion of her form, her relation to an inexplicit background, is the sign of this image's formal imbrication in a world. The abstraction of novelistic description, Sam Spade entering a kitchen, Elizabeth Bennet seeing a house, John Ashbery's woman reading, sinks the thing in a world. These are descriptions of how things show up within a world, as condensing or embodying a range of implicit relations. "A handsome modern house": the thing shows up as a dense point in a network of cultural associations, as a *thickening* of worldly connections.[4] To someone familiar with a world, the house does not first show up as a gray rectangle subsequently interpreted as a house, but gets immediately recognized as a "handsome modern house." These descriptions describe the way things appear as connected to other things in a world, as a knot of cultural associations and connections. When Ashbery writes of the "leaving-out" process he refers to the abstraction of this art of representing the thing as a part of a world. The art of this kind of description is the art of making what is unsaid about things "pull us back" to a world.

In contrast, to attempt a full description of an object's material shape is to attempt to cut off the thing's formal involvement with innumerable other things in a world. The description of a house as a rectangular stone building thirty feet high precipitates it from its intraworldly connections, poses it as a complete and distinct object. When absorbed in a novel we sometimes skip through this kind of description, and the mass market paperbacks that solicit this absorption contain very little of it. It seems to interrupt our absorption, to eject us from the world. Description that defamiliarizes, description that attempts to represent a thing as if it had never been seen before, recovers a distinctness, a completeness, a wholeness for the thing at the price of distancing it from a world. As Ashbery writes at the opening of 1970's *Three Poems*, "I thought that if I could put it all down, that would be one way. And next the thought came to me that to leave all out that would be another, and truer way" (*The Mooring*, 309). Ashbery wants the truth that is revealed by what is left out. In his mature poetry he chooses the art of describing a thing's partiality, its place as part of a world.

This art presents a different challenge for Ashbery than it does for Austen or Hammett, who, after all, represent the familiar things of a familiar world. The task of describing the familiar thing of an unfamiliar world is a bit harder. How does one describe an alien thing in terms of its involvement in an alien world? This is a problem science fiction has wrestled with since its inception. There seems to be no way around the process of first describing the thing, say a teleporter, in terms of its physical shape, then explicitly rendering the background norms and conventions most relevant to the use of the teleporter, and then referring to it simply as a teleporter, or by some colloquial-sounding contraction. This process interrupts the mimesis of a world so jarringly that it is often felt necessary to motivate this device by introducing a time or space traveler from our own world who needs to have everything made explicit. Since science fiction writers are typically interested in the content of some alien or future society or technology, this mimetic disruption is an acceptable cost.

But Ashbery wants to describe unrecognizable things as they appear in unknown worlds. Two separate problems, two steps can be isolated in the process of producing these things. The first step is to create things that are not recognizable as parts of our world, and the poems constantly display Ashbery's inventiveness in this respect. His poetry contains such things as "The money fish strapped to my thigh" (*Whispers*, 37); "The nice octagon trainer" (*Bird*, 111); "The flowers of the lady next door, beginning to take flight" (*Name*, 19); "The new apartment building, now vacant, circl[ing] like a moth" (*Name*, 75). These things, made by fusing familiar objects to create strikingly unfamiliar images, recall the famous definition of literary value by Lautreamont, an important influence on Ashbery, who titled one of his books *Hotel Lautreamont*. Lautreamont writes of the "beauty" of "the chance juxtaposition of an umbrella and a sewing machine on a dissecting table" (217). But Ashbery doesn't value this kind of beauty. Lautreamont-style juxtaposition is important to Ashbery as a step in the process of producing a different kind of value. He wants to give the "money fish" and the "octagon trainer" a world, to describe them as a thickening of the relations and associations of a world. He wants the relation between "octagon" and "trainer" to be arbitrary in a different way than Lautreamont's "chance meeting"; he wants to mimic the arbitrariness of cultural conventions. He doesn't want the chance meeting of an umbrella and a sewing machine on a dissecting table, but the chance meeting of a stove and a refrigerator in a kitchen. He wants to give the relation between an octagon and a trainer the same kind of relation that obtains between "milk and cookies" (*Selected*, 172). When an umbrella shows up against the bright, white, blank ground of the dissecting table, its shape appears whole, complete, distinct, independent. But when Sam Spade sits down in a kitchen chair the shape remains partial, indistinct, and dependent, its edges fold into tables, linoleum, refrigerators. Ashbery wants things to appear as dense points in a matrix of cultural relations, not as objects thrown on a dissecting table.

Instead of a combination umbrella and sewing machine, Ashbery tries to make his things recognizable as the tools of a different world. But how can one represent a "money-fish strapped to my thigh" as a kind of tool? How does one make the relation between a "pansy jamboree" and a "thigh-bone guitar" look like the relation between milk and cookies? How does one distinguish the literary production of an alien thing from the arbitrary yoking together of familiar words or things? Ashbery solves this problem by describing these unfamiliar things in terms of the genre of the familiar. His rigorous investigation of novelistic description furnishes him with a variety of techniques in the art of the unsaid, with a range of methods for inventing things that show up in imaginary worlds. Ashbery has a surrealist knack for creating otherworldly images; he uses the conventions of novelistic realism to make them take root in other worlds.

But before proceeding to investigate the poet's use of these conventions, I want to make explicit the sense of the shape of Ashbery's career that organizes this discussion. I am arguing that an important goal of his poetry is the representation of things from other worlds, and that the curious properties of these poetic things open a new horizon for literary value. But I think his approach to this goal has altered over the course of his career. The poems explored in detail above are taken from his early and mid career; most of the poems explored below are from his late career, with the majority dating from the last fifteen years. The early Ashbery approached the familiarizing procedures I am discussing in a thematic and prospective way. When I say of the poem about the woman reading cited above that it is like a manual for describing worldly things, I refer to this thematic dimension of the early poetry. By the late period, Ashbery doesn't need to speculate about how to make the kinds of things that interest him. The method, the machine, the formula is in place, and is capable of producing unlimited examples. In addition to this difference is another: the focus on the (other)worldly thing moves from the periphery to the center of his poetic project. Whereas the early poetry is remarkably various in its aims, the late Ashbery is remarkably consistent. It is possible that the readings offered above of *Three Poems* or "Forties Flick" would not be possible except from the perspective of the late work.

John Vincent, who has written extensively and beautifully on the later books, believes he needs to defend these poems from the common critical sense that there are too many of them and that they are too much alike (1–26).[5] By contrast, I think the standard critical reaction to the late work is correct as description—that it is formulaic and unlimited similar poems could be quickly produced by the formula—but wrong as value judgment. My wager is that once readers understand the formula Ashbery has discovered in the context of the Romantic effort to defeat time, they won't be inclined to dismiss the poems produced by it.

Ashbery's formula for inventing otherwordly things relies upon the novel, and his most striking novelistic technique is the incorporation of dialogue in his poems. Dialogue represents the most economical means of registering "all that remains unsaid," all that does not need to be said about a thing between the inhabitants of a world: "Did you say, hearing the schooner overhead, we turned back to the weir?" (*Selected*, 312); "The witch stirred the soup with a magic spoon. She said 'We can make this happen'" (*Name*, 74); "You know the kind of thing I mean. Zombie set-to's, that kind of thing" (*Bird*, 111); "'You remembered . . . to bring . . . the gold stuff?' 'Oh sure, but I'm not a catalog'" (*Hotel Lautreamont*, 108); "The bird-sellers walk back into it. 'We needn't fire their kilns. . . . Grettir is coming back to us'" (*Houseboat Days*, 5); "Probably the rain never got loose, for all you know" (*Hotel*, 113). To judge the contribution of dialogue to Ashbery's characteristic effect, compare these examples with the opening line of a celebrated W. S. Merwin poem: "In a dream I returned to the river of bees" (100). Merwin's monologic, oracular voice presents the dream image to us in all its stark juxtaposition. If this were an Ashbery poem, the line might read, "I returned to the river of bees," and the second line might begin with quotation marks, and someone saying "What time did you get there? I must have missed you."

Simply placing the alien thing in the mouth of a speaker registers something very simple: what the speaker expects the addressee to recognize. The reply shows what the addressee does in fact recognize. Dialogue reveals the presence of the background against which things show up. What voices are these? Who is the "you" in an Ashbery poem, who is the "I"? Anyone. These anonymous voices represent the anyone of another world.[6]

Ashbery uses dialogue to show "all that remains unsaid" about a thing, to provide the thing with a background, to demonstrate its *familiar* shape. His method is the opposite of the defamiliarization procedure. Ashbery seeks to familiarize his images. By placing a thing in dialogue, placing it between people, he transforms it from a surprising juxtaposition to a familiar thing instantly recognizable to the "anyone" of a world. Another way to put this is to say that dialogue kills Ashbery's figures. He is always looking for ways to kill his figures, and another of his characteristic techniques involves imitating the dead metaphors of our own world.

Just as he investigates the novelistic "leaving out process," Ashbery's exploration of familiar clichés and sayings provides him with a model for inventing the dead metaphors of other worlds. His poetry constitutes a kind of museum of figures, metaphors, juxtapositions, all kinds of surprising language that has become unsurprising: "where the rubber meets the road" (*Bird*, 51); "train of thought" (*Bird*, 74); "having taken a proverbial powder" (*And the Stars Were Shining*, 41); "you know, the nuts and bolts" (*Bird*, 118); "jump through hoops" (*Whispers*, 88); "the 'sands of time,' as they call them" (*Name*, 96). Like his use of otherworldly things in general, Ashbery's use of clichés runs from the archaic expressions of our own past to the sayings of imaginary worlds: "Perhaps we'll, heh heh, temper the wind to the shorn lamb a bit" (*Houseboat Days*, 64); "It gave me the widdershins" (*Bird*, 111); "Fixed names like 'doorstep in the wind'" (*Selected*, 288); "No more apples on the dashboard" (*Hotel*, 137); "I was wondering if this was a 'harvest home,' a phrase I had often heard" (*Name*, 4); "Time to pull in one's horns, me buckoes, if you catch my drift" (*Hotel*, 109); "We babbled about the wind and the sky and the forests of change" (*Selected*, 83); "She had a saying, never stay in the pantry while the mill is operating" (*Bird*, 95); "As Henny Penny said to Turkey Lurkey, something is hovering over us" (*Name*, 19).

The form of the saying is another genre of the familiar. In the saying, juxtaposition passes over into worldly connection; the striking juxtaposition of sand and time, forests and change, becomes an association like milk and cookies. The ritual, another form of the familiar, provides an especially vivid example of the thing that condenses or embodies the background practices and norms of a world: "They are giving that party, to turn on that dishwasher" (*Selected*, 211); "A rite of torpor" (*Selected*, 44); "A pansy jamboree" (*Girls*, 43); "I was a phantom for a day. My friends carried me around with them" (*Whispers*, 32). The form of the ritual, game, or holiday sinks an unrecognizable thing in an alien world's matrix of associations and traditions.

Another of Ashbery's familiarizing procedures relies on a feature of poetic form. Paradoxically, the relative brevity of the lyric renders it uniquely suited to the novelistic mimesis of other worlds. The science fiction novel, as I noted above, registers a certain tension between the mimesis of things as they show up for the inhabitants of another world, and the process of making the background norms and practices of that world explicit. This process of making explicit frames the novel. To put it in terms of the Austen example I've been using, first one gets the thirty-foot-high stone rectangle, then one is told that people sleep and eat in this kind of thing, and then a character comes along who enters a "handsome modern house." Everything that shows up must first be presented as a distinct object that is then explicitly related to other things and practices. On the basis of this kind of exposition, a little space is cleared for novelistic mimesis, for things to emerge in relation to what is unsaid.

In contrast, Ashbery's lyrics open and close in the middle of things. Perhaps the closest analogue for an Ashbery line is a sentence drawn from the middle of a science fiction novel, from the space cleared for the novelistic. Consider the following sequence of examples, in which Ashbery lines alternate with science fiction sentences: "Something more three dimensional must be breathed into action" (*Name*, 98); "He held the fireball close the better to encompass the activating syllables";[7] "Only danger deflects the arrow from the center of the persimmon disk" (*Selected*, 219); "The fog balled, lengthened into an arrow, plunged with intense speed at the nose" (Vance, 120); "My megaunits are straining at the leash" (*Bird*, 174); "How did you become infected with the creature?" (Vance, 275); "Like a bottle imp towards a surface which can never be approached" (*Selected*, 225); "My eh, other lobe is onto us";[8] "Scramble the 'believer' buttons" (*Name*, 77); "While the raft floated placidly along the river, the sun gave an alarming pulse" (Vance, 236); "The due date kept flashing past the diamond slot" (*Name*, 67).

It might illuminate the shared features of these examples to subject the science fiction sentences to the kind of questions critics often put to Ashbery's lines. What are the "activating syllables" of the first science fiction sentence? What is their relation to a "fireball?" Why does the character hold the fireball close? The Jack Vance novel from which this is taken painstakingly details a set of background structures so this action, these things can show up as condensing and embodying this background. (This world is the earth of the distant future, a future technology has been recovered by the postapocalyptic inhabitants as magic, certain syllables call forth fire, and so on.) What logic associates "due date" and "diamond slot" in the Ashbery line? What does Ashbery's speaker mean by "believer buttons?" Are "megaunits" something the speaker owns, or part of the speaker's body, or something else? How does it make sense for them to "strain against a leash"? These questions, like the questions raised by the science fiction sentence, pull us towards a world. These things arise in relation to what is unsaid; they condense and embody norms, associations, customs, and standards. Ashbery manipulates the various genres of the familiar (dialogue, ritual, saying, novelistic sentence) to make these unrecognizable things recognizable as the things of a world.

Science fiction commits itself to a careful reconstruction of the other world, its things arise in relation to the unsaid only after first making the background explicit. Ashbery proceeds differently. His lines open in the middle of things. As one poem puts it, the "things to be sung of" are "science fiction lumps," the thickening of the associations of an alien world (*Self-Portrait*, 20–21). His things show up like the temple of a vanished cult or the artifact of an unknown culture. They embody norms, associations, and customs of which we know nothing.

Why is this important to him? If Ashbery had some particular vision of another world he could, like a science fiction novelist, simply tell us what that world is like. Why does he value the apparition of an otherworldly thing in the absence of the exposition of another world? The answer lies in Ashbery's fascination with a peculiar feature of the encounter with a thing from an unfamiliar culture. One way to show what this encounter is like is to show what it is not. And a way of showing what this encounter is not lies ready to hand in the oddly consistent critical encounter with Ashbery's things.

Ashbery's poetry consists of "strange juxtapositions" between familiar things. This formulation, from W. H. Auden's introduction to Ashbery's first volume in 1956, has shaped much of the subsequent criticism (16). The influence of this reading is all the more striking in that Auden was an unsympathetic reader who, as Ashbery remarks, "never liked" the poems and made little effort to understand them. Yet four decades later James Longenbach writes of Ashbery's "virtuoso manipulations of disjunction" (32), Vernon Shetley analyzes Ashbery's "style of chaotic juxtaposition" (124), and Mutlu Blasing writes that Ashbery "figures the self in and as disjunction" (106). Consider again the line: "The due date kept flashing past the diamond slot." According to the criticism, the interest of such a line is not the relation that brings "due date," "diamond," and "slot" together, but the absence of a relation. For critics from Auden to Andrew Ross, to read Ashbery is to encounter a lack of association between familiar things, rather than to encounter a thing composed of unfamiliar associations.

What is the difference between these encounters? The difference turns on the relation of a thing to its context. For the critics, the things that show up in Ashbery's lines have no relation to a context. Marjorie Perloff, in a series of books and essays, has presented the fullest account of "Ashbery's ability to modulate linguistic units into repeated new and startling juxtapositions" (*Poetic License*, 283). He "presents us with clear visual images" that are "parts that belong to no whole" (*Poetics of Indeterminacy*, 267, 273). "In Ashbery's verbal landscape, fragmented images appear one by one . . . without coalescing . . . there is no world, no whole to which these parts belong. Totality is absent" (10). In these poems, "even familiar things become unfamiliar" (274).

Ashbery's images are like movable parts for Perloff. A jamboree, a pansy, a due date are recognizable, self-identical things that have the same shape in any context. The self-identity of these "clear images" unmoors them from any single context. The formal identity that renders them iterable prevents them from adhering to any one place. Possessing a form independent of context, they have "no connection to the context in which they appear" (283). Thus the images combined in an Ashbery line have what Perloff calls an "accidental" relation to each other (283). Like the sewing machine and umbrella that show up on a dissecting table, the relation between these images is "undecidable." The very idea of a stable context, of a whole that fuses these drifting images together, is destroyed. As William Flesch writes, Ashbery's images are like a "quotation out of context" that "undoes all context" (58). When one line refers to a lake as a "lilac cube," Perloff notes Ashbery's "refusal to spell out" the connection between lilac and cube (*Poetics of Indeterminacy*, 270). Instead of a description of a single unrecognizable thing, a lake that is a lilac cube, Perloff sees the juxtaposition of three references to recognizable things: the color lilac, a cube, and a lake, three movable parts that could show up anywhere, in any combination, and appear here as if by accident.

But if Perloff sees the "refusal to spell out" the logic that associates these images as the sign of a purely accidental association, Ashbery sees what he calls the "leaving out process" as a way of describing a thing formed by worldly associations. He intends his manipulations of various genres of the familiar to demonstrate that these elements, lilac, cube and lake, pansy and jamboree, octagon and trainer, are associated in and by a world. The "leaving out process" means refusing to spell out these associations in the text in order to show that the relevant context for the "lilac cube lake" is not the text, not the line or the poem, but a world, a culture.

The description cannot be disassociated from this context, from this world, because it is not fully distinct from that world. It lacks the self-identical shape that would render it the same thing outside that world. As Ashbery writes, "The lady on the next bar-stool / but one didn't seem to understand / you when you spoke of 'old dark house' movies / she thought there must be an old dark house somewhere" (*Name*, 82). Films in the old dark house genre have been set in castles, asylums, hotels, monasteries, and apartment buildings. The associations and conventions that make a film recognizable as an "old dark house movie" (sliding panels, lost travelers, madmen) are not available to someone unfamiliar with the genre. Nor are these associations made explicit in the description. Like Perloff, the person in the poem sees this description as a juxtaposition of "old dark house" and "movie" and is thus baffled when there is no old dark house in the movie.

This description lacks self-identity. It's not that it means different things in different contexts; it's that it isn't the same thing in different contexts. There is no route from old dark house movie to old dark house movie, no connection between old dark house movie as a juxtaposition of clear images and old dark house movie as a description of a worldly thing. The absence of an old dark house doesn't necessarily prevent a movie from being an old dark house movie. The description "old dark house movie" is literally not the same when disassociated from its context in a world. It isn't a juxtaposition of "clear images" legible to any English speaker but a kind of thickening of worldly conventions. "The lady didn't seem to understand you." This person, like the critics, mistakes the kind of thing the description "old dark house movie" is. It's not that she doesn't know what the *words* in the description mean; it's that she doesn't recognize the *genre* of the description. If she had recognized the kind of description it is, she would not have seen it as a juxtaposition of movable parts, wouldn't have assumed that an old dark house movie is a movie about an old dark house.[9]

By describing things in terms of the genres of the familiar, Ashbery indicates that the elements of these descriptions are fused by a worldly logic that is not identical to semantic or syntactic logic. Ashbery describes things as parts of worlds. They are indistinct from those worlds. They don't have the same form outside of those worlds. They have no self-identity; the principle of their identity is identical with the world they are part of. Ashbery's descriptions are not composed of "clear images." They are not like the description of a thirty-foot-high stone rectangle, a movie with an old dark house in it, "petals on a wet black bough" (Pound), "a shape with lion body and the head of a man" (Yeats).[10] As Bill Brown argues, we need a perceptual clarity, a full material description in order to prize the worldly thing from its context, to give the thing the self-identity, the distinct form that renders it iterable across different contexts. ("The sensuousness praxis is indistinguishable from the resignifying praxis" ("How to Do Things with Things," 954).) Things, from handsome modern houses to old dark house movies, can be described in this way. But this sensuous description of independent, distinct forms is just what Ashbery's descriptions, as we have seen, do not give us. The "leaving out process" leaves out this kind of description. The element that establishes the self-identity of the thing is missing, left out.

"The due date flashed past the diamond slot." Where are the clear images here? What are the movable parts? What is being juxtaposed with what? Recognizing the description's genre, we will avoid making the mistake of the speaker in the poem quoted above. Just as there might not be an "old dark house" in an "old dark house movie," there might not be a "due date" in "the due date flashed past the diamond slot." This line is not a juxtaposition of clear images, but a worldly thing. "Due date" doesn't find itself next to "diamond slot" by accident; the elements of this sentence are fused by the associations of an unknown world. The genre of the saying, the ritual, or the novelistic sentence presents things as dense points in a network of associations. Ashbery's lines, as he writes in one poem, "offer something strange to the attention, a thing/that is not itself" (*Self-Portrait*, 19). These kinds of things, the poem goes on to say, are "things to be sung of." The worldly thing, the thing that is not itself, is not iterable. It cannot be lifted from its context, from its part in a world.

But doesn't Ashbery show us these things outside of their worlds? After all, his whole effort, unlike the science fiction novelist, is to show us the thing without showing us the world. If the worldly thing can't leave its world, and if Ashbery describes things without describing their worlds, then are the critics really wrong? Even if Ashbery does present his lines in terms of the genres of the familiar, can we encounter them as anything other than juxtapositions of familiar images?

To encounter a thing that can't leave its world without encountering its world is neither an unthinkable nor an unfamiliar experience. Ashbery compares his things to the tools of an unknown culture. If we dig up an ancient tool in the Egyptian desert, our sense of its form, which way is up and which way is down, depends on our sense of what it was used for, what rituals it was part of. Our sense of its world determines our sense of its form as a thing, as a tool. Our problem interpreting the artifact is not caused by our encountering it outside its context. If we approached the thing as if it were separate from its world we could simply give it a complete material description and no-one would think anything was missing. The problem is rather that in seeing it as a worldly thing, we never see it as separate from its context. When we uncover the tool of an unknown culture, it's not quite right to say that the context is absent. Rather, we should say that the context's mode of presence has changed. When we know the context, we see its form. When we don't know the context, *the presence of the unknown context renders the thing formless.* The formlessness of the tool *is* the presence of its unknown world.

The tool's finder has a choice. She can either see the thing as an odd-looking lump of bronze, in which case that odd form comes into distinct perceptual focus. Or she can see it as the artifact of another culture, in which case it becomes formless. It loses its form for the simple reason that what counts as crucial or important in its form as artifact can't be read directly off its shape as odd-looking lump of bronze. This is the same problem the person unfamiliar with American films has in trying to see what an old dark house movie looks like. Ashbery's speaker and the archeologist both have a *superficial* problem: they aren't trying to discover what the thing *means*, what its historical, social, political significance is, but simply what it *looks like*. The problem here runs quite counter to what various critics, drawing on Jameson's account of postmodernism, see as the "depthlessness" or "pure surface" of Ashbery's lines.[11] What does the surface look like? What does an old dark house movie look like? What is the "octagon trainer's" shape as a tool? Which way is up, which way is down? In these artifacts of enduring indeterminacy, Ashbery has achieved Kant's crucial criteria for an image that "keeps" the interpreter in vital suspension between chaos and recognition.

In a process that works exactly opposite to Heidegger's procedure in his celebrated "The Origin of the Work of Art," the form of the tool provides the template for the perfect object of sustained aesthetic attention. Heidegger saw Van Gogh's representation of a piece of "equipment"—peasant shoes—as the means by which viewers gained a deep sense of the world of the peasant. In an even more emphatic example, Heidegger uses the Greek temple as an instance of how the work is not simply a part of a world, but participates in the world's construction. The structure of the temple can be seen in the most literal way as inculcating the norms of a world by directing the body's gaze and movements along certain trajectories. As has been widely recognized, Heidegger's effort in this essay is to challenge the Kantian vision of art as performing an operation on individual experience with a vision of art as folding individuals into a world. Here, however, Ashbery ingeniously scavenges the principles of world construction for a Kantian aim. These poems offer us the position of an archeologist forever suspended in intense concentration on the worldly object. Ashbery's characteristic withholding of information about this world shows us that this experience of suspension, and not the unfolding of archeological comprehension or cultural insertion, is what's ultimately at stake. If, as Proust and Kant show us, perceptual intensity is what the desire to know feels like and what the achievement of knowledge diminishes, then Ashbery has created the blueprint of an image that will forever solicit the invigorating desire to know, and forever defer pacifying knowledge.

It may seem as if Ashbery unjustifiably moves between two different registers when he compares the verbal description of a worldly thing to a "complicated set of tools whose use cannot be discovered" (cited in Perloff, *Poetics of Indeterminacy*, 262). But both a familiarizing description and a tool represent a thickening of worldly associations. It might be easiest to see a familiar description as a worldly thing when the description *is* the thing it refers to, as is the case with a saying like "sands of time." But any familiarizing description is put together by a world. The description and the tool are the same kind of artifact. The words "old dark house movie," like the physical elements of a tool, are fused by worldly associations. If the person who uncovers the tool is like a science fiction novelist (or like an archeologist) she'll want to dig deeper, to begin to piece together the practices and norms of the culture, to begin to establish a link between the form of the material and the form of the tool.[12] But if she appreciates the kind of value Ashbery cultivates, she'll leave immediately, perhaps taking a photo of the tool with her to stick on her refrigerator.

My sense of the special kind of reference performed by Ashbery's descriptions can be clarified in contrast to John Shoptaw's different reading of what Ashbery leaves out of the poems. In *On the Outside Looking Out*, Shoptaw also perceives that Ashbery's fragmentary lines 'belong' to a context outside the poetic text, which he understands as the poet's homosexuality. He argues that Ashbery's poetic words and phrases allude to this context through a process of "cryptography" whereby references to queer sexuality are "displaced" by homological or homophonic words and phrases (5). This process of encoding, where a word in the poem takes the place of another word, is quite different from the logic I have in mind. Shoptaw's argument rests on the assumption that the context in which the lines are embedded, while not present in the poem, is or can be known to us. Thus, for him, Ashbery's allusions "misrepresent familiar sources" (12). Ashbery's cryptography is thus, for Shoptaw, a special case of defamiliarization, the process of making a familiar thing strange. Where Shoptaw imagines that one semantic unit takes the place of another semantic unit, such that the poem can be "decoded" by a process of substituting the displaced parts back into the poem, I am interested in how the things Ashbery describes exist in a part-to-whole relation with a missing context, an unknown world.

Like a photo of an alien artifact on a refrigerator, the description presented in an Ashbery line is an organization, a knot, a thickening of unknown associations, norms, and traditions. Consider this line from *Girls on the Run*: "The whistle charged doom / its impact was tremendous" (50). Ashbery "refuses to spell out" what is happening here. But this leaving out doesn't mean that the only connection here is syntactic. Perloff might ask: is the doom charged with whistles or is the whistle charging doom? But when we recognize the genre of this description, we are not uncertain of what is happening here because the juxtaposition of "whistle" and "doom" could represent either of these things. We are uncertain because the description embodies unknown associations. The presence of these unknown associations, this unknown world, appears in and as the formlessness of the thing described.

What part of this unknown world appears in the formlessness of the thing? All of it. When one identifies the lump of bronze as a tool of an unknown culture, one exchanges a distinct object for a formless whole. As Ashbery puts it in one poem: "As long as one has some sense that each thing knows its place ... getting to know each ... must be replaced by imperfect knowledge of the featureless whole" (*Self-Portrait*, 16).[13] As another poem states, "everything is like something else" (*Bird*, 79). Merleau-Ponty writes about a thing that is "not a chunk of absolutely hard, indivisible being, but a sort of straits" through which constellations of associations pass (250). Colors, paintings, songs, phrases, tools: the things in an Ashbery poem are not solids, but windows through which "everything" passes. This "everything" is a culturally defined everything, the "everything" of a particular world. As Daffy Duck says, "La Celestina has only to warble the first few bars / of 'I thought about you' for *everything*—a mint-condition can / of Rumford's baking powder, a celluloid earring, Speedy Gonzalez ... to come clattering through" (*Selected*, 227).

Daffy's "everything" is not the everything of a language or a dictionary, not the material everything of the universe, but the everything of a culture. The surfaces of Ashbery's things are continually disturbed by the ripples made by everything passing through: "a pansy jamboree," "the forests of change," "the due date flashing past the diamond slot"; a whole unknown world, a whole matrix of associations vibrates on the formless surface of these things. To adapt Pound's famous phrase, Ashbery's otherworldly thing is a space through which, into which, and out of which the everything of another world constantly rushes.

※

A totality is present in the thing's formlessness. In its ability to contain a totality, the otherworldly thing represents a totally dense form of value. In the context of the Romantic tradition analyzed by this book, the value of an image absolutely resistant to the habituation that is the hallmark of neurobiological time is obvious. But the fact that this resistance to habituation is powered by the structures of habituation themselves is not simply a particularly satisfying instance of poetic subversion. In Ashbery's images the frame of the biological individual merges with the frame of the collective, the historical, and the social. If Orwell's virtual art depended on excluding history—stopping historical time in order to stop experiential time—in Ashbery we have discovered a positive relation between the social and the aesthetic, between historical time and neurobiological time. The form-devouring worlds that inhabit Ashbery's things generate a new kind of value. I want to begin to pursue the relation between history and Romantic timelessness by exploring a late poem that illuminates the value of this value.

"Outside my window the Japanese driving range / shivers in its mesh veils. . . . Why is it here? / A puzzle. And what was it doing before, then? An earlier / puzzle" (*Wakefulness*, 46). In 1998, a Japanese driving range that suddenly shows up outside the poet's window takes the place of 1977's "temple of a vanished cult." Ashbery associates the driving range's alluring formlessness ("I like it," he says), with its relation to its unknown world ("What were you doing before you got here?"). It is a "puzzle." Its surface a shifting veil, the "featureless whole" of a foreign world floods its form.

Here Ashbery presents his vision of how otherworldly things store value in terms of the kind of thing that frequently shows up in contemporary America. In addition to Japanese things, his recent poetry contains South Korean ("South Korean Soap Opera"[14]) and Chinese ("Chinese Whispers") things. Things produced in these particular countries (Japanese cars, Korean DVD players, Chinese films) have occupied a central and controversial place in American consciousness over the decades spanned by Ashbery's career. And in these late works, Ashbery presents the odd relation between thing and context in his poems as an insight into the possibilities of literary value in the context of globalization.

Ashbery sees the thing from another culture as the model for a new form of value, a new store of value. Earlier writers believed a thing's universal value depends on the extent to which it is possible to extract it from its cultural context. For Ezra Pound, the clarity and distinctness of the Chinese ideogram renders it valuable. You don't need to know Chinese to understand the form; Pound's version of ideogrammic value depends on the formal clarity that enables the symbol to leave its context.[15] We have seen that Ashbery's critics have read his poetry in precisely these terms. Lautreamont's operating table, the blank space on which things from incommensurable worlds come together, and which Foucault has described as figuring the basic principle of modern taxonomy, remains for critics like Perloff the model for Ashbery's page.[16]

In contrast to Pound's ideogram or Lautreamont's umbrella, Ashbery's Japanese driving range does not become valuable by a process of alienation; this value does not depend on alienating the thing from the scene, the world of its production. It is not because the Japanese thing has been severed from Japan that it takes on value in America. It shines with a universal value outside Ashbery's window precisely because it cannot be severed from Japan, because the foreign culture is present in the thing's formlessness. In Ashbery's poetry, the most universal value is also the most foreign. "Whatever charms is alien" (*Name*, 50). But unlike the value of the exotic foreign thing, the value of an Ashbery thing depends on its retaining its familiar shape. The driving range, the "octagon trainer," the "pansy jamboree" retain the shape they have for the members of their culture of origin, persons for whom the thing is a thickening of everyday associations. All of Ashbery's efforts, the entire "art of the unsaid," is directed towards showing us *this* shape. The source of the alien thing's universal value is the way it is seen by people for whom it is not exotic, but familiar.

This value, the value of presenting the familiar shape of an unfamiliar world, overturns a basic modern understanding of value. A common definition of modernity equates it with the rise of capitalism as the dominant mode of valuation. And the capitalist market, according to the modern understanding, endows the object with the ability to leave, or to become alienated from, its context. From Marx's vision of free trade "pitilessly tearing asunder" traditional relations (*The Communist Manifesto*, 15), to Karl Polanyi's idea that capitalism "disembeds" human relations from human cultures, to Deleuze's concept of capitalism's "deterritorializing" power, the universal value of the capitalist commodity is obtained by violently severing it from its context in the lifeworld of a culture. A thing's global market value stands utterly opposed to its cultural value, the value the thing has in relation to the norms and traditions of a particular place. Universal value and cultural value stand as stark alternatives, opposed historically, in Marx's dialectic, and spatially, in recent theories locating the possibility of the resistance to capital on the indigenous periphery of the global market.

This opposition between universal and cultural value also structures recent debates about the value of literary study in a time characterized by globalizing and transcultural processes and dynamics. Wai Chee Dimock articulates a pervasive worry when she argues that our time reveals a profound threat to literary value. Globalization, according to Dimock, by eroding the boundaries of cultures and nations, erodes the (national, cultural) disciplinary structures within which the study and custodianship of literary value has resided (219). For Dimock, to respond to this situation by entrenching the value of the texts we study in their old, monocultural contexts is to take the side of reaction. Such an entrenchment equates the "humanities with 'homeland defense'" (223). "Nowhere is 'American' more secure than when it is offered as American literature . . . nowhere is it more affirmed as inviolate" (223). The way forward for literary study is to alienate the work from "its" culture, and to interpret literature's value and meaning on a global, transcultural scale. The global value of this literature is necessarily opposed to the cultural value obtained by reading texts within the narrow context of a particular culture.

Other critics worry that the problem globalization presents to literary study does not lie in the temptation to cling to cultural value, but in the temptation to discard it in favor of universal value. Some critics connect the impulse to discover a universal, transcultural mode of valuing literature with the "homogenizing" tendencies of capitalism.[17] Rey Chow finds Lautreamont's operating table beneath the demand to find a space where works drawn from different cultures might be compared. And beneath the apparently flat, blank table of comparison, she sees the ideology of a Eurocentric modernism. By muting cultural difference, "this ideology demands that others be like us" (300). Chow finds inspiration for an adequate response of the humanities to globalization in new modes of comparativism. "Unlike old fashioned comparative literature based on Europe, none of the [new comparative] studies vociferously declares its own agenda as international or cosmopolitan; to the contrary, each is firmly located within a specific cultural framework" (301).[18] This practice opposes "universal" modes of valuing because they "tend to subsume otherness" (304).[19]

What value can literature have today? It can possess a cultural value, the familiar value a work has in its cultural lifeworld. Or it can have a universal value, the value of the defamiliarized work, the work that travels across cultures and nations. The critics that have attempted to articulate the threat globalization presents to literary value, and to propose solutions, diagnose our situation in terms of this choice between universal value and cultural value. But perhaps this opposition is inadequate to the possibilities. Ashbery, I want to suggest, invents a form of literary value that escapes this choice. In Ashbery's objects, universal value does not succeed in driving out cultural value. But neither do these poems present the resistance of the cultural, the rooted, the contextual, to the global. In these works, universal value and cultural value are not alternatives. Here, cultural value becomes a powerful technology for producing universal value.

For Ashbery, to value a thing from another culture is to observe how its formlessness absorbs the everything of an unknown world like a sponge. A Japanese driving range, a Paris street, an octagon trainer, "aw nerts." Here cultural difference is a step in a production process, a process that generates a value accessible by anyone. Ashbery's poetry presents the theater of a new, global product. In the fluid, volatile surfaces of his things, we are invited to behold the mystery of a commodity that does not alienate the world of its production, but contains it. In so doing, he lifts the multicultural condition out of historical time, out of phenomenological time, out of capitalist time, and places it in the no-time of the aesthetic.

❖

I have just characterized Ashbery's production of a virtual commodity as intimating a new relation to history. But this characterization immediately raises a critical question. Am I serious? I devoted a substantial portion of my second chapter to discussing the epistemological weakness of commodity theory in literary criticism. And yet now I am celebrating poems that seem, if anything, far less defensible as an account of commodity exchange than Jameson's. Any economist would surely say that the value of an Asian commodity such as, for example, the Sony PlayStation derives not from its capacity to encapsulate the whole of Japanese society, but from its ability to deliver a function consumers value[20] at a competitive price. Furthermore, this function has nothing to do with an ability to counter experiential time by maintaining an always-new image. Indeed, the displacement of the PlayStation by the PlayStation 2 and then the PlayStation 3 might be taken as proof that the opposite is in fact the case. What, then, is the relation of Ashbery's cultured images to global commodity exchange?

The answer is that Ashbery's images are not *representations* of actual commodities but *creations* that selectively and transformatively incorporate elements of actuality in the process of making something new.[21] His lines open a relation to our multicultural world, a relation that depends on their capacity for becoming different than the world, but that has the potential to yield new knowledge about it. The fact that Ashbery's line marries universal and pluralist modes of valuation does not mean that these modes are not opposed in our world. They are. That these lines are something else added to existing states of affairs—rather than entailed by them—is simply what it means to say that Ashbery has created something new. And yet meditating on his creation illuminates surprising capacities of our multicultural situation.

Ashbery identifies plausible features of the real-world encounter with the thing from another culture in order to suggest the ability of this encounter to realize a kind of value that is not typically associated with it. The logic of the poet's relation to global commodities thus resembles Proust's relation to music. As I argued in my first chapter, Proust seizes on empathy—our capacity to sense another mind in our encounter with artistic form—to achieve the aim of "permanent novelty." By imaginatively placing ourselves in the composer's position, Proust thinks we can trade our own perceptual habits for theirs, and thus encounter the world with "new eyes." Ashbery approaches the formlessness the worldly object attains by virtue of its inextricability from its unknown context in a similar vein. The experience of such an object, properly framed, would be an experience of deferred knowledge, of suspension in the moment before the object resolves into stable form. And this moment, as we have seen, is the moment of peak perceptual intensity.

The image of the thing from another culture thus contains a potential immunity to familiarization, a shield against the normal course of perceptual time. This immunity remains virtual or potential for a number of reasons, above all because of the absolute dominance of a very different mode of valuing commodities in our world. I don't imagine that we experience Chinese or Japanese products in the way Ashbery imagines, nor do I think it especially likely that we ever will. Actual global products tend not to be designed in a way to highlight their imbrication with their home culture, and the consumer experience of them tends not to be framed by an orientation to this imbrication. Further, in those cases where commodities are so framed—in shops catering to tourists for example—knowledge about the home culture is not foreclosed in the way Ashbery's effect requires. Such a foreclosure happens only when the product gleams on the store shelf next to products from a dozen other countries, with the small "made in China" sticker on the back the only evidence of its origin. The cultural status of the object is emphatically not what is advertised in such instances.

Thus the cultural orientation to objects urged by multicultural thinkers and activists and the economic orientation instituted by global markets remain stubbornly opposed. And yet I think Ashbery's quest for something unnatural and unworldly does illuminate aspects of our actual world. This curious potential feature of the experience of the global commodity is supported by deep phenomenological insight into our habits of seeing. In addition, the capacity of the multiculturalist insistence on the imbrication of commodities with their culture to help us imagine what stopped time would feel like is, like Proust's exposition of empathy, something we simply didn't know before.

I have argued that Ashbery, Orwell, Nabokov, De Quincey, Keats, and Proust attempt to make the unimaginable imaginable by fashioning virtual images of unfading vivacity. If I have consistently cast doubt on the prospect of actualizing these images, I have also tried to demonstrate that articulating a productive relation between these virtual images and reality is within our grasp. The relation between Humbert's nymphet and recent addiction research, or between Apollo's song and musicology, is eminently actualizable, and this actualization is the work of criticism. In the process of surveying this tradition, I have attempted to indicate how this work might proceed. Like Proust's imaginary septet, De Quincey's immortal laudanum bottle, and Orwell's fictional regime, Ashbery's fantastic commodities enable us to challenge our current descriptions of actual phenomena from new perspectives, with unexpected associations. I think this strategy represents a viable way forward for criticism in the context of the modern research university. I want to conclude this book's analysis of the literary effort to defeat time with some reflections on the method of that analysis.

# CONCLUSION: FROM REPRESENTATION TO CREATION

HAD I ADOPTED a more conventional approach in this book, I might have attempted to locate *Lolita* with respect to midcentury youth culture, to embed Keats in the early nineteenth-century effort to distinguish the aesthetic from the commercial, to understand Ashbery's poetry as a reflection of twenty-first-century consumerism. Such an approach would be carefully attuned to literature as an index of actual social, political, cultural, and historical forces. My reasons for rejecting such an approach are not theoretical. I would hardly wish to deny that literature is produced by real people, struggling in real conditions, at particular moments in time. The problem with criticism that seeks to understand and excavate these conditions is purely practical, and derives from the actual conditions in which twenty-first-century criticism finds itself.

When literary critics describe actual states of affairs, our claims are necessarily parasitic on the methods and models of other disciplines, except in cases where we choose to make use of models long abandoned by those disciplines. Neither option has proved particularly successful at defending the value of humanistic scholarship at what is perhaps the lowest point of its postwar intellectual prestige.[1] This concrete situation, and not abstract theoretical considerations, provides the impetus for a new approach. One response has been to sever our involvement with other disciplines as much as possible, focusing on narrowly literary topics or composing narrowly literary history. This retreat, however, risks sacrificing much of the interest of literature. But when we are attuned to the ways in which our objects of study achieve discontinuity with actuality, our descriptions gain a genuine autonomy that makes possible a new and productive relation to other disciplines. If someone wants to know how humans experience time, they will probably consult a psychologist. If they want to know how people have measured time, they will consult a historian of science. If they want to know how people value time, they will consult an economist or sociologist. But if they want to know how to stop time, then they will come to us. We won't be able to stop it for them. But we will send them back to psychology, biology, and economics with new eyes, new motives, and a new sense of what is imaginable.

I don't pretend that the approach I have chosen is as viable for every work as historicist methods. This shift from representation to creation entails a bias in selecting the object of study. Some works are more energetic in their efforts to break free of the actual than others. Works that manifest that virtual dimension which the previous chapters have explored in terms of the ekphrastic impulse are particularly valuable for the kind of approach I am advocating. This virtuality places the old question of the autonomy of the work of art on an entirely new plane. Precisely by denying that its work consists in the making available of an actual object of aesthetic experience, the novel or poem relinquishes its claim to art's distinctive sociological status as analyzed by critics from Adorno to Bourdieu to McGurl. The virtual work of art is a kind of thinking, a kind of tinkering, a kind of engineering. Its autonomy is that of thought moving in the space between reality and desire. The critic's work is to give this free thought a form by which it can be brought into contact with the disciplined thinking of the research institution.

There is no necessary conflict between this commitment to the radical autonomy of literary thinking and a commitment to the value of the knowledge produced by humanists working within the contemporary university. Quite the opposite. In this book, as in a surprising range of emerging criticism, claims for the latter turn out to depend on the former. In the process of describing the effort to imagine an artifact that can successfully stop time, I have engaged with disciplinary discourses at a variety of levels. In some cases, as with Ashbery's commodity, the complexities of the virtual object consumed my attention, and I have done little more than to indicate the relations this object opens with multiculturalism, phenomenology, and economics. In other cases, as with Keats's imaginary music or Nabokov's objects of obsession, I have pursued these relations in some detail. Sometimes I have attended to disciplines relatively distant from traditional literary study. In other cases, the

## CONCLUSION: FROM REPRESENTATION TO CREATION    141

discourses in question have been closer to home, as when I argued that reading Kant in the context of the Romantic effort to defeat time enables us to take seriously formulations neglected by the history of philosophy. Throughout, the central focus of this book has been to delineate the time-stopping forms projected by temporal works. But perhaps *Writing Against Time*'s primary interest for criticism lies in the proof it furnishes of the real disciplinary relations made possible by ideal objects.

✺

I want to conclude by locating my methodological intervention as a response to what I perceive as the current impasse in the struggle to define criticism's institutional orientation. In gesturing towards today's reigning historicism as the path this book has not taken, I do not mean to suggest that this historicist common sense is naive about its disciplinary situation. In fact, historicism as practiced by critics such as Virginia Jackson or Robert Mitchell represents one of the two dominant, and dialectically related, modes of interdisciplinary criticism over the past forty years. I want to briefly rehearse the history of these two positions. The first, now less common, is the view that literary criticism's unique relation to the disciplines derives from its status as a species of creative writing. The second, and currently ascendant view, is that literary criticism uses literature as evidence in producing descriptions of actual states of affairs. These positions are mirror images of each other, and are equally limited attempts to deal with the fact that ambitious criticism is constantly drawn into the domain of other disciplines without the specialized competencies required to produce new disciplinary knowledges. I will here pay particular attention to the first position, because it represents a neglected stage in criticism's recent history, because it registers the fundamental issues unusually vividly, and because throughout this book I have already described and challenged some of the key exponents of the second.

In the late 1970s, Geoffrey Hartman emerged as the most visible spokesman for the view that literary theory had become a genre of creative writing. What has been less often recognized is the sociological acuity which Hartman brought to his analysis of the turn to theory in criticism. In *Criticism in the Wilderness*, his most sustained consideration of these issues, Hartman declares: "Literary criticism is now crossing over into literature" (213). For Hartman, this passage is above all "a political movement that attacks the isolation of the critic: isolation within the university" (9). Hartman sees this isolation as the inevitable result of the efforts of early- and mid-century critics and administrators to define literary study as a discipline.[2] The transformed mode of literary criticism we now know as "theory" is for Hartman a particular mode of interdisciplinarity. And here we have the crux of Hartman's insight: Literary criticism's anxieties about its status as a discipline and its relation to other disciplines drive it to become—literature. Literary criticism's solution to its particular interdisciplinary problem—that of transcending the boundaries of the English department—is to become creative writing.

The novelty of Hartman's vision of criticism as a literary genre lies in his defining it in terms of a relation to modern academic disciplines as opposed to other literary genres.[3] Criticism now "crosses the line into philosophy . . . linguistics, sociology" (240). If the question for Dryden or Johnson was where criticism stands vis-à-vis poetry or drama, the question for Hartman is where criticism stands vis-à-vis the specialized discourses of other departments. He describes the literary quality of criticism's relation to these discourses as "creative ferment," and opposes criticism to interdisciplinary writing characterized by "systematic exploration and synthesis" (241). Thus theory consists of sentences about economics which cannot be taken seriously in economics departments (Hartman's example is marxism); sentences about psychology which cannot be taken seriously in psychology departments (Hartman's example is Lacanian psychoanalysis); sentences about language which cannot be taken seriously by philosophers of language (Hartman's example is deconstruction) (82–85). To this list we can now add sentences about science which cannot be taken seriously in science departments.[4] To say that theoretical sentences can't be taken seriously is to say that they cannot be legitimated as knowledge according to the standards that govern knowledge production in the disciplines. How then can theoretical sentences be taken? As literature. Literary scholars break free of their isolation and travel into the spheres of the disciplines surrounded and protected by the aura of style. Their extra-disciplinary sentences cannot be taken seriously. But they can, Hartman predicts, be taken—as writing.

Hartman describes this style in terms of the fascinating linguistic surface of theoretical sentences. His sense of how theory's style crosses disciplinary borders differs dramatically from an older academic tradition, perhaps best represented by William James's use of style against the developing technicality of philosophy and psychology in the early twentieth century.[5] Hartman, by contrast, celebrates unserious technicality. He speaks of an "*extraordinary language* movement within modern criticism" (85). He sets up a genealogy and a trajectory for this movement that progresses from "the freakish style of Carlyle and Nietzsche," to "Benjamin's packed prose," to "the outrageous verbalism of Derrida, or the ridiculous terminology of psychoanalysis" (85). For Hartman, the power of theory is above all a "verbal power" (85). Theory's way of transcending the regimes of truth that support and separate the disciplines is the way of style. Hartman presents this way as a remedy both for literary criticism's ancient anxiety about its possibly redundant relation to its subject—literature—and for its more recent anxiety about its possibly superfluous position in the research university. By writing theory, literary critics unlock the slumbering linguistic power of the disciplines.[6]

I have one qualification to Hartman's description. It seems to me that Hartman's focus on the purely linguistic quality of theory—its "verbal power"—neglects a key source of theory's allure, a source suggested by his own discussion. I refer to the as-if relation to interdisciplinary knowledge that theory holds out.[7] It seems to me that theory's special mode of transcending disciplinary borders constitutes a significant part of its special appeal. What literature professor has not desired (to adapt a line by Althusser) the imaginary relation theory offers to the real conditions of knowledge in the research university?[8] Nor is this appeal restricted to those already professionally committed to literary studies. I remember, as an undergraduate writing a paper in my first literary theory course in the late nineties, experiencing the attraction of a kind of knowledge production that *feels like* creative writing; of a kind of creative writing that *feels like* producing knowledge.

But is this as-if sustainable? Hartman sees the emergence of philosophy or economics into style as the emergence of philosophical and economic sentences into pure linguistic surface. But it is not clear that this idea of style as pure linguistic surface is coherent without something like a deconstructive account of language. What does seem clear is that the idea that a deconstructive sentence can count as *good* style depends on assenting at some level to either the deconstructive account of writing as the pure play of signifiers, or the deconstructive account of what writing does to propositions, or both.[9] In the absence of such assent, it is true, Hartman would have no problem convincing most American philosophers that Derrida's text is not philosophy but writing. But I think he would have a rather more difficult time convincing a philosopher, an undergraduate, or a journalist that Derrida's text is *good* writing.

At one point in his book, Hartman suggests that theory opens an unserious mode of interdisciplinarity through style. At other points, however, he suggests that theory's style enters the disciplines as an antagonist, contesting disciplinary knowledge on its own grounds, beating it, and taking away its privilege.[10] How can style do this? I can see but one way. The belief that Derrida's style corrects philosophy depends on believing Derrida's ideas about the instability of context and the slide of signifiers. My point is that a (deconstructive) proposition about what thinking of propositions as writing accomplishes explains why Hartman thinks theory's sentences can count as good style. In moments like these, good style turns out to mean effective style. And style's efficacy in challenging the disciplines' propositions depends on style's status as performed or enacted proposition.

Now we don't have to believe Hartman thought of deconstruction as a coherent philosophy of language, nor do we have to come to a decision as to whether it is or it isn't. What is important is that in embracing deconstruction, Hartman does not offer a philosophical defense of deconstruction's tenets.[11] He defends deconstruction as style. But when he suggests that deconstruction's style presents a *philosophical* challenge to Anglo-American philosophy, he suspends his certainty that deconstruction consists of unserious statements about language. Indeed, I suspect that the very haziness with which Hartman regards the propositions about language that underlie his vision of effective style is crucial to that vision. This fuzziness allows him to become the visionary of a new genre rather than the advocate of a particular philosophy.

If the suspended propositionality of deconstruction qualifies criticism's claim to be creative writing, the suspended propositionality of marxism qualifies its claim to be knowledge. In a recent article in *Critical Inquiry*, Frederic Jameson argues that marxist historicism—not deconstruction or phenomenology—is the paradigm of theory ("How Not to Historicize Theory"). While many varieties of contemporary historicism are not aligned with Jameson's version of marxism, both his influence and the peculiar qualities of his approach justify his claim for its paradigmatic status.

An irony of this historicism is that it often presents itself as a hard-nosed, demystifying strategy, a turn away from the frivolity of high theory and the enchantments of the aesthetic. And yet, for reasons I discussed at length in my second chapter, the labor theory of value on which research programs like Jameson's rely is often used—along with creationism—as the classic example of an indefensible theory. As we have seen, Jameson makes no effort to defend the theoretical basis of his criticism, other than sporadic and implausible attempts to suggest that contemporary economists are also somehow committed to the labor theory. Jameson himself describes his relation to social science as "tourism," which suggests that he regards the evasion of serious engagement with other disciplines as a kind of intellectual vocation (*Postmodernism*, 267). His work reveals that if a certain haziness about deconstruction's propositions supports Hartman's 1980 contention that theory is style, a certain haziness about marxism's propositions supports Jameson's 2008 contention that theory is knowledge. The famous motto "always historicize!" rests on undefended, and—judging from the past century of debate—probably indefensible, propositions about economics, history, and politics.[12]

The wide and shallow influence of Jameson's sense of the political stakes of historical criticism, and the narrow but deep penetration of marxist commodity theory into mainstream literary historicism, makes his work a particularly salient example. But the problem is not specific to Jameson's brand of marxism. While a great deal of historicist scholarship cannot be accused of fuzziness about the nature of its claims, *ambitious* historicism does tend to have this problem. If a critic wants simply to describe the fiber used to make the paper on which Shakespeare's Quartos were printed, she needn't make use of the Jamesonian historicist paradigm. But to the extent that the critic wants to make further (economic) claims about the relations that organize that production, (philosophical) claims about the ways those relationships shape reading, or (psychological) claims about the forms of life that mode of reading supports, then she risks succumbing to the disciplinary problematic sketched above and facing the choice between uncritical parasitism on other fields or recourse to the low-prestige models cast off by economics, psychology, and the history of science. There are examples of ambitious historicism which reverse the trend, creating strong extra-disciplinary relations by identifying historical forces best illuminated by literary critical methods. One need only mention Said's *Orientalism* to recall the high-water mark of postwar literary studies' intellectual impact, when the claims of a literary critic were taken seriously across half a dozen disciplines. But one would struggle to find more than one or two such examples from the past twenty years, an era in which Said has been eclipsed by Sokal as the symbol of literary criticism's intellectual power.

And despite frequent claims to have learned from the Sokal Hoax how to break from the bad past, this sorry episode has not appeared to have had a beneficial effect on the most energetic contemporary opponent to historicism, the new scientifically-inflected criticism. As critics like Jonathan Kramnick and Ruth Leys have pointed out, a certain haziness clings to much of the new work on literature and science. Either supposedly authoritative scientific models are imported wholesale without any indication of the debates that accompany them in their home disciplines (Kramnick's target), or experimental results are interpreted by critics without acknowledgement of how widely they diverge from the experimenters' own interpretations (Leys's target). Rather than offering a viable third way, much of the criticism engaged with neuroscience replicates the problems we have observed in Hartman's and Jameson's methods. Current interdisciplinary criticism largely consists of discipline-specific sentences that cannot be taken seriously outside the English department, and that people in the English department cannot find a good way of taking unseriously.

The two modes of criticism briefly surveyed above represent symptoms of the same pathology. It infects deconstructive claims about literature as revealing the truth of language, marxist claims about science fiction novels as revealing the truth about society, and cognitive studies claims about writing as revealing the deep truth about the brain. In each case, an attempt to repress or transmute criticism's virtual relation to the disciplines resurfaces as disciplinary embarrassment. This pathology is characteristic of interpretive programs that understand literature as a reflection or extension of the actual. It manifests in a dramatic and undefended discrepancy between the literary critic's picture of language, economics, or biology, and that of linguists, economists, and biologists. Sometimes the gap between criticism's virtual world and the actual world becomes amusingly obvious. In "Paranoid Reading," Eve Sedgwick commented on the irony of the fact that D. A. Miller's Foucaultian *The Novel and the Police* was published in 1988, after two terms of Reagan. Sedgwick reads Miller's passionate denunciation of the dangers of a modern welfare state that bathes its citizens in ever-greater mental, medical, and educational care with disbelief. "As if!" she writes, reflecting on the difficulty of getting her insurance company to pay for therapy (19).

I believe that a solution to this dilemma lies not in evading criticism's virtual dimension but rather in embracing it by placing it back where it belongs: in our object of study. I want to suggest that seeing how the literary image differs from the actual is the first step in describing the *relation* of the work to the actual. And it is in this relation that our best hope for working out a viable mode of interdisciplinary research lies, a mode that isn't simply parasitic on the claims of other disciplines, but that offers meaningful interventions in shared questions.[13] A striking variety of work along these lines is currently under way, enough, indeed, to discern a genuinely new critical mode. Steven Justice, for example, has shown that medieval accounts of miracles don't simply reflect the medieval tendency to experience everything in terms of god's supernatural presence in the world, but create something that was hard for medieval people to believe. Rei Terada has examined the way Coleridge's interest in delicate, evanescent images shows us the therapeutic value in perceiving what's not there. Mark Hansen has described how new media art creates new modes of embodiment. Rita Felski has adumbrated the claim of the escape that literature offers by reversing the procedures of critical demystification. Oren Izenberg has explored the way modern poetry's contribution to ethics is expressed by virtual poems projected but not embodied by actual language. And in bringing literature's ideal images of timelessness into relation with the discourses of the actual, I have tried to suggest something of the knowledge-generating potential of that much-maligned organ, the Romantic imagination.

#  REFERENCE MATTER

# NOTES

INTRODUCTION: WRITING AGAINST TIME

1. Blakey Vermule claims, "The reasons that we care about literary characters are finally not much different from the question of why we care about other people" (xiii).

2. In addition, the reader brackets those parts of his immediate experience—the sound of cars driving by outside, the color of the sunlight on the page—that he understands not to be relevant to this projected experience. Theo Davis cogently argues that this bracketing does not distinguish literary from nonliterary experience (9–30). To focus on what's relevant and to bracket what's irrelevant is simply what it means to pay attention to something. Walter Benn Michaels has identified a tradition of postwar American art and writing that does seek to make the audience's total experience relevant, as in John Cage's famous *4'33"*. But the cannier representatives of this tradition understand that this kind of unfiltered experience is quite different from everyday experience. (Cage, for instance, consistently compares the effect of his work to Buddhist meditative practice.) Of course, to claim that the brain processes real and fictional images similarly does not mean that we recognize a flower in a poem and a flower in life *as* images in the same way. But given the emphasis placed on the role of interpretation in perception by the phenomenological tradition, we might not want to draw too firm a boundary between the real and the fictional here either.

3. See Timothy Schroeder and Carl Matheson, 33. For the classic treatment of this issue see Kendall Walton's discussion of "quasi-fear" (195–204).

4. See Alvin Goldman, "Imagination," 48.

5. While I take up the question of the relation of science to literature below, given the passions aroused by the introduction of brain research into literary studies, it may be best to briefly characterize my approach at the outset. Like other critics, I have been dissatisfied with the often reductive way scientific models have been applied to texts, the simplification of scientific debates that this application typically entails, and the absence of a meaningful effort to bring literary insights to bear on scientific problems. But to reject the findings of new brain sciences wholesale seems to me to be undesirable both intellectually and in terms of the long-term health of the discipline. In my view, recognition of the problems of what one might call "cognitive studies 1.0" clears the way for a more balanced and genuinely interdisciplinary sense of the place and value of scientific

research for humanistic scholarship. This involves discriminating between those literary problems science can genuinely help illuminate and those problems it can't. In its scientifically informed sections, *Writing Against Time* seeks to model a new kind of relation between literary studies and science by tracking literary projects whose Romantic ambition forces us to move between registering how science can specify certain cognitive limits, and how literature, in seeking to burst those limits, casts an unexpected light back on scientific problems.

My engagement with science in this book reflects my sense of it as an important, though inevitably minor, addition to the critic's traditional intellectual tools. Substantial parts of the second chapter have been written in collaboration and consultation with neuroscientists, psychologists, and historians of science, and elements of that chapter's argument have appeared in a prominent neuroscience journal. (See Michael Clune, John Sarneki, and Rebecca Traynor). Readers primarily interested in the relation of the humanities and sciences may wish to turn to that chapter, although portions of this introduction and the first chapter also make use of scientific material.

6. See Paul Ricoeur for a rich interpretation of Augustine's vision of time with particular reference to narrative problems.

7. See Andrew Bennett for a penetrating look at the eighteenth-century debate over Shakespearean immortality (34–36).

8. I do not want to elide the important differences between these two poems. If the bird of beaten gold in "Sailing to Byzantium" represents a commitment to enduring inorganic form, "Byzantium" at moments expresses an almost Keatsian effort to imagine "life-in-death." See Daniel Albright's *Quantum Poetics* for an acute discussion of the liquid "wave-form" characteristic of the latter type of Yeatsian image.

9. In one way of course, Sylvia Plath here develops the particular variant of the ekphrastic tradition I analyze in relation to John Keats's "Ode on a Grecian Urn" in my first chapter. But unlike the voice that issues from the urn in the final lines of the "Ode," the seeming speech of Plath's sculpture addresses *itself*: "We have come so far, it is over." The sculpture's voice does not pretend to have anything for us (the readers). This lyric "overhearing" (John Stuart Mill), embedded in a fiction that conceals speech itself, thus makes this a kind of hyper-lyric, multiplying the signs of its closedness to audience.

10. For a discussion of Jennifer Moxley's *The Line*, her key work in this respect, see my "Theory of Prose." Gwendolyn Brooks's *Annie Allen* and *In the Mecca* represent her most powerful reworking of the classical tradition of immortality (collected in *Blacks*, 77-140, 401-58).

11. For a brilliant recent meditation on obscurity in poetry, see Daniel Tiffany's *Infidel Poetics*. For a good discussion of the new resonance of Edmund Burke's materialist aesthetics for criticism inspired by developments in cognitive science, see Alan Richardson's *The Neural Sublime*.

12. See Jean-Jacques Nattiez for the most extensive critical treatment of Swann's musical experience. Nattiez is particularly good at teasing out the interpretive issues which underlie the critical effort to identify the sources of the sonata. I disagree with his reading of the passage in question on one fundamental point. While Nattiez attends

to Proust's representation of the process by which Swann understands the phrase, he fails to register the "disenchantment" which accompanies knowledge here. Perhaps this oversight is due to his interest in seeing Proustian music in terms of truth—a perspective, as we shall see in the next chapter, more appropriate to the narrator's experience of the septet than of Swann's experience of the sonata.

13. Alva Noe, who comes out of the phenomenological tradition, here exemplifies a tendency of that tradition that accounts for its near absence from much of what follows. Husserl and Heidegger, though in different ways, emphasize the way our encounters with things are shaped by a temporal horizon consisting of the memory of past encounters and the anticipation of future uses or significances. (See Hubert Dreyfus for a lucid discussion.) This emphasis on time's constitutive role in perception becomes so marked that, as Noe shows, the prospect of a truly novel encounter becomes almost inconceivable within this tradition. For a vivid recent example of the extent to which Heideggerian criticism radically diminishes the significance of the present, see Vivasvan Soni's recent book. Here the investigation of human happiness takes the form not of the question, am I happy? but of the prospective-retrospective, will I have been happy? (74). See my *American Literature and the Free Market* for an extended treatment of this issue with particular reference to Heidegger. Phenomenology's very antipathy to novelty gives it a central role in the fourth chapter of this book, where it will be found to play a surprising role.

14. This sense that perceptual vivacity is associated with the effort to understand thus distinguishes the kinds of habit-defeating sensations that interest Proust from the kinds of "visceral" modernist shock effects—of disgust, chaos, horror, etc.—that Rita Felski explores in her recent study (105–31), and that Walter Benjamin attributes to Baudelaire in his classic essay. (Note how distant the emphases of Baudelaire's description of Wagner's music quoted above are from the terms of Benjamin's discussion.) I also want to distinguish the dynamic I focus on from the structure of sublime experience, in which it is partially embedded for some critics. Thomas Weiskel's three-stage model of the Romantic sublime, for instance, consists of: a) a habituated state, b) the traumatic shattering of habit by alterity, and c) sublimation in a feeling of enhanced subjective power (described by Gary Lee Stonum, 68–70). The tradition I focus on places less emphasis on the final stage, the discovery of blocked powers of mind most fully articulated in Immanuel Kant's discussion of the mathematical sublime. An intense feeling of life in perception replaces the expansive awareness of one's cognitive powers seen by Kant and others as the payoff of the sublime. Thus Kant's account of the beautiful is more relevant to the problems associated with this tradition, and I take it up at length in my first chapter. The situation is complicated, however, with respect to Burke, whose interest in technical means of forestalling habituation in his discussion of the sublime will turn out to anticipate Kant's description of duration in his analysis of the beautiful, even as other central elements of Burke's discussion are dismissed in the *Critique of Judgment*. Partly because of the complex history of which these instances are but the tip of the iceberg, I have not used the term *beautiful* in preference to *sublime*, preferring to focus on the language of duration, form, and perception to cut across traditional aesthetic distinctions in setting out as clearly as possible the paradoxical effort that concerns us.

15. Other relevant studies include Harold Bloom's exploration of the fraught relations the survival of past poets presents for the living, and Leo Bersani's critical analysis of the impulse to look to posterity as a remedy for death.

16. See Niklaus Largier for an interesting reading of the impact of contemporary transformations of religious life on aesthetics in this period; see Martin Jay for a useful history of the concept of experience. Karl Polanyi offers a particularly powerful economic history relevant to aesthetic questions. Alan Richardson develops a useful account of the medical and scientific context (*British Romanticism and the Science of Mind*). Jerome Christensen offers an interesting recent example of what a non-historicist study of Romanticism might look like.

17. As I hope will be clear from the preceding discussion, this distinction between those who value intense experience and those who value increased knowledge should not be taken to imply that cognition and sensation are separable for writers who seek the extension of the first impression. The relation between knowledge and experience does, however, take a distinctive form for these writers. I examine the difference between the cognitive effort to grasp the form of the image, and the cognitive effort to discover new meanings in the interpretation of a familiar image, in my discussion of Kant in the first chapter.

18. Lisa Zunshine, in *Why We Read Fiction,* describes the pleasure of reading in terms of the exercise of cognitive faculties for negotiating interpersonal relations as presented in cognitive science. Mark Turner has drawn on cognitive science to describe metaphor as what he calls "conceptual blending." Gabrielle Starr, in "Multisensory Imagery," shows how art capitalizes on the way the brain processes different sensory modalities to orchestrate combinations of modalities that produce a richer mental image.

19. By harping on the limits of form with regard to the problem explored by this book, I certainly do not mean to dismiss the commitment to form that vitalizes some of our most powerful criticism. Two particularly interesting recent examples are Frances Ferguson's *Pornography, the Theory*, which examines the relation of form and action, and Aaron Kunin's "Character's Lounge," which undertakes a formal analysis of the work of character.

20. This virtuality in part motivates my description of the tradition I study as "Romantic," since critics from William Hazlitt to D. G. James to Simon Jarvis have seen a lack of fit between ambition and realized form as a central feature of Romantic poetry. Hazlitt claims that "poetry represents forms chiefly as they suggest other forms" (cited in François, 452). James writes, "We observe [Romanticism] casting around, perhaps desperately, for expressive form; and we also observe it failing to obtain what it wants" (xi). Jarvis explores the Romantic ambivalence about achieved form in terms of the tension between "idolatry" and iconoclastic "imagination" in Wordsworth. Insofar as the Romantic virtuality I examine is concerned with the difference between actual and virtual forms of perception, it echoes and develops Milton's description of pre- and post-lapsarian sensation in *Paradise Lost*. As Frank Kermode puts it, Milton's poem is haunted by "a strong sense of the woeful gap between the possible and the actual in physical pleasure" (594).

CHAPTER 1: IMAGINARY MUSIC

1. While Thomas Nagel's essay as a whole focuses on the epistemological consequences of the difference between first- and third-person perspectives, in citing him I am most interested in the related but distinct question of our imaginative capacity, which his example raises in an especially vivid way. See Mark Bruhn for a very different discussion of the constraints on imagination that applies Mark Turner's work on conceptual schema to Wordsworth's imagery.

2. In addition to Carl Dahlhaus's, two other broad studies exploring the relations between literature and music are particularly relevant to the argument I pursue. Marc Berely examines the history of poets' "claim to song as an important trope that serves to define their conception of themselves as poets" (3). He situates this trope in terms of the Platonic distinction between "practical" and "speculative" music, a distinction he tracks through early modern and Romantic poetries. Lawrence Kramer provides a stimulating comparison between the aesthetic strategies of nineteenth-century poets and composers. But his suggestive observations on the virtual songs in Wordsworth's "The Solitary Reaper" and Whitman's "The Music Always Round Me" are closest to the emphases of my discussion (139–41). Finally, a brief passage from William James's *Varieties of Religious Experience* will serve both to illustrate the ubiquity in nineteenth-century culture of beliefs about music similar to those Dahlhaus finds in Nietzsche, and to suggest the way a conviction of the superiority of music to verbal expression could be linked to alternative conceptions of human time. "Many mystical scriptures," James writes, "are indeed little more than musical compositions.... Music gives us ontological messages which non-musical criticism is unable to contradict.... That doctrine, for example, that eternity is timeless, that our 'immortality,' if we live in the eternal, is not so much future as already now and here" (421–22). James's decision to read texts about immortality as a kind of music complements the decision by Proust and Keats to make immortality imaginable through the ekphrasis of music.

3. Sybil de Souza provides a cogent discussion of these issues. She points out that in an early manuscript Marcel listens to a "quartet," and attributes the change to his need for a piece with greater "complexity" (117). In addition to Beethoven, she points to quartets by Debussy and Franck as possible models for Vinteuil's late work.

4. My reading of Swann's experience of the phrase as an "impression" should be contrasted with the sense Jesse Matz gives this term. Matz focuses on a category of Proustian experience, the most celebrated instance of which is Marcel's tasting of the madeleine. For Matz, this "impression" is "extra-temporal," because it forges so strong a connection between a present and past moment that they become identical. This should be contrasted with a moment like Swann's encounter with the phrase, which is extra-temporal in the sense of an arrest, a swelling of the experience of the present. This presentness is extra-temporal in being lifted from succession, rendered immune to anticipation and remembrance. Compared with the timelessness of the phrase, the extra-temporality of the madeleine, as Matz ably analyzes it, is more central both to the critical tradition on Proust as well as to the structure of *In Search of Lost Time* as a whole. Georges Poulet expresses a typical and influential view when he writes that

Proust seeks to "bring back the past into the present, the past not as past, not as a series of points of time, but as a simultaneous whole possessed in its entirety" ("Timelessness and Romanticism," 22). One way of thinking about these two strains of Proustian timelessness is to suggest that they emphasize different aspects of Augustine's problem. If the sonata is an instance of the effort to "lay hold of the heart" and prolong the vital experience of the present moment, the madeleine symbolizes the effort to overcome the human condition as "stretched" between past and future and to grasp the entire shape of a life in an instant.

5. See Jean-Jacques Nattiez for an account of Proust's "musical semiology" (63).

6. Paul de Man suggests another reason for why Proust might prefer virtual music to actual language as his preferred means of communication. De Man's celebrated reading of Proust's representation of reading emphasizes the degree to which the multiple temporalities involved in the encounter with a text resists Proust's intentions. "*À La Recherche du Temps Perdu* narrates the flight of meaning, but this does not prevent its own meaning from being, incessantly, in flight" (78). I regard de Man's insight as complementary to Proust's own sense, expressed in the passage describing Marcel's weariness with Bergotte, that literature's temporality resists the heart's desire.

7. For Kant's influence, see the classic discussions in M. H. Abrams's *The Mirror and the Lamp* and *Natural Supernaturalism*. Kant remains a central topic for scholars of Romantic literature. Compelling philosophical—as opposed to historical—treatments include Frances Ferguson's *Solitude and the Sublime*, and Rei Terada's *Looking Away*.

8. But the conception of Kantian pleasure as a drily disinterested state lingers. See, for example, Simon Jarvis's claim that for Kant pleasure is "either empirical gratification" or "disinterested delight" (*Wordsworth*, 125). The view I expound here brings Kantian disinterest closer to Simon Jarvis's compelling characterization of Wordsworth's idea of happiness.

9. An example is Kant's argument that there is pleasure in discovering the orderliness of nature. Henry Allison writes that Kant "admits that there is no pleasure involved in the apparent organizability of nature in terms of genera and species. But he also insists that there once was, and he explains the lack of pleasure currently felt on the grounds that it has become so familiar to us that we no longer take special notice of it, that is, we have lost sight of its contingency" (55).

10. See also Guyer, who notes that music "provides one of [Kant's] few illustrations of his key concept" (82).

11. Phillip Fisher's excellent study of the aesthetics of wonder contains a discussion of duration that contrasts with the Kantian aesthetic in clarifying ways. Like Kant, Fisher highlights the relation between pleasurable, intensified aesthetic awareness and the effort to understand, but the relation works quite differently for him. Fisher's account of wonder is of an instant of illumination, an intensified awareness that illuminates that which will then be explored by thought. In wonder, the form of the object is instantaneously available to perception, a feature of Fisher's account that explains his privileging of visual art. To extend the duration of pleasure is thus to attend closely to details of the object. "In the attention brought about by wonder, the capacity to notice the actual

details of the object is a strategy on the part of pleasure that seeks to last as long as possible" (39). But for Kant, lingering on details is not a strategy designed to extend pleasurably intense perception. As in Swann's first encounter with the sonata as an indistinct excitation that gradually assumes determinate shape, for Kant apprehension of the form is the *result* of the process of attention, not its starting point. Rather, the mental effort to grasp the details and their relation to the whole, to discern the very shape of the details, itself produces heightened attention. Whereas in the instances I explore, the cognitive effort and the intensity of perception are identical, for Fisher they are distinct but related. The "experience of duration, of not getting it, is the background of the sudden moment of saying 'I get it'" (65). It is the moment when one "gets it" that Fisher describes as the experience of wonder, whereas the authors I study view the duration of the gradual resolution of the object into determinate form as the apex of perceptual experience.

12. It might be argued that the effort to discover new meanings in the image is not ultimately different in kind from the effort to understand or to grasp the image's form. This is a complex question, but the short answer is that for the writers I study—Kant, most articulately, but also Proust, Keats, or Nabokov—the cognitive grappling with the form is strongly distinguished from an interpretive activity aimed at associating the form with new significances. I resist the Kantian temptation to describe the vitalizing struggle with form as a different kind of cognition—a different kind of understanding— from that involved in the pursuit of new meanings in familiar forms. Certainly writers like Proust and Keats treat it as such. But whether their practice is philosophically or psychologically justified is a question that lies outside the scope of this book. (I explore this question further, in relation to Shklovsky's critics, in Chapter 3, note 4, below.) In any case, whether the knowledge at issue in the initial grappling with form is like or unlike the knowledge at issue in reinterpreting familiar forms should not obscure the fact that nothing like a simple distinction between "experience" and "knowledge" is involved here. If this book succeeds at producing new knowledge of familiar works, it will be as a result of attending to the kind of thinking that animates intense perceptual experience.

13. By bringing empirical psychology into contact with Kant's formulations, I may be thought to violate the spirit of a critical project the philosopher famously distinguishes from psychology. But, as Gary Hatfield argues, we cannot take Kant's repudiation of eighteenth-century rationalist psychology as a general antipathy to psychological observation as such. In fact, Kant regularly "appeal[s] to experience to ground some basic claims," and he takes "reflection on ordinary experience" as a "starting point for philosophy" (216). Of course, whether the neurobiological descriptions of the human sense of time of which I have made use are ultimately compatible with Kant's transcendental description of mind is a different question. As a general matter, Hatfield cautiously foresees a potential convergence between the new sciences of mind and the Kantian framework. But this problem lies well beyond the scope of my study.

14. The relatively few commentators who have dwelled on Kant's concern with the duration of aesthetic pleasure do not seem to see this as creating a problem for form. Thomas Pfau, for example, notices that Kant values the prolongation of pleasure, but thinks that aesthetic form as such is what guarantees prolongation for Kant. This does

not seem right to me. Kant's position seems to require a very special kind of form: a form that will prolong pleasure and defeat habit.

15. See James Heffernan for a similar reading of the poem as a critique of the capacity of visual art to represent or embody transcendence. "Figures simultaneously quickened by desire and arrested by art . . . will become unbearably frustrated" (113).

16. The positions I associate with Murray Krieger, Helen Vendler, and Georges Poulet do not, of course, exhaust the critical accounts of this central Romantic poem. I want to indicate just three additional essays that have a special bearing on my argument. Marshall Brown interprets the urn's "unheard music" in terms of form, which he understands as the "enabling virtualities under the world of appearances" (473). This is also a Kantian reading, but unlike my interest in Kant's discussion of the duration of pleasure in the *Critique of Judgment*, Brown's interest lies in developing his sense of experience—organizing form by analogy to the categories of the *Critique of Pure Reason*. Gabrielle Starr, in "Poetic Subjects and Grecian Urns: Close Reading and the Tools of Cognitive Science," investigates the tension in the poem's activation of visual and auditory imagery. In arguing for the effect of this tension on the reader, Starr relies on scientific models to describe the constraints on imagination in poetic reception. Her essay, which shows Keats cannily adapting to those constraints in the "Urn," offers a useful counterpoint to my interest in Keats's effort to overcome such constraints in "Hyperion."

Finally, Anne-Lise François offers a complex and fascinating account of Keats's tendency—in the "Urn" and elsewhere—to represent musical form through visual image. "To see it may be all one can do with singing, first because there is no such thing as an uncrossed act of perception [i.e., one that doesn't involve multiple senses], no such thing as 'pure listening,' and then (and on the contrary) because only thus can utterance become 'singing'—pure in the sense of devoid of communicative content" (460). François does not, however, understand Keats's poetic desire as a straining towards an impossible fullness of perception. Where I see the poetry as animated by the prospect of achieving ideal form, even as the poet takes up complex psychological attitudes towards this prospect, François sees Keatsian form as creating pleasure in a deliberate suspension of movement towards the fuller modes of perception the poetry intimates.

17. Suzanne Langer, one of Henri Bergson's most distinguished readers, has seen his entire philosophy of time as a philosophy of music, considered as the art of duration (104–20).

18. See Roger Shattuck for an account of the impact of Proust's reading of Bergson on *In Search of Lost Time*.

19. In conjoining Kant and Bergson, I have not forgotten that the latter frames his project in opposition to the treatment of time in *The Critique of Pure Reason*. But Kant's description of the duration of pleasure in *The Critique of Judgment* follows, as Paul Guyer implicitly recognizes, a distinct logic, and it is on the ground of the duration of aesthetic attention that Kant and Bergson's ideas become commensurable. This surprising result is but one of the fruits of recovering this neglected dimension of Kant's aesthetics. The use of the word *indeterminacy* in discussions of Kant and Bergson can, however, be misleading in a literary context, where it can be confused with the very

different deconstructive sense of the term. The latter's sense of indeterminate or undecidable texts typically depends on iterability, which in turn depends on clearly distinct words and letters. *Indeterminacy* in this sense obviously will not answer to the Bergsonian demand for *indistinction*, nor make texts plausible vehicles for the effort explored here. I take up the question of iterability at length in my fourth chapter.

20. For an extensive discussion of the parallels between musical forms and Keats's prosody, see John A. Minahan. For a classic discussion of the rhythm in "Hyperion" centering on its "management of the pause," see Walter Jackson Bate (408–10). And for a suggestive recent approach to poetry's actual (as opposed to virtual) melodics, see Simon Jarvis, "The Melodics of Long Poems." For an interesting recent collection of essays on the poetics of sound in Romanticism, see Susan Wolfson. Finally, Jerome Christensen reads Wordsworth's poetics in a manner that suggests interesting parallels to the "choreographing of expectations" musicologists find in their object of study. Meter, for Wordsworth, disciplines poetic enjoyment through "regular bursts of pleasurable surprise" (201). But on repeated readings the surprise of such music would, of course, be diminished, and thus fall short of the ideal music imaged by Keats.

21. In fact Bennett goes further, and suggests that the idea of posthumous life through the text projects an infinite deferral of reading to the *next* generation.

22. A particularly relevant example of a critical account prefigured by this poem is W.J.T. Mitchell's influential description of ekphrasis as a relation to the other, animated by desire (for dominance) and fear (of being dominated). Mitchell identifies the speaking subject of the ekphrastic relation as male. While this seems appropriate for an example like "Ode on a Grecian Urn," here the genders are reversed, and Keats processes the mingled threat and desire elicited by Apollonian song primarily through a female perspective. In addition, the complexity with which the poem offers us the view that ekphrastic beauty is bound up with power radically undermines Mitchell's presentation of this as the buried truth of ekphrastic poetry. For a quite different discussion of the potential political significance of Keatsian beauty, see Noel Jackson's recent essay. Jackson argues that Keats's acceptance of the impossibility of extending the "time of beauty" is accompanied by a devotion to the possibilities opened by the unpredictable microknowledges that intense attentiveness to the present might foster.

23. In her original account, Marjorie Levinson suggests that Keats breaks off because "Hyperion"—the work most praised by Keats's contemporaries—promises to be his most masterful poem and thus elicits a fear of success, an anxiety about entering maturity and adult temporality (181). More representative of the critical tradition is Bloom's conviction that the poem is in fact substantially, if not formally, whole. "Hyperion is already a complete poem once Apollo has realized himself" (*The Visionary Company*, 388).

CHAPTER 2: THE ADDICTIVE IMAGE

1. For the best study of the Sokal Hoax, see John Guillory.
2. David Chalmers's discussion of zombies illustrates how scientific descriptions of human functioning work without making a place for consciousness.
3. This is why it strikes me that pursuing consciousness (or qualia) as it has been

conceptualized in philosophy of mind is a dead end for literary studies. For an interesting attempt, see Oren Izenburg's "Poems Out of Our Heads." I will argue in this chapter that establishing the relevance of consciousness to literary studies involves moving past epiphenomenality.

4. We might contrast Edgar Allan Poe's writing on morphine or Denis Johnson's writing on heroin to the hallucinogen literature of the mid-twentieth century, which does not register the same dramatic discrepancy between the experience of empirical users and the literary representation of that experience. But both the objects (which are affirmed to be non-addictive) and the emphases of hallucinogen writing differ from the work with which I am concerned. The well-known tendency of narcotics to dull perception over time is well-represented in literary texts, and is curiously marked in those works that are also replete with descriptions of the perception-intensifying effects of the addictive substance. See for example, William S. Burroughs's description throughout *Naked Lunch* of heroin addiction as a nearly catatonic state.

5. One must distinguish Thomas De Quincey's account of the first time he became intoxicated on opium from his reflections on the possible origins of his propensity to addiction in various incidents in his childhood. Alina Clej is quite right to point out the confusion of this latter speculation on psychological origins, but wrong to include De Quincey's description of the first time he actually takes opium—that "cardinal event"—in her discussion of how in De Quincey the "origin of things . . . melts into a haze" (62).

6. De Quincey writes of the *Confessions* that "opium is the true hero of the tale" (86), and he develops this hero in several directions simultaneously. The supernatural description of the drug itself and of the first time he took it exists alongside numerous descriptions of its effects when ingested. Sometimes these effects are rendered in terms of a suspension of time. Under opium's influence, he writes, "over every form . . . brooded a sense of eternity and infinity" (82). But the most celebrated passages of the *Confessions*—the description of De Quincey's dreams under the influence of opium—have no analogue in either empirical descriptions of actual addicts, nor in other literary descriptions of narcotics. The point of view I adopt here suggests that the figuration of the dream sequences derive not from the effects of the ingested drug on De Quincey's brain, but from the power of opium as object of perception to alter the possibilities of the literary image.

7. Yet the skeptical reader might well ask, given the suspicion I cast on the phenomenological accuracy of De Quincey's descriptions of opium's effects, why I should regard his description of the persistence of his first time as an accurate account of the experience of an addict? One way of answering this objection would be to point to the large number of texts that offer an account of the persistence of the first time similar to De Quincey's—and I provide several such examples. But I think a better response to the question of why we should believe in the truth of De Quincey's representation of the immortality of the first time is the pragmatic one. We should believe it if it will show us something new about addiction. If this chapter succeeds, it will do so by sketching the reasons we should attend to the part of *The Confessions* I highlight on such pragmatic grounds.

8. Several critics have drawn attention to the relation between opium and art in *The*

*Confessions*. Margaret Russett argues that De Quincey's representation of opium was shaped by his reading of Wordsworth's poetics, and claims that "addiction . . . is mimesis in reverse, life endlessly imitating art" (18). Drawing on Russett's account, Jerome Christensen notices that for De Quincey opium gives a "vitally formal, that is poetic, pleasure" (202), and argues that poetry and opium are for De Quincey interchangeable terms. "Nothing in their exquisitely pleasurable effects distinguishes the two, except that poetry does not ordinarily lead to addiction . . . what keeps poetry from producing the deleterious effects of opium is not any element intrinsically superior or different . . . but that the former is regulated by meter" (201). I agree with these critics that De Quincey's deep engagement with Romantic poetics shapes his representation of addiction in a fundamental way. But I take a nearly opposite view of the dynamics of this relation. They think that what interests De Quincey as a writer on addiction is its aesthetic aspects, but go on to argue that what opium does for De Quincey is simply a deficient copy of what poetry does. I argue that specific perceptual and temporal features of opium addiction serve De Quincey as the model for a truly effective poetry.

9. My description here of *Lolita*'s representation of obsession in terms of an image that marks a break with habitual perception might be usefully contrasted with one of the most interesting accounts of obsession in recent criticism. Bill Brown, in *A Sense of Things*, focuses his discussion of Frank Norris's novels on "the relation between Norris's representation of habits and his habits of representation" (53). While Brown sees some modes of addiction in these works—such as Vandhover's gambling—in the traditional terms of habit (54), he departs from this analysis when he reads Trina's "addiction" to gold in *McTeague* as a break in habitual perception. But whereas in the works I consider this break is valued in Kantian aesthetic terms as an enhancement of the feeling of life, Brown convincingly argues that for Norris it has a primarily epistemological valence. Trina's obsessive handling of gold thus represents an effort to know it, "as though you had to grasp the same coffee mug over and over to verify its three dimensionality" (67). If gold for Trina comes to seem like the most solid, earthly, and knowable object in the world, De Quincey and Nabokov persist in describing the objects of their pathological attention as "magical," "immortal," and "bewitched."

10. As will become clear, I do not apply the term "addiction" to Humbert's condition loosely, but because the structure of this fictional character's obsession with nymphets both mirrors and usefully illuminates the disorder that is currently the object of scientific investigation. I do not claim that this term should or could be usefully applied to actual pedophiles, a question well beyond the scope of this study.

11. See also the discussion of Davidson and addiction in Jon Elster's *Strong Feelings* (170–72).

12. Samuel Beckett, in his early study of Proust, suggests another connection between the two novels when he calls the images "fetishes," like the famous madeleine Proust associates with the overcoming of time through involuntary memory (30–31).

13. Eric Naiman has recently shown how the criticism consistently overstates the erotic impact of Vladimir Nabokov's prose, forgetting the gap between word play and actual sexual satisfaction (42). Humbert's pathology turns that gap into a gulf.

14. While I will not linger over this question, I will note that the assumption by several critics that Humbert is an unreliable narrator is related to the assumption of Nabokov's artistic mastery. I will subject this latter assumption to scrutiny below. Here I want simply to suggest the implications of this scrutiny for the critical commonplace of Humbert's unreliability. If Humbert has been seen as an effective artist who aestheticizes his pathology, I see Humbert/Nabokov as an ambitious artist modeling his art on pathology.

15. See Abrams's survey of a century of responses to Wordsworth's poetry in *Natural Supernaturalism* for particularly vivid examples of lives transformed by literature in the most dramatic ways (134–40).

16. See Felski's account of artistic "shock" for a good account along these lines (105–31).

17. Michael Wood does not take up the question of time with respect to *Lolita*, but discusses related dynamics in *Speak, Memory* and *Ada*. For Wood, the virtual, unachieved quality of time stopping in Nabokov is one of the "doubts" his title refers to. His reading, however, gives Nabokov's corpus a kind of closure that my account questions. In Wood's hands, Nabokov's failure to make effective time-resistant writing is woven into a story about the tragedy of time's inescapability. Wood recognizes the virtuality of the passages that claim to arrest time, but still wants an achieved text. Nabokov's text is thus not the text that stops time but the text that bemoans time's persistence. I want to pursue the value of the virtual text, the text that does not give up on its impossible desire, a little further.

18. If Marc Redfield insists on a straightforward identification of addiction and commodity fetishism, this relationship is more subtle and modulated in De Quincey's best critics. Russett, for example, reads opium as a "figure for alienated labor" that "spiritualizes market exchange" (135) in part through reconciling economic and aesthetic value (141). The status of her discussion of the "equivocation at the commodity's heart" itself equivocates between a description of De Quincey's own understanding of economics—derived largely from Ricardo—and an analysis of the actual social and economic conditions he inhabits (149). Jerome Christensen's description of De Quincey's addiction cites Fredric Jameson directly, to whom I turn below (196), but also investigates the relationship between De Quincey's representation of addiction and Wordsworth's account of meter in ways that cannot be assimilated to Jameson's understanding of the link between economic conditions and aesthetic form. But despite the fact that these critics' readings of opium are quite different than Redfield's, the way the economic context is brought to bear—and the ghostly presence of commodity theory in the elaboration of that context—renders these accounts useful examples of the pervasive effects of the interdisciplinary model I wish to contest.

19. See my *American Literature and the Free Market* for a detailed discussion of the extent to which Adorno's aesthetics are dependent on the labor theory of value (147–65). The necessity of freeing marxist literary studies from its commitment to the labor theory of value does not, in my view, entail a rejection of the marxist tradition. In the same pages I defend the enduring value of several of Marx's basic insights about economic relations for thinking about postwar writing.

20. It might be pointed out that a number of models that have held sway in neoclassical economics—the efficient markets hypothesis, the image of homo economicus as rational chooser—rest on shaky empirical and argumentative foundations. But those who hold leftist alternatives to these models would hardly want to proceed by imitating the weakness of their opponents in this respect. Indeed, left economics has been increasingly successful in challenging many neoclassical models precisely by subjecting them to empirical testing.

21. Richard Godden's recent *PMLA* piece, one of the rare attempts by a marxist critic to engage economics, unfortunately relies on Postone's concept of "abstract" labor, a concept that suffers from the same flaws addressed by John Roemer. For a left economist's perspective on these issues, see Gregory La Blanc.

22. For three different perspectives on the low *academic* prestige of scholarship like Jameson's, see Michael Berube, Mark Bauerlein and Ian Hunter. This is a different question from the abuse this work routinely suffers in journalism, mass media, and the culture at large, which to some extent may still be entangled with the politics of the "culture wars" of the 1990s. Just because Jameson's views are in fact mistaken does not mean that views like his are not often dismissed for politicized reasons that have little to do with their intellectual merit. This tendency does, however, seem to be in decline. An attitude like that expressed by Jesse Prinz—"conservative in science, radical in politics"—appears to be in the process of replacing the earlier alignment of epistemological softness with left politics. (See also Bruno Latour.)

23. Jameson's student Nicholas Brown has responded to an earlier version of the argument I make here by claiming that Jameson and other marxist critics are not interested in economic questions at all, but only in "cultural interpretation." If true, this would furnish such critics with a defense for their disinterest in defending positions that only appear economic. But I find Brown's claim implausible, given that the entire thrust of marxist criticism has been to erase the boundary between purely economic and purely cultural questions. There is an urgent political as well as intellectual need for a strong anticapitalist critique, and a criticism that deploys the labor theory of value without attempting to defend it does nothing to answer this call.

24. For two useful overviews of this history, see Carlton Erikson and Nancy D. Campbell.

25. See B. L. Carter and S. T. Tiffany. I adapt portions of this account from my "Cue Fascination," coauthored with Rebecca Traynor and John Sarneki. As noted in that piece, its central idea is drawn from my work on the literary image of addiction.

26. See Richard B. Rosse et al.

27. See Norman Earl Zinberg.

28. See A. S. Freeman, L. T. Meltzer, and B. S. Bunney, and P. A. Garris et al.

29. See the anthology by Ned Block, Owen Flanagan, and Guven Guzeldere titled *The Nature of Consciousness* for a useful selection of major contributions to the debate from the mid-1970s to the mid-1990s.

30. For a recent impressive attempt, see Jesse Prinz on consciousness as a means of focusing information processing. He admits that what interests people in phenomenal

consciousness itself—"what it feels like" to be attentive rather than the content of the attention—is not explained by his model.

31. Phillip Fisher finds support for a radical equation of consciousness and novelty in Wittgenstein's late writing. "Wittgenstein's point is that there can be no 'feeling of the ordinary'.... What Wittgenstein contrasts to the ordinary is the feeling of surprise ... *we notice something in so far as it is unexpected*" (20, my emphasis).

32. Leys is the most recent humanist to cast a critical eye on this study; she also takes up the response by Gallagher that I discuss below.

33. Again, I wish to emphasize that in raising the possibility that a conscious fascination with the addictive object plays a nontrivial role in addiction, I do not mean to cast doubt on the robust evidence for the role of purely automatic and "robotic" responses. Nor do I mean to suggest that this fascination is more important than these responses (although I do think its features and implications make it more philosophically *interesting*). As A. David Redish, Steve Jensen, and Adam Johnson demonstrate, addiction is a complex disorder in which a variety of different mechanisms play a part. I hope to have made a preliminary case for why it might make sense to explore the fascination described in the literature further. Establishing the existence and importance of this fascination in a scientifically rigorous way would undoubtedly involve reckoning with the kinds of problems that always arise when dealing with first-person reports. For an interesting approach to these problems, see Antoine Lutz et al.

CHAPTER 3: BIG BROTHER STOPS TIME

1. See also Hannah Arendt's definition of totalitarianism as an "experiment in constantly transforming reality into fiction" (*The Origins of Totalitarianism*, 511).

2. See also John Dewey's discussion of "mechanical" habit, which he distinguishes from "artistic" forms of habit in *Human Nature and Conduct: An Introduction to Social Psychology*, 58–74.

3. The classic study of the twentieth-century impulse to collapse the border between art and life is Peter Burger's *Theory of the Avant-Garde*. Burger's treatment of "shock" as device recognizes Shklovsky (18). In that he interprets defamiliarization in cognitive terms, Burger's position is similar to the readings of Shklovsky I analyze below. For a recent study on practices that merge life and art see Michael Sheringham. On the association of the collapse of art and life with totalitarianism see Benjamin and Arendt, and also Andrew Hewitt.

4. Here we come up against an ambivalence noted in the previous chapter, in that the "knowledge" produced by the aesthetic can refer either to the understanding of the form as it unfolds over the duration of the initial encounter, or to the uncovering or association of additional significances. If Ginzburg, like many critics, tends to oppose defamiliarization as "knowledge" to defamiliarization as "intense experience," we have seen that the latter is itself the result of a striving for a certain kind of cognitive mastery, and vanishes once that new knowledge is achieved. Ginzburg would be more accurate if he said that he, like Winckelmann, values the knowledge that comes at the end of the process of grappling with an art work, not the evanescent intensification of the feeling

of life characteristic of that process's earlier stages. Here I would like to introduce a further distinction that will specify more clearly the real difference between Ginzburg and myself. Ginzburg values the knowledge which is secured after the stage of "impressionistic immediacy," *and which takes no note of that stage, or of the process by which the knowledge emerges.* By contrast, my own claims for the knowledge generated by analysis of the Romantic effort to defeat time depends on close attention to this stage, and to writers' efforts to extend it. In other words, I do not disagree with Ginzburg about the value of the knowledge given by art; I do disagree with him about where to look for it.

5. Cristina Vatulescu attempts to historicize Shklovsky's aesthetics. In her intriguing investigation of the "estranging" or "surrealist" techniques of the Soviet secret police, she proposes a different relation between the aesthetic and totalitarianism than that developed here. While the secret police in her account attempt to disorient prisoners by putting them in spaces where familiar objects have actually been replaced by strange objects, Shklovsky (at least in "Art as Technique") and Orwell are interested in making one see familiar objects *as if for the first time.* This is a key distinction. It accounts for the emphasis on the temporality of perception in the works I examine, the link they forge between perceptual intensity and "an eternal present." When Winston falls into the hands of the secret police towards the end of 1984, the regime's procedure shifts to one roughly analogous to those Vatulescu describes. In these scenes, O'Brian aims not to make Winston see familiar objects in a new way, but to make him see terrifying and strange objects (as when he shows him a rat about to gnaw off his face), or to make him see things that are not actually visible (as when he tries to get Winston to see more fingers than he is holding up).

6. *Limited Inc.* contains Jacques Derrida's fullest exposition of his theory of iterability.

7. See also Peter Steiner's characterization of Shklovsky's theory of perception as "mechanistic" (44–68).

8. In the interrogation sequence, O'Brian seeks to "cure" Winston of his belief in the past (247–48). Exactly what the regime objects to in Winston can be seen by comparing him before and after his reprogramming in the Ministry of Love. When he is finally released, he has lost his desire for a past or future, but he still cannot get used to the taste of gin (293). Winston's desire for a past and a future, which represents a fundamental opposition to the regime, should be distinguished from his passionate awareness of the surface of the world ("rocks are hard, water is wet"), which is elicited by the regime through the technique of prohibition.

9. See Jameson's discussion of Michel Foucault's "total" disciplinary systems in *Postmodernism* (5).

CHAPTER 4: THE CULTURED IMAGE

1. Cited in Perloff, 262. I take up Marjorie Perloff's influential reading of John Ashbery's poetry as "disjunct" below. For the relation of Ashbery and Roussel, see also Charles M. Cooney. Cooney's approach is broadly consistent with Perloff's in describing Ashbery's poetry as "radically disjunct" (89).

2. In the following I use *world* and *culture* as synonymous, in the phenomenological

sense of Thomas Kuhn, who defines a world as "the entire constellation of beliefs, values, techniques and so on shared by members of a given community." Hubert Dreyfus usefully glosses Kuhn's definition by contrasting "the physical world" with "the world of physics." It is the latter sense of *world* I intend (88–90). And while I use *world* and *culture* to refer to the same thing, there are shades of emphasis. For example, in discussing Ashbery's use of invented or imaginary cultures, and to indicate the affinity of his project with that of an important strain of science fiction, I have sometimes preferred *world* to *culture*.

3. Henrik Birnbaum introduces this term in "Familiarization and its Semiotic Matrix." As will become clear, I apply this term within a phenomenological critical framework, in contrast to Birnbaum's semiotic approach. The special features of the "familiar" which phenomenology draws out will prove crucial to understanding the value this process has in Ashbery.

4. My understanding of the thing of novelistic realism as condensing the norms and values of a world is indebted to Heidegger's discussion of the thing as a "gathering" of the principles that structure the experience of a given culture ("The Thing," 161–85).

5. John Vincent's main argument—that the basic unit of Ashbery's poetic practice is the book—moves in the opposite direction of mine. I hold that the basic unit of Ashbery's practice is the line. I think the widespread feeling that individual lines in Ashbery poems (especially late Ashbery poems) are interchangeable with lines in any other late Ashbery poem provides evidence for my view.

6. Vincent explores what Bonnie Costello calls the "fruitful ambiguity of the second person" in Ashbery, identifying *you* with either the reader or Ashbery's lover or friend (145–60). I think that reading the second person in terms of Ashbery's investigation of novelistic and dialogic techniques suggests a third alternative: *you* can refer to someone addressed by a speaker in a poem, a person known to the speaker, and a person unknown to both reader and poet.

7. Jack Vance, *Tales of the Dying Earth*, 271. This novel, a genre classic, was first published in 1964, and has exerted a powerful influence on science fiction and fantasy works from Gene Wolfe's *Book of the New Sun* to Gary Gygax's *Dungeon and Dragons* role-playing games.

8. William Gibson, *Neuromancer*, 168.

9. In "Hegel," Ashbery presents the same problem from the opposite perspective: "She said she had 'dishpan hands'/ No-one quite understood what she was talking about" (*Can You Hear, Bird?* 56).

10. I note that the canonical poems from which these two modernist examples are drawn suppress or flatten the background. Yeats's "shape" is seen against a desert; Pound turns the worldly background of a subway station into a flat "black bough."

11. John Bayley, 198. See also Andrew Ross.

12. For an influential description of this procedure, see Paul Ricoeur's account of the "trace" in *Time and Narrative*, Vol. 3, 78–104, 119–25.

13. In this movement from part to whole I note the difference of Ashbery's project from that of the subgenre of science fiction Jameson has described as characterized by

the "unknowability thesis" regarding alien cultures (*Archeologies of the Future*, 107–18). Science fiction from Lem to Clarke, on Jameson's account, focuses on the epistemological problem of how one can know a truly other culture, and regards the impossibility of this knowledge as pure deprivation. For Ashbery, the very lack of knowledge about the alien world of the object serves as the technology that makes that world present, as a totality, in the formlessness of the alien thing.

14. *Hotel Lautreamont*, 78.

15. The relatively unproblematic *availability* of Chinese poetry for Pound has led to a number of works exploring the relation of modernism to orientalism. (See especially Eric Hayot). Here I simply wish to note the difference between a stance where the Eastern object becomes a more or less clearly delimited, more or less eternal, fixed, unchanging object of Western knowledge, and the radical alterity at stake in Ashbery's rendering of the Eastern thing as fluid, open, unfixed.

16. Perloff, in her recent *21st Century Modernism*, has revised her earlier classification of Ashbery as postmodern, and joined James Longenbach in arguing for this poetry's deep continuity with modernism. Her reading of Ashbery's poetics remains unrevised, but she now (correctly) locates the dynamics she finds in Ashbery in the work of modernists like Eliot and Pound. On Foucault's treatment of Lautreamont's table, see Rey Chow, 293. For an interesting reading of Ashbery's project as an attempt to carry forward the modernist project as defined by Jurgen Habermas, see David Herd. Herd thinks Ashbery's "occasional poetry" seeks to recreate a world for modern people who have lost one. Referring to Habermas's sense of the "background" of norms which allow communication, Herd argues that these poems, in their attention to "details of everyday life," create a background adequate to our dynamic modern occasion. The problem with this argument is that the "background" does not consist of an accumulation of "details," but rather of the norms, beliefs, and values that enable the details to show up for people in certain ways. The poems withhold this background, and their characteristic effect depends on this withholding.

17. William Maxwell notes that "homogenization" is the "defining fear of globalization studies in the 1990's" (361).

18. For Chow, to work within the terms of a specific culture is not to accept a fixed, static, or essentialist idea of that culture. On the contrary, the work Chow celebrates reveals the traces of other cultures, the hybridity and impurity of any given culture. But global commensurability is neither the starting nor the ending point of this kind of scholarship. The culture within the frame of study may be mixed and impure, but the "specific cultural framework" remains the horizon of interpretation and value. For a more radical effort to rethink the processes of intercultural contact, see Charles Hallisey's brilliant essay.

19. Gayatri Spivak makes a similar point when she advocates comparativism as resisting "globalization [as] the imposition of the same system of exchange everywhere" (72).

20. Economists will, of course, disagree about the *source* of this value, with some arguing value derives from the consumers' rational knowledge of their desires, and others arguing it derives from social and cultural forces, advertising, or product placement

in the store or on an internet site. (See my *American Literature and the Free Market* for a fuller discussion of these issues.)

21. For the classic account of Romantic anti-mimetic aesthetics, see Abrams's *The Mirror and the Lamp*. See also Brian McHale's influential description of the distinction between modern and postmodern fiction in terms of a shift between epistemological and ontological concerns.

CONCLUSION: FROM REPRESENTATION TO CREATION

1. Despite what is often claimed, this crisis in the value of literary *scholarship* is distinct from the relative health of public interest in literature, as measured both by the steady increase in book sales in recent years and by the stability of student enrollments in English majors over the past two decades. (On the latter, see especially the 2009 MLA "Report to the Teagle Foundation on the Undergraduate Major.")

2. In attacking I. A. Richards's model of practical criticism, Geoffrey Hartman argues that literary studies should not be a discipline but a literary genre (298). For an interestingly related later view, this time with respect to art criticism, see W.J.T. Mitchell's idea of "indiscipline" as "turbulence or incoherence at the inner and outer boundaries of disciplines." ("Interdisciplinarity and Visual Culture," 541).

3. For an excellent study of the establishment of criticism as a genre see Patrick Parrinder. Parrinder places Dryden at the origin of this establishment in English literature (6–18).

4. See John Guillory's "The Sokal Hoax and the History of Criticism" for examples of the last category. My use of *serious* and *unserious* to describe the literary strategies Hartman has in mind is indebted to Susan Sontag's usage in her classic "Notes on 'Camp,'" in which she calls for "a new, more complex relation to the serious" (288).

5. See, for example, Francesca Bordogna (260–63).

6. For Hartman there is a deep continuity between criticism's practice in this regard and that of Romantic literature itself, which he sees as periodically resurrecting the forms of old knowledge as new style.

7. It is important to distinguish the as-if relation of theory's (fully-formed) concepts to disciplinary regimes from Kant's account of aesthetic form as quasi- or as-if concepts in the *Critique of Judgment*. In a boldly revisionist reading of Adorno carried out over a series of essays and books, Robert Kaufman has recently explored the possible contribution of aesthetic form to social theory along Kantian lines, arguing that art presents the occasion for the generation of new critical concepts.

8. For an early instance of this desire, see David Wellbery's reading of the figure of Arnheim in Musil's *Man Without Qualities* as showing how "disciplinary complexity generates the phantasm of personally embodied interdisciplinary integration." Arnheim's speech is "systematically nonserious" (986).

9. For classic statements of deconstruction's theory of language and writing, see Jacques Derrida, *Limited Inc.*, and Paul de Man, *Allegories of Reading*. These two works offer distinctive descriptions of the way propositions are transformed by writing: de Man focuses on the materiality of the signifier and Derrida on the iterability of the sign.

These distinctions could be multiplied with reference to other works by the same authors, or by other deconstructive critics. Such distinctions are quite irrelevant for Hartman who, in this work at least, typically declines to explicitly engage with deconstructive arguments even as his description of style ultimately depends, in a general way, on *some* version of deconstruction.

10. While this ambiguity characterizes *Criticism in the Wilderness* as a whole, particular chapters tend to lean one way or the other. Contrast his second and third chapters' emphasis on criticism's "freakish" verbal power, for instance, with the claims for theory's ability to correct the disciplines in his "Coda."

11. Hartman distinguished himself from Yale colleagues like Paul de Man and D. A. Miller by describing himself as "barely deconstructionist" (Hartman cited in Vincent Leitch, 281). Hartman's reluctance to commit to the deconstructive theory he often worked with might be usefully illuminated by considering it in the context of a career that Leitch describes as spent "avoiding such commitments." Hartman "worked to remain independent" (160–61). This disposition fits nicely with the logic of the position Hartman advances in *Criticism in the Wilderness.*

12. It is not clear to me that the presuppositions that have tended to displace Jameson's among historicists are any more defensible or are, in fact, defended. See Virginia Jackson's "Please Don't Call It History" for a striking articulation of a theory of literary history that can only be described as nominalist. Here Jackson lays out a historicism that would castigate as "idealist" any effort to understand artifacts outside a narrowly defined historical context, but she doesn't defend it, nor even manifest an awareness that so counterintuitive a notion of history needs defense. By contrast, Wai Chee Dimock defends her nearly opposite vision of literary history with a surprising, though cogent and persuasive, understanding of the relation between text and context.

13. As I hope this study has shown, engaging in such work does not mean automatically deferring to the supposedly greater wisdom of other disciplines. Agreement of economists, neuroscientists, historians, or philosophers with the literary critic's claims is not necessary to validate them. I have taken pains to indicate places where scientists and philosophers disagree among themselves and where they disagree with me, as well as to indicate why I continue to hold my positions in the face of such disagreement. But my disagreement with Redish et al., for example, is also evidence of engagement, and rejecting what I have identified as the several pathologies of interdisciplinary criticism seems necessary to create the possibility of such engagement. Also, as I hope this study has shown, a belief in the potential of criticism's responsible interdisciplinary engagement does not diminish the value of an inquiry whose main ambition is to illuminate the operations of some of our most powerful literary artifacts.

# BIBLIOGRAPHY

Abrams, M. H. *The Mirror and the Lamp*. Oxford: Oxford University Press, 1971.
———. *Natural Supernaturalism*. New York: Norton, 1973.
Adorno, Theodor. *Aesthetic Theory*. Translated by Robert Hullot-Kantor. Minneapolis: University of Minnesota Press, 1998.
Albright, Daniel. *Quantum Poetics*. Cambridge: Cambridge University Press, 1997.
Alexandrov, Vladimir. *Nabokov's Otherworld*. Princeton: Princeton University Press, 1991.
Allison, Henry. *Kant's Theory of Taste*. Cambridge: Cambridge University Press, 2001.
Altieri, Charles. *Painterly Abstraction in Modernist American Poetry*. Cambridge: Cambridge University Press, 2009.
Arendt, Hannah. *The Origins of Totalitarianism*. 1951. New York: Harcourt Brace, 2004.
———. *The Human Condition*. 1958. Chicago: University of Chicago Press, 1998.
Ashbery, John. *Houseboat Days*. New York:  , 1975.
———. *Self-Portrait in a Convex Mirror*. New York: Penguin, 1976.
———. *Selected Poems*. New York: Penguin, 1986.
———. *And the Stars Were Shining*. New York: Farrar, Straus and Giroux, 1995.
———. *Can You Hear, Bird?* New York: Farrar, Straus and Giroux, 1997.
———. *The Mooring of Starting Out: The First Five Books of Poetry*. New York: Ecco Press, 1998.
———. *Wakefulness: Poems*. New York: Farrar, Straus and Giroux, 1999.
———. *Girls on the Run*. New York: Farrar, Straus and Giroux, 2000.
———. *Hotel Lautreamont*. New York: Farrar, Straus and Giroux, 2000.
———. *Your Name Here*. New York: Farrar, Straus and Giroux, 2001.
———. *Chinese Whispers*. New York: Farrar, Straus and Giroux, 2002.
Auden, W. H. "Introduction," in John Ashbery, *Some Trees*. New Haven, CT: Yale University Press, 1956.
Augustine. *Confessions*. 397–98. Translated by Henry Chadwick. Oxford: Oxford University Press, 2009.
Austen, Jane. *Pride and Prejudice*. 1813. New York: Penguin Classics, 2002.
Baars, Bernard. "In the Theater of Consciousness: Global Workspace Theory, a Rigorous Scientific Theory of Consciousness." *Journal of Consciousness Studies* 4.4 (1997): 280–314.
Bate, Walter Jackson. *John Keats*. Cambridge, MA: Harvard University Press, 1963.

Baudelaire, Charles. "Richard Wagner and Tannhäuser in Paris," in *The Painter of Modern Life and Other Essays*. Translated by Jonathan Mayne. London: Phaidon, 1995.

Bauerlein, Mark. "Diminishing Returns in Humanities Research." *Chronicle of Higher Education* (July 20, 2009). http://chronicle.com/article/Diminishing-Returns-in/47107/ (accessed Aug. 1, 2010).

Bayley, John. "The Poetry of John Ashbery," in *John Ashbery*. Edited by Harold Bloom. New York: Chelsea House, 1985.

Becker, Gary, and Kevin Murphy. "A Theory of Rational Addiction." *Journal of Political Economy* 96 (1988): 675–700.

Beckett, Samuel. *Proust*. 1931. New York: Grove Press, 1994.

Benjamin, Walter. *Illuminations*. Translated by Harry Zohn. New York: Schocken Books, 1969.

Bennett, Andrew. *Keats, Narrative and Audience*. Cambridge: Cambridge University Press, 1994.

———. *Romantic Poets and the Culture of Posterity*. Cambridge: Cambridge University Press, 1999.

Berely, Marc. *After the Heavenly Tune*. Philadelphia: Duquesne University Press, 2000.

Bergson, Henri. *Matter and Memory*. 1896. Translated by N. M. Paul and W. S. Palmer. New York: Zone Books, 1988.

Berridge, Kent C., and Terry E. Robinson. "Parsing Reward." *Trends in Neuroscience* 26.9 (2003): 507–13.

Bersani, Leo. *A Future for Astynax*. New York: Columbia University Press, 1984.

Berube, Michael. "What's the Matter with Cultural Studies?" *Chronicle of Higher Education* (Sept. 15, 2009). http://chronicle.com/article/Whats-the-Matter-With/48334/ (accessed Aug. 1, 2010).

Birnbaum, Henrik. "Familiarization and Its Semiotic Matrix," in *Russian Formalism: A Retrospective Glance*. Edited by Robert Louis Jackson and Stephen Rudy. New Haven, CT: Yale University Press, 1985.

Blasing, Mutlu. *Politics and Form in Postmodern American Poetry*. Cambridge: Cambridge University Press, 1995.

Block, Ned, Owen Flanagan, and Guven Guzeldere, eds. *The Nature of Consciousness: Philosophical Debates*. Cambridge, MA: MIT Press, 1997.

Bloom, Harold. *The Visionary Company*. Ithaca, NY: Cornell University Press, 1961.

———. *The Anxiety of Influence*. Oxford: Oxford University Press, 1973.

———. "Introduction," in *George Orwell's 1984*. New York: Chelsea House, 1987.

Bloom, Paul. *How Pleasure Works*. New York: Norton, 2010.

Bolano, Roberto. *By Night in Chile*. Translated by Chris Andrews. New York: New Directions, 2003.

Boon, Marcus. *The Road of Excess*. Cambridge, MA: Harvard University Press, 2005.

Bordogna, Francesca. *William James at the Boundaries: Philosophy, Science, and the Geography of Knowledge*. Chicago: University of Chicago Press, 2008.

Bourdieu, Pierre. *Distinction: A Social Critique of the Judgement of Taste*. Cambridge, MA: Harvard University Press, 1984.

Bree, Germaine. *Marcel Proust and Deliverance from Time*. New Brunswick, NJ: Rutgers University Press, 1955.
Brooks, Cleanth. *The Well-Wrought Urn*. New York: Mariner, 1956.
Brooks, Gwendolyn. *Blacks*. Chicago: Third World Press, 1992.
Brown, Bill. "How to Do Things with Things." *Critical Inquiry* 24 (Summer 1998): 935–64.
———. *A Sense of Things: The Object Matter of American Literature*. Chicago: University of Chicago Press, 2004.
Brown, Marshall. "Unheard Melodies: The Force of Form." *PMLA* 107.3 (May 1992): 465–81.
Brown, Nicholas. "Response to Neoliberal Aesthetics." *Nonsite* 1 (Winter 2011).
Bruhn, Mark. "Romanticism and the Cognitive Science of Imagination." *Studies in Romanticism* 48 (Winter 2009): 543–64.
Burger, Peter. *Theory of the Avant-Garde*. Translated by Michael Shaw. Minneapolis: University of Minnesota Press, 1999.
Burke, Edmund. *A Philosophical Enquiry into the Origin of Our Ideas of the Sublime and Beautiful*. 1757. Oxford: Oxford University Press, 2009.
Burroughs, William. *Naked Lunch*. New York: Grove Press, 1959.
Cameron, Sharon. *Lyric Time*. Baltimore: Johns Hopkins University Press, 1979.
Campbell, Nancy D. *Discovering Addiction: The Science and Politics of Substance Abuse Research*. Ann Arbor: University of Michigan Press, 2007.
Carr, David. *Night of the Gun*. New York: Simon and Schuster, 2008.
Carroll, Noel. "Art and Human Nature." *Journal of Aesthetics and Art Criticism* 62.2 (2004): 95–107.
Carter, B. L., and S. T. Tiffany. "Meta-analysis of Cue-Reactivity in Addiction Research." *Addiction* 94.3 (1999): 346–47.
Caruth, Cathy. *Unclaimed Experience*. Baltimore: Johns Hopkins University Press, 1996.
Cavell, Stanley. *Must We Mean What We Say?* Cambridge: Cambridge University Press, 1969.
Chalmers, David. *The Conscious Mind*. Oxford: Oxford University Press, 2007.
Childress, Anna Rose, A. Thomas McLellan, Ronald Ehrman, and Charles P. O'Brien. "Classically Conditioned Responses in Opioid and Cocaine Dependence: A Role in Relapse?" *NIDA Research Monograph* 84 (1988): 25–43.
Chow, Rey. "The Old/New Question of Comparison in Literary Studies." *ELH* 71 (2004): 289–311.
Christensen, Jerome. *Romanticism at the End of History*. Baltimore: Johns Hopkins University Press, 2004.
Clarke, Arthur C. *Rendezvous with Rama*. New York: Bantam, 1969.
Clej, Alina. *A Genealogy of the Modern Self: Thomas De Quincey and the Intoxication of Writing*. Stanford: Stanford University Press, 1995.
Cloninger, C. Robert "Neurogenetic Adaptive Mechanisms in Alcoholism." *Science* 236 (1987): 410–16.
Clune, Michael. "Theory of Prose." *NO: A Journal of the Arts* 6 (Jan. 2008): 48–62.

———. *American Literature and the Free Market, 1945–2000*. Cambridge: Cambridge University Press, 2010.

Clune, Michael, John Sarneki, and Rebecca Traynor, "Cue Fascination." *Behavioral and Brain Sciences* 31.4 (Aug. 2008): 458–59.

Cohen, G.A. *Karl Marx's Theory of History*. Princeton, NJ: Princeton University Press, 2000.

Coleridge, Samuel Taylor. *Biographia Literaria*, in *Collected Works*. Vol. 7. Princeton, NJ: Princeton University Press, 1985.

Conant, James. "Rorty and Orwell on Truth," in *On Nineteen Eighty-Four: Orwell and Our Future*. Edited by Abbott Gleason, Jack Goldsmith, and Martha C. Nussbaum. Princeton, NJ: Princeton University Press, 2005.

Cooney, Charles M. "Intellectualist Poetry in Eccentric Form: John Ashbery, French Critical Debate, and an American Raymond Roussel." *Contemporary Literature* 48 (June 2007): 61–92.

Crabbe, J. C. "Genetic Contributions to Addiction." *Annual Review of Psychology* 53.1 (2002): 435–62.

Culler, Jonathan. "The Literary in Theory," in *What's Left of Theory?* Edited by Judith Butler. New York: Routledge, 2000.

Dahlhaus, Carl. *From Romanticism to Modernism*. Berkeley: University of California Press, 1989.

Davidson, Donald. "How is Weakness of the Will Possible?" (1969), in *The Essential Davidson*. Oxford: Oxford University Press, 2006.

———. "What Metaphors Mean" (1974), in *The Essential Davidson*. Oxford: Oxford University Press, 2006.

Davis, Theo. *Formalism, Experience, and the Making of American Literature*. Cambridge: Cambridge University Press, 2007.

De Man, Paul. *Allegories of Reading*. New Haven, CT: Yale University Press, 1979.

De Quincey, Thomas. *Confessions of an English Opium Eater*. 1821. New York: Penguin, 2003.

De Souza, Sybil. "Why Vinteuil's Septet?" in *Critical Essays on Marcel Proust*. Edited by Barbara Bucknall. New York: G.K. Hall, 1987.

Deleuze, Gilles, and Felix Guatarri. *A Thousand Plateaus*. Minneapolis: University of Minnesota Press, 2001.

Dennet, Daniel. *Consciousness Explained*. New York: Back Bay, 1992.

Derrida, Jacques. *Limited Inc*. Evanston, IL: Northwestern University Press, 1988.

Dewey, John. *Human Nature and Conduct: An Introduction to Social Psychology*. 1922. New York: Legacy, 2007.

———. *Art as Experience*. 1932. New York: Perigee, 2005.

Dimock, Wai Chee. "Scales of Aggregation: Prenational, Subnational, Transnational." *American Literary History* 18.2 (Mar. 2006): 219–28.

———. *Through Other Continents*. Princeton, NJ: Princeton University Press, 2008.

Doherty, Brigid. "'See: We Are All Neurasthenics!' or, The Trauma of Dada Montage." *Critical Inquiry* 24 (Autumn 1997): 104–18.

Dreyfus, Hubert. *Being-in-the-World: A Commentary on Heidegger's Being and Time.* Cambridge, MA: MIT Press, 1990.
Durantaye, Leland. "Eichmann, Empathy and *Lolita*." *Philosophy and Literature* 30.2 (Oct. 2006): 311–28.
Eagleman, David M. "Human Time Perception and its Illusions." *Current Opinion in Neurobiology* 18 (2008): 131–36.
Eliot, T. S. *Four Quartets.* New York: Harcourt Brace, 1943.
Elster, Jon. *Making Sense of Marx.* Cambridge: Cambridge University Press, 1985.
———. *Strong Feelings: Emotion, Addiction, and Human Behavior.* Cambridge, MA: MIT Press, 2000.
Epstein, Richard. "The Case of George Orwell," in *On Nineteen Eighty-Four: Orwell and Our Future.* Edited by Abbott Gleason, Jack Goldsmith, and Martha C. Nussbaum. Princeton, NJ: Princeton University Press, 2005.
Erikson, Carlton, *The Science of Addiction.* New York: Norton, 2007.
Felski, Rita. *Uses of Literature.* Oxford: Blackwell, 2008.
Ferguson, Frances. *Solitude and the Sublime.* New York: Routledge, 1992.
———. *Pornography, the Theory.* Chicago: University of Chicago Press, 2004.
Fingarette, Herbert. *Heavy Drinking: The Myth of Alcoholism as a Disease.* Berkeley: University of California Press, 1989.
Fisher, Phillip. *Wonder, the Rainbow, and the Aesthetics of Rare Experiences.* Cambridge, MA: Harvard University Press, 1998.
Flesch, William. "Quoting Poetry." *Critical Inquiry* 18 (Autumn 1991): 42–63.
Foucault, Michel. *The History of Sexuality: An Introduction.* Translated by Robert Hurley. New York: Vintage, 1990.
François, Anne-Lise. "'The feel of not to feel it,' or the Pleasures of Enduring Form," in *A Companion to Romantic Poetry.* Edited by Charles Mahoney. Oxford: Wiley-Blackwell, 2010: 445–66.
Freedman, Carl. "Antinomies of *1984*," in *Critical Essays on George Orwell.* Edited by Bernard Oldsey and Joseph Browne. Cambridge: Cambridge University Press, 1986.
Freeman, A. S., L. T. Meltzer, and B. S. Bunney. "Firing Properties of Substantia Nigra Dopaminergic Neurons in Freely Moving Rats." *Life Sciences* 36.20 (1985): 1983–94.
Fried, Michael. *Absorption and Theatricality.* Chicago: University of Chicago Press, 1980.
———. *Art and Objecthood.* Chicago: University of Chicago Press, 1998.
Friedman, Milton. *Essays in Positive Economics.* Chicago: University of Chicago Press, 1953.
Gadamer, Hans. *Truth and Method.* 1975. New York: Continuum, 2004.
Gallagher, Shaun. "Where's the Action? Epiphenomenalism and the Problem of Free Will," in *Does Consciousness Cause Behavior?* Edited by Susan Pockett, William P. Banks, and Shaun Gallagher. Cambridge, MA: MIT Press, 2006.
Garris, P. A., M. Kilpatrick, M. A. Bunin, D. Michael, Q. D. Walker, and R. M. Wightman. "Dissociation of Dopamine Release in the Nucleus Accumbens from Intracranial Self-Stimulation." *Nature* 398 (Mar. 1999): 67–69.

Geertz, Clifford. *The Interpretation of Cultures.* New York: Basic Books, 1973.
———. "Blurred Genres: The Refiguration of Social Thought." *American Scholar* 49 (Spring 1980): 165–79.
Genette, Gerard. *The Aesthetic Relation.* Ithaca, NY: Cornell University Press, 1999.
Gibson, William. *Neuromancer.* New York: Ace, 2004.
Gigante, Denise. *Life: Organic Form and Romanticism.* New Haven, CT: Yale University Press, 2009.
Ginzburg, Carlo. "Making Things Strange." *Representations* 56 (Fall 1996): 8–28.
Gleason, Abbott. "Puritanism and Power Politics during the Cold War: George Orwell and Historical Objectivity," in *On Nineteen Eighty-Four.* Edited by Abbott Gleason, Jack Goldsmith, and Martha C. Nussbaum. Princeton, NJ: Princeton University Press, 2005.
Godden, Richard. "Labor, Language, and Finance Capital." *PMLA* 126.2 (Mar. 2011): 412–21.
Goldman, Alvin. "Imagination and Simulation in Audience Response to Fiction," in *The Architecture of the Imagination.* Edited by Shaun Nichols. Oxford: Oxford University Press, 2006.
———. *Simulating Minds.* Oxford: Oxford University Press, 2008.
Graff, Gerald. "Fear and Trembling at Yale." *American Scholar* (1977): 467–78.
Grossman, Allen. *The Long Schoolroom.* Ann Arbor: University of Michigan Press, 1997.
Guerlac, Suzanne. *Thinking in Time: An Introduction to Henri Bergson.* Ithaca, NY: Cornell University Press, 2006.
Guillory, John. "The Sokal Affair and the History of Criticism." *Critical Inquiry* 35 (Winter 2002): 109–27.
Guyer, Paul. *Kant and the Claims of Taste.* Cambridge: Cambridge University Press, 1997.
Hadot, Pierre. *Philosophy as a Way of Life.* Translated by Michael Chase. Oxford: Blackwell, 1995.
Hallisey, Charles. "Roads Taken and Not Taken in the Study of Theravada Buddhism," in *Curators of the Buddha.* Edited by Donald Lopez. Chicago: University of Chicago Press, 1995.
Hammet, Dashiell. *The Complete Novels.* New York: Library Classics of the United States, 1999.
Hansen, Mark. *Bodies in Code.* New York: Routledge, 2006.
Hartman, Geoffrey. *Criticism in the Wilderness.* New Haven, CT: Yale University Press, 1980.
Hatfield, Gary. "Empirical, Rational, and Transcendental Psychology," in *The Cambridge Companion to Kant.* Edited by Paul Guyer. Cambridge: Cambridge University Press, 1992.
Hayles, Katherine. *How We Became Posthuman.* Chicago: University of Chicago Press, 1999.
Hayot, Eric. *Chinese Dreams: Pound, Brecht, Tel Quel.* Ann Arbor: University of Michigan Press, 2003.
Heffernan, James. *Museum of Words.* Chicago: University of Chicago Press, 1993.

Heidegger, Martin. "The Thing," in *Poetry, Language, Thought*. 1951. Translated by Albert Hofstadter. New York: HarperCollins, 2001.
———. "The Origin of the Work of Art," in *Off the Beaten Track*. 1956. Translated by Julian Young and Kenneth Haynes. Cambridge: Cambridge University Press, 2002.
Herbert, Frank. *Dune*. 1965. New York: Ace, 2005.
Herd, David. *John Ashbery and American Poetry*. Manchester, UK: Manchester University Press, 2000.
Hewitt, Andrew. *Fascist Modernism: Aesthetics, Politics, and the Avant-Garde*. Stanford: Stanford University Press, 1996.
Holquist, Michael, and Ilya Kliger. "Minding the Gap: Towards a Historical Poetics of Estrangement." *Poetics Today* 26.4 (Winter 2005): 613–36.
Horkheimer, Max and Theodor Adorno. *The Dialectic of Enlightenment*. Stanford: Stanford University Press, 1997.
Hunter, Ian. "The History of Theory." *Critical Inquiry* 33 (Autumn 2006): 78–112.
Huron, David. *Sweet Anticipation: Music and the Psychology of Expectation*. Cambridge, MA: MIT Press, 2008.
Hyman, Steven E. "Addiction: A Disease of Learning and Memory." *American Journal of Psychiatry* 162.8 (2005): 1414–22.
Ingle, Stephen. *The Social and Political Thought of George Orwell*. New York: Routledge, 2006.
Izenberg, Oren. "Poems Out of Our Heads," *PMLA* 123.1 (Jan. 2008): 216–22.
———. *Being Numerous*. Princeton, NJ: Princeton University Press, 2011.
Jackson, Noel. "The Time of Beauty." *Studies in Romanticism* 50.2 (Summer 2011): 309–32.
Jackson, Virginia. *Dickinson's Misery*. Princeton, NJ: Princeton University Press, 2005.
———. "Please Don't Call It History." *Nonsite* 2 (Fall 2011). http://nonsite.org/the-tank/ (accessed Jan. 12, 2012).
James, D. G. *The Romantic Comedy*. Oxford: Oxford University Press, 1947.
James, William. *Pragmatism and Other Writings*. New York: Penguin, 2000.
———. *The Varieties of Religious Experience*. 1902. New York: Penguin, 2005.
Jameson, Fredric. *The Prison House of Language*. Princeton, NJ: Princeton University Press, 1972.
———. *Postmodernism, or, the Cultural Logic of Late Capitalism*. Durham, NC: Duke University Press, 1991.
———. *Archeologies of the Future*. London: Verso, 2007.
———. "How Not to Historicize Theory." *Critical Inquiry* 33 (Spring 2008): 563–82.
Jarvis, Simon. *Wordsworth's Philosophic Song*. Cambridge: Cambridge University Press, 2007.
———. "The Melodics of Long Poems." *Textual Practice* 24.4 (Oct. 2010): 607–21.
Jay, Martin. *Songs of Experience*. Berkeley: University of California Press, 2006.
Johnson, Denis. *Jesus' Son: Stories*. New York: Picador, 1991.
Jones, Wendy S. "Emma, Gender, and the Mind-Brain." *ELH* 75.2 (Summer 2008): 315–43.
Justice, Steven. "Did the Middle Ages Believe in Their Miracles?" *Representations* 103 (Summer 2008): 1–29.

Kahneman, Daniel, and Amos Tversky. "The Framing of Decisions and the Psychology of Choice." *Science* 211 (Jan. 30, 1981): 453–58.
Kant, Immanuel. *Critique of Pure Reason*. 1781. Translated by Werner S. Pluhar. Indianapolis, IN: Hackett, 1996.
———. *Critique of Judgment*. 1790. Translated by Werner S. Pluhar. Indianapolis, IN: Hackett, 1987.
Kapur, Shitij, Romina Mizrahi, and Ming Li. "From Dopamine to Salience to Psychosis—Linking Biology, Pharmacology and Phenomenology of Psychosis." *Schizophrenia Research* 79.1 (2005): 59–68.
Kaufman, Robert. "Adorno's Social Lyric and Literary Criticism Today," in *The Cambridge Companion to Adorno*. Edited by Tom Huhn. Cambridge: Cambridge University Press, 2004.
Keats, John. *Keats's Poetry and Prose*. Edited by Jeffrey N. Cox. New York: Norton, 2008.
Kermode, Frank. "Adam Unparadised," in *Paradise Lost*. Edited by Scott Elledge. New York: Norton, 1993.
Koch, Christof. *The Quest for Consciousness: A Neurobiological Approach*. Boston: Roberts and Company, 2004.
Kotler, M., H. Cohen, R. Segman, I. Gritsenko, L. Nemanov, B. Lerer, I. Kramer, M. Zer Zion, I. Kletz, and R. P. Ebstein. "Excess Dopamine D4 Receptor (D4DR) Exon III Seven Repeat Allele in Opioid-Dependent Subjects." *Molecular Psychiatry* 2 (1997): 251–54.
Kramer, Lawrence. *Music and Poetry: The Nineteenth Century and After*. Berkeley: University of California Press, 1984.
Kramnick, Jonathan. "Against Literary Darwinism." *Critical Inquiry* 37 (Winter 2011): 315–47.
Krieger, Murray. *The Play and the Place of Criticism*. Baltimore: Johns Hopkins University Press, 1967.
Krishnan, Sanjay. "Opium and Empire." *boundary 2* 33.2 (2006): 203–34.
Kunin, Aaron. "Shakespeare's Preservation Fantasy." *PMLA* 124.1 (Jan. 2009): 92–106.
———. "Character's Lounge." *MLQ* 70.3 (Sept. 2009): 18–42.
La Blanc, Gregory. "Commentary: Economic and Literary History: An Economist's Perspective." *New Literary History* 31 (2000): 355–77.
Langer, Suzanne. *Feeling and Form*. New York: Scribners, 1953.
Largier, Niklaus. "Mysticism, Modernity, and the Invention of Aesthetic Experience." *Representations* 105 (Winter 2009): 37–60.
Latour, Bruno. "Why Has Critique Run Out of Steam?" *Critical Inquiry* 30 (Winter 2004): 225–48.
Lautreamont, Comte de. *Maldoror*. 1868. Translated by Paul Knight. New York: Penguin, 1978.
Leitch, Vincent. *American Literary Criticism from the Thirties to the Eighties*. New York: Routledge, 1988.
Lende, Daniel H. "Wanting and Drug Use." *Ethos* 33.1 (2005): 100–124.

---. "Addiction: More Than Innate Rationality," *Behavioral and Brain Sciences* (Aug. 2008): 453–54.

Levinson, Marjorie. *The Romantic Fragment Poem.* Chapel Hill: University of North Carolina Press, 1986.

Leys, Ruth. "The Turn to Affect: A Critique." *Critical Inquiry* 37.3 (Spring 2011): 434–72.

Libet, Benjamin, Curtis A. Gleason, Elwood W. Wright, and Dennis K. Pearl. "Time of Conscious Intention to Act in Relation to Onset of Cerebral Activity (Readiness-Potential)." *Brain* 106 (1983): 623–42.

Longenbach, James. *The Resistance to Poetry.* Chicago: University of Chicago Press, 2004.

Lukacs, Georg. *The Historical Novel.* Translated by Hannah Mitchell and Stanley Mitchell. Lincoln: University of Nebraska Press, 1983.

Lutz, Antoine, Jean-Phillipe Lachaux, Jacques Martinerie, and Francisco J. Varela. "Guiding the Study of Brain Dynamics by Using First-Person Data: Synchrony Patterns Correlate with Ongoing Conscious States During a Simple Visual Task." *Proceedings of the National Academy of Sciences* 99.3 (2002): 1586–91.

Marx, Karl. *The Communist Manifesto.* Translated by Samuel Moore. London: Charles Kerr, 1998.

Massumi, Brian. *Parables for the Virtual.* Durham, NC: Duke University Press, 2002.

Matz, Jesse. *Literary Impressionism and Modernist Aesthetics.* Cambridge: Cambridge University Press, 2007.

Maxwell, William. "Global Poetics and State-Sponsored Transnationalism." *American Literary History* 18.2 (Spring 2006): 70–82.

McGurl, Mark. *The Program Era.* Cambridge, MA: Harvard University Press, 2009.

McHale, Brian. *Postmodernist Fiction.* New York: Routledge, 1987.

McLane, Maureen. *Romanticism and the Human Sciences.* Cambridge: Cambridge University Press, 2000.

Merleau-Ponty, Maurice. *Basic Writings.* Translated by Thomas Baldwin. New York: Routledge, 2004.

Merwin, W. S. *The Second Four Books of Poems.* Port Townsend: Copper Canyon Press, 1993.

Meyer, Steven. *Irresistible Dictation.* Cambridge, MA: Harvard University Press, 2001.

Michaels, Walter Benn. "Neoliberal Aesthetics." *Nonsite* 1 (Winter 2011). http://nonsite.org/issues/issue-1/ (accessed Jan. 15, 2012)

Mill, John Stuart "Thoughts on Poetry and Its Varieties," in *Dissertations and Discussions, Politics, Philosophy, and History.* Edited by Ned Block, Owen Flanagan, and Gwen Gezuldere. Vol. 1. London: John Parker and Son, 1859.

Miller, D. A. *The Novel and the Police.* Berkeley: University of California Press, 1989.

Minahan, John A. *Word Like a Bell: John Keats, Music and the Romantic Poet.* Kent: Kent State University Press, 1992.

Mitchell, Robert. "Suspended Animation, Slow Time, and the Poetics of Trance." *PMLA* 126.1 (Jan. 2011): 107–22.

Mitchell, W.J.T. "Ekphrasis and the Other," in *Picture Theory.* Chicago: University of Chicago Press, 1994.

———. "Interdisciplinarity and Visual Culture." *Art Bulletin* 77.4 (Dec. 1995): 541–44.

Modern Language Association. *Report to the Teagle Foundation on the Undergraduate Major*. New York: MLA Publications, 2009.

Mooney, Susan. *The Artistic Censoring of Sexuality*. Columbus: Ohio State University Press, 2008.

Moxley, Jennifer. *The Line*. Sausalito, CA: Post Apollo Press, 2007.

Nabokov, Vladimir. *Lolita*. 1955. New York: Vintage, 1997.

Nagel, Thomas. "What Is It Like to Be a Bat?" (1974), in *The Nature of Consciousness: Philosophical Debates*. Edited by Ned Block, Owen Flanagan, and Guven Gezuldere. Cambridge, MA: MIT Press, 1997.

Naiman, Eric. *Nabokov, Perversely*. Ithaca, NY: Cornell University Press, 2010.

Nattiez, Jean-Jacques. *Proust as Musician*. Cambridge: Cambridge University Press, 1989.

Nehamas, Alexander. *Only a Promise of Happiness: The Place of Beauty in a World of Art*. Princeton: Princeton University Press, 2007.

Nietzsche, Friedrich. *The Will to Power*. 1906. Translated by Walter Kaufman. New York: Vintage, 1968.

Noe, Alva. *Action in Perception*. Cambridge, MA: MIT Press, 2004.

———. "Experience of the World in Time." *Analysis* 66.289 (Jan. 2006): 26–32.

Nussbaum, Martha. *The Therapy of Desire*. Princeton: Princeton University Press, 1994.

Orwell, George. *1984*. New York: Signet, 1949.

Parrinder, Patrick. *Authors and Authority*. New York: Columbia University Press, 1991.

Pater, Walter. *The Renaissance*. 1873. Oxford: Oxford University Press, 1998.

Perloff, Marjorie. *Poetic License*. Evanston, IL: Northwestern University Press, 1990.

———. *The Poetics of Indeterminacy: Rimbaud to Cage*. Evanston, IL: Northwestern University Press, 1999.

———. *21st Century Modernism*. Oxford: Blackwell, 2002.

Pfau, Thomas. "The Voice of Critique: Aesthetic Cognition After Kant." *MLQ* 60.3 (Summer 1999): 321–52.

Plath, Sylvia. *Collected Poems*. New York: Faber, 1981.

Polanyi, Karl. *The Great Transformation*. 1944. New York: Beacon, 2001.

Poulet, Georges. "Timelessness and Romanticism." *Journal of the History of Ideas* 15.1 (Jan. 1954): 3–22.

———. "The Phenomenology of Reading." *New Literary History*. 1.1 (Oct. 1969): 53–68.

Pound, Ezra. *Poems and Translations*. New York: Library of America, 2003.

Prinz, Jesse. "A Neurofunctional Theory of Consciousness," in *Cognition and the Brain*. Edited by Andrew Brook and Kathleen Akins. Cambridge: Cambridge University Press, 2005.

Proust, Marcel. *In Search of Lost Time*. 1913–27. 4 vols. Translated by D. J. Enright, Terrence Kilmartin, and C. K. Scott Moncrieff. New York: Everyman's Library, 2001.

Redfield, Marc. "Introduction," in *High Anxieties: Cultural Studies in Addiction*. Edited by Janet Farrell Brodie and Marc Redfield. Berkeley: University of California Press, 2002.

Redish, A. David, Steve Jensen, and Adam Johnson. "A Unified Framework for Addiction." *Behavioral and Brain Sciences* 31.4. (Aug. 2008): 415–37.
Richardson, Alan. *British Romanticism and the Science of Mind*. Cambridge: Cambridge University Press, 2001.
———. *The Neural Sublime*. Baltimore: Johns Hopkins University Press, 2010.
Ricoeur, Paul. *Time and Narrative*. Vol. 3. Translated by Kathleen McLaughlin and David Pellauer. Chicago: Chicago University Press, 1984.
Rimbaud, Arthur. *Collected Poems*. Translated by Oliver Bernhard. New York: Penguin, 1983.
Robinson, Thomas E., and Kent C. Berridge. "The Neural Basis of Drug Craving: An Incentive-Sensitization Theory of Addiction." *Brain Research Reviews* 18.3 (1993): 247–91.
———. "Incentive-sensitization and drug 'wanting'" (reply). *Psychopharmacology* 171.3 (2004): 352–53.
Roemer, John. *Analytical Marxism*. Cambridge: Cambridge University Press, 1986.
Rorty, Richard. *Contingency, Irony, and Solidarity*. Cambridge: Cambridge University Press, 1989.
Ross, Andrew. *The Failure of Modernism: Symptoms of American Poetry*. New York: Columbia University Press, 1986.
Ross, Don. "Economic Models of Pathological Gambling," in *What is Addiction?* Edited by Don Ross, Harold Kincaid, David Spurrett, and Peter Collins. Cambridge, MA: MIT Press, 2010.
Rosse, Richard B., Maureen Fay-McCarthy, Joseph P. Collins, Debra Risher-Flowers, Tanya N. Alim, and Stephen I. Deutsch. "Transient Compulsive Foraging Behavior Associated with Crack Cocaine Use." *American Journal of Psychiatry* 150 (1993): 155–56.
Russett, Margaret. *De Quincey's Romanticism*. Cambridge: Cambridge University Press, 1996.
Sacks, Oliver. *Musicophilia*. New York: Vintage, 2008.
Said, Edward. *Orientalism*. New York: Vintage, 1979.
Sandison, Alan. *The Last Man in Europe*. New York: Scribners, 1974.
Scarry, Elaine. *Dreaming by the Book*. Princeton: Princeton University Press, 1999.
Schiller, Friedrich. *On the Aesthetic Education of Man*. 1794. Translated by Elizabeth M. Wilkinson and L. A. Willoughby. Oxford: Oxford University Press, 1967.
Schroeder, Timothy, and Carl Matheson. "Imagination and Emotion," in *The Architecture of the Imagination*. Edited by Shaun Nichols. Oxford: Oxford University Press, 2006.
Schultz, Wolfram "Predictive Reward Signal of Dopamine Neurons." *Journal of Neurophysiology* 80 (1998): 1–27.
Searle, John. "The Mystery of Consciousness Continues." *New York Review of Books* (June 9, 2011): 47–51.
Sedgwick, Eve. "Epidemics of the Will," in *Tendencies*. Durham, NC: Duke University Press, 1993.

———. "Paranoid Reading and Reparative Reading," in *Novel Gazing*. Durham, NC: Duke University Press, 1997.
Shakespeare, William. *Shakespeare's Sonnets*. 1609. Edited by Stephen Booth. New Haven, CT: Yale University Press, 1977.
Shattuck, Roger. *Proust's Way*. New York: Norton, 2001.
Shelley, Percy Bysshe, *Selected Poetry and Prose*. London: Wordsworth Editions, 1998.
Sheringham, Michael. *Everyday Life: Theories and Practices from Surrealism to the Present*. Oxford: Oxford University Press, 2006.
Shetley, Vernon. *After the Death of Poetry*. Durham, NC: Duke University Press, 1993.
Shklovsky, Viktor. "Art as Device," in *Theory of Prose*. 1929. Translated by Benjamin Sher. Normal, IL: Dalkey Archive Press, 1991.
Shoptaw, John. *On the Outside Looking Out*. Cambridge, MA: Harvard University Press, 1995.
Simmons, Dan. *Hyperion*. New York: Spectra, 1990.
Sloboda, John. *Exploring the Musical Mind: Cognition, Emotion, Ability, Function*. Oxford: Oxford University Press, 2005.
Snyder, Bob. *Music and Memory*. Cambridge, MA: MIT Press, 2001.
Soni, Vivasvan. *Mourning Happiness*. Ithaca, NY: Cornell University Press, 2010.
Sontag, Susan. "Notes on 'Camp,'" in *Against Interpretation*. New York: Picador, 1966.
Spivak, Gayatri. *Death of a Discipline*. New York: Columbia University Press, 2003.
Stafford, Barbara Maria. *Echo Objects*. Chicago: University of Chicago Press, 2007.
Starr, Gabrielle. "Poetic Subjects and Grecian Urns: Close Reading and the Tools of Cognitive Science." *Modern Philology* 105.1 (2007): 48–61.
———. "Multisensory Imagery," in *Introduction to Cultural Cognitive Studies*. Edited by Lisa Zunshine. Baltimore: Johns Hopkins University Press, 2010.
Steiner, Peter. *Russian Formalism: A Metapoetics*. Ithaca, NY: Cornell University Press, 1984.
Sterling, Bruce. *Schizmatrix Plus*. New York: Ace, 1996.
Stonum, Gary Lee. *The Dickinson Sublime*. Madison: University of Wisconsin Press, 1990.
Terada, Rei. *Looking Away: Phenomenality and Dissatisfaction*. Cambridge, MA: Harvard University Press, 2009.
Tiffany, Daniel. *Infidel Poetics*. Chicago: University of Chicago Press, 2009.
Trungpa, Chogyam. *The Myth of Freedom*. Boston: Shambhala Books, 1976.
Turner, Mark. *The Artful Mind*. Oxford: Oxford University Press, 2006.
Vance, Jack. *Tales of the Dying Earth*. 1964. New York: Orb, 2000.
Varela, Francisco J. "Neurophenomenology: A Methodological Remedy for the Hard Problem." *Journal of Consciousness Studies* 3 (June 1996): 330–49.
Varela, Francisco J., Evan Thompson, and Eleanor Rosch. *The Embodied Mind: Cognitive Science and Human Experience*. Cambridge, MA: MIT Press, 1991.
Vatulescu, Cristina. "Tracking Estrangement Through Literary and Policing Practices." *Poetics Today* 27.1 (Spring 2006): 35–66.
Vendler, Helen. *The Odes of John Keats*. Cambridge, MA: Harvard University Press, 1985.

Vermule, Blakey. *Why Do We Care About Literary Characters?* Baltimore: Johns Hopkins University Press, 2010.
Vincent, John. *John Ashbery and You.* Athens: University of Georgia Press, 2007.
Walton, Kendall L. *Mimesis as Make-Believe.* Cambridge, MA: Harvard University Press, 1993.
Wellbery, David. "The General Enters the Library: A Note on Disciplines and Complexity." *Critical Inquiry* 35 (Summer 2009): 982–94.
Williams, Raymond. "George Orwell," in *George Orwell's 1984.* Edited by Harold Bloom. New York: Chelsea House, 1987.
Wimsatt, W. K., and Monroe Beardsley. "The Affective Fallacy," in *The Verbal Icon: Studies in the Meaning of Poetry.* Lexington, KY: University Press of Kentucky, 1954.
Wolfson, Susan, ed. "'Soundings of Things Done': The Poetry and Poetics of Sound in the Romantic Ear and Era." *Romantic Circles Praxis Series* (2008). http://www.rc.umd.edu/praxis/sound.ns/potkay.html.
Wood, Michael. *Nabokov: The Magician's Doubts.* Princeton: Princeton University Press, 1994.
Wright, Erik Olin. *Classes.* Oxford: Blackwell, 1985.
Yeats, William Butler. *Collected Poems.* New York: Scribners, 1996.
Zinberg, Norman Earl. *Drug, Set, and Setting: The Basis for Controlled Intoxicant Use.* New Haven, CT: Yale University Press, 1986.
Zunshine, Lisa. *Why We Read Fiction.* Columbus: Ohio State University Press, 2006.
———, ed. *Introduction to Cognitive Cultural Studies.* Baltimore: Johns Hopkins University Press, 2010.

# INDEX

Abrams, M. H., 156n7, 162n15, 168n21
Addiction: and consciousness, 76–86; habit and, 65–66, 78, 164n33; incentive salience and, 78–79; literary criticism and, 71–75; as model for literature, 57–86
Adorno, Theodor, 27, 72, 140, 162n19, 168n7
Albright, Daniel, 152n8
Alexandrov, Vladimir, 68
Allison, Henry, 36–38, 40–41, 156n9
Altieri, Charles, 40
Arendt, Hannah, 6–7, 16, 88, 90, 164n1, 164n3
Ashbery, John, 115–38; and archeology, 116, 128–29; *Chinese Whispers*, 116, 132; *Girls on the Run*, 116, 123; *Hotel Lautremont*, 120, 122–23, 127; *Houseboat Days*, 119, 122–23; and the novel, 117–25; and science fiction, 120, 124–25; *Self Portrait in a Convex Mirror*, 117, 125, 128, 131, 166n13; *Your Name Here*, 120, 122–24, 127
Auden, W. H., 125
Augustine, St., 3–5, 69, 152n6, 156n4
Austen, Jane, 57, 117, 120, 124

Baars, Bernard, 82–84
Bate, Walter Jackson, 159n20
Baudelaire, Charles, 9, 14, 19, 29, 34, 38–40, 64, 153n14
Bauerlein, Mark, 163n22
Bayley, John, 166n11
Becker, Gary, 74
Beckett, Samuel, 161n12
Benjamin, Walter, 64, 67, 90, 143, 153n14, 164n3
Bennett, Andrew, 16, 52–53, 152n7, 159n21

Berely, Marc, 155n2
Bergson, Henri, 23, 34, 44–46, 158nn17–19
Berridge, Kent C., 78–80, 83
Bersani, Leo, 33, 154n15
Berube, Michael, 163n22
Birnbaum, Henrik, 166n3
Blasing, Mutlu, 125
Block, Ned, 81, 163n29
Bloom, Harold, 87, 154n15, 159n23
Bloom, Paul, 19
Bolano, Roberto, 7, 16
Boon, Marcus, 60
Bordogna, Francensca, 168n5
Bourdieu, Pierre, 37, 140
Bree, Germaine, 28
Brooks, Cleanth, 43
Brooks, Gwendolyn, 8, 152n10
Brown, Bill, 128, 161n9
Brown, Marshall, 158n16
Brown, Nicholas, 163n23
Bruhn, Mark, 155n1
Burger, Peter, 164n3
Burke, Edmund, 3, 10–12, 152n11, 153n14
Burroughs, William, 160n4

Cameron, Sharon, 67
Campbell, Nancy D., 163n24
Carr, David, 61
Carter, B. L., 163n25
Caruth, Cathy, 64
Chalmers, David, 58, 81, 159n2
Chow, Rey, 134, 167n16
Christensen, Jerome, 71, 154n16, 159n20, 161n8, 162n18
Clej, Alina, 71, 160n5

# INDEX

Coleridge, Samuel Taylor, 10–11, 59, 61, 147
Commodity: Ashbery's invention of, 132–37; Marxist theory of, 71–75
Conant, James, 88–89
Consciousness: and literary study, 34–35, 82, 86; and science, 81–86
Cooney, Charles M., 165n1

Dahlhaus, Carl, 25–26
Davidson, Donald, 65, 104–6, 161n11
Davis, Theo, 151n2
Defamiliarization, 18, 20, 103–4, 111–13. *See also* Shklovsky, Viktor
de Man, Paul, 156n6, 168n9
de Souza, Sybil, 155n3
Deleuze, Gilles, 34, 134
Dennet, Daniel, 58
De Quincey, Thomas, 60–62, 64, 70–72, 75–78, 84, 90, 137, 160nn5–7
Derrida, Jacques, 104, 143–44, 165n6, 168n9
Dewey, John, 15, 18, 164n2
Dimock, Wai Chee, 134, 169n2
Doherty, Brigid, 64
Dreyfus, Hubert, 94, 153n13, 166n12
Durantaye, Leland, 67

Eagleman, David M., 3–4, 13
Ekphrasis, 20, 43–55, 159n22. *See also* Literature, and the virtual
Eliot, T. S., 6, 167n16
Elster, Jon, 73, 161n11
Epstein, Richard, 87
Erikson, Carlton, 163n24

Felski, Rita, 147, 153n14, 162n16
Ferguson, Frances, 154n19, 156n7
Fisher, Phillip, 156n11, 164n31
Flesch, William, 126
Foucault, Michel, 94–95, 133, 165n9, 167n16
Francois, Anne-Lise, 154n20, 158n16
Freedman, Carl, 92
Freeman, A. S., 163n28
Fried, Michael, 18, 27
Friedman, Milton, 74

Gadamer, Hans, 36
Gallagher, Shaun, 85–86, 164n32

Garris, P. A., 163n28
Genette, Gerard, 40
Gibson, William, 166n8
Gigante, Denise, 52–53
Ginzburg, Carlo, 103–4, 164n4
Gleason, Abbott, 100
Godden, Richard, 163n21
Goldman, Alvin, 1, 30, 151n4
Grossman, Allen, 34
Guerlac, Suzanne, 34, 45
Guillory, John, 159n1, 168n4
Guyer, Paul, 39, 41, 48, 156n10, 158n19

Habit, 2, 10–11, 25–32, 49–51. *See also* Defamiliarization; Novelty; Time
Hadot, Pierre, 16
Hallisey, Charles, 167n18
Hammet, Dashiell, 118
Hansen, Mark, 147
Hartman, Geoffrey, 141–46, 168n2, 168n6, 169n9, 169n11
Hatfield, Gary, 157n13
Hayles, Katherine, 34
Hayot, Eric, 167n15
Heffernan, James, 158n15
Heidegger, Martin, 93–94, 115, 129, 153n13, 166n4
Herbert, Frank, 60
Herd, David, 167n16
Hewitt, Andrew, 164n3
Holquist, Michael, 106–7
Horkheimer, Max, 27, 72
Hunter, Ian, 163n22
Huron, David, 47

Imagination, 4–5, 20, 23–26, 147
Immortality: classical, 6–9, 15–16, 34, 52, 70; Romantic, 9–21
Ingle, Stephen, 88
Izenberg, Oren, 33, 147

Jackson, Noel, 159n22
Jackson, Virginia, 141, 169n12
James, D. G., 154n20
James, William, 100, 142, 155n2
Jameson, Frederic, 72, 74–75, 103–5, 111, 129, 144–46, 163n23, 165n9, 166n13

Jarvis, Simon, 154n20, 156n8, 159n20
Jay, Martin, 154n16
Johnson, Denis, 160n4
Jones, Wendy S., 57
Justice, Steven, 146

Kahneman, Daniel, 74
Kant, Immanuel, 20, 23, 141, 153n14, 156nn8–10; on aesthetic pleasure, 36–39, 46, 50; on disinterest, 37, 95; on duration, 39–42, 51, 69, 129–30
Kapur, Shitij, 79
Kaufman, Robert, 168n7
Keats, John, 57, 90, 103, 137, 139; "Bright Star," 4–6, 9, 26, 33, 42, 47, 51; "Hyperion," 42, 47–55; "Ode on a Grecian Urn," 42–46, 158n16
Kermode, Frank, 154n20
Kliger, Ilya, 106–7
Kramer, Lawrence, 155n2
Kramnick, Jonathan, 19, 145–46
Krieger, Murray, 43–46, 51
Krishnan, Sanjay, 71
Kunin, Aaron, 6, 154n19

La Blanc, Gregory, 163n21
Langer, Suzanne, 158n17
Largier, Niklaus, 154n16
Latour, Bruno, 163n22
Lautreamont, Comte de, 120, 133–34
Leitch, Vincent, 169n11
Lende, Daniel H., 76, 80
Levinson, Marjorie, 33, 159n23
Leys, Ruth, 34–35, 145–46
Li, Ming, 79
Libet, Benjamin, 84–85
Literature: and economics, 27, 71–75, 132–37; and history, 15–17, 18–19, 27, 69–70, 144–45; 169n12; interdisciplinary study of, 19, 136–47; and science, 1–4, 30–31, 57–60, 76–86, 151–52n5; and the virtual, 32–42
Longenbach, James, 125, 167n16
Lukacs, George, 72
Lutz, Antoine, 164n33

Marx, Karl, 133–34, 162n19
Massumi, Brian, 34–35, 84

Matheson, Carl, 1, 151n3
Matz, Jesse, 155n4
Maxwell, William, 167n17
McGurl, Mark, 140
McHale, Brian, 168n21
McLane, Maureen, 47
Merleau-Ponty, Maurice, 131
Merwin, W. S., 122
Meyer, Steven, 58–59
Michaels, Walter Benn, 151n2
Mill, John Stuart, 152n9
Miller, D. A., 146, 169n11
Minahan, John A., 159n20
Mitchell, Robert, 32–33
Mitchell, W. J. T., 159n22, 168n2
Mooney, Susan, 67
Moxley, Jennifer, 8, 152n10
Music: and literature, 23–55; nuance ineffability, 50–51; and philosophy, 25–26, 41–42, 48

Nabokov, Vladimir, 20, 30, 63–78, 87, 90, 103; aesthetics of, 66–68, 71–72; and ethics, 65–67; on psychoanalysis, 64–65
Nagel, Thomas, 24–25, 155n1
Naiman, Eric, 161n13
Nattiez, Jean-Jacques, 152n12, 156n5
Nehamas, Alexander, 13
Nietzsche, Friedrich, 9, 16, 23, 26, 28, 143
Noe, Alva, 13, 15, 58, 153n13
Novelty: and consciousness, 82–83, 164n31; permanent, 19–20, 25–31; and phenomenology, 153n13. *See also* Addiction; Time
Nussbaum, Martha, 16

Orwell, George, 87–114; aesthetics of, 99–101; and the human, 101, 113–14; on prohibition, 90–94; on sexuality, 94–95

Parrinder, Patrick, 168n3
Pater, Walter, 10, 59
Perloff, Marjorie, 104–5, 126–27, 130–31, 165n1, 167n16
Pfau, Thomas, 157n14
Plath, Sylvia, 8, 152n9
Polanyi, Karl, 133, 154n16

Poulet, Georges, 9, 29–30, 44, 155n4
Pound, Ezra, 128, 132–33, 166n10, 167n15
Prinz, Jesse, 163n22, 163n30
Proust, Marcel, 11–12, 38–41, 90, 100–103, 130, 136, 155n4; and the reasonable solution to the problem of time, 17–18; and the unreasonable solution to the problem of time, 25–32

Redfield, Marc, 71, 162n18
Redish, A. David, 77, 80, 85
Richardson, Alan, 152n11, 154n16
Ricoeur, Paul, 152n6, 166n12
Rimbaud, Arthur, 33–34, 60
Robinson, Thomas, 78–79, 83
Roemer, John, 73, 163n21
Rorty, Richard, 87–89
Ross, Andrew, 125, 166n11
Ross, Don, 80
Rosse, Richard B., 163n26
Russett, Margaret, 71, 161n8

Sacks, Oliver, 48
Said, Edward, 145
Sandison, Alan, 99–100, 103
Sarneki, John, 152n5, 163n25
Scarry, Elaine, 2–3, 19, 57, 102–3, 108
Schiller, Friedrich, 9
Schroeder, Timothy, 1, 151n3
Searle, John, 35
Sedgwick, Eve, 71, 146
Shakespeare, William, 6, 8–9, 11, 70, 99, 152n7
Shattuck, Roger, 158n18
Shelley, Percy B., 10, 16–17, 32, 62
Sheringham, Michael, 164n3
Shetley, Vernon, 125
Shklovsky, Viktor, 3, 10–11, 59, 89, 101; on the history of art, 18, 108–9; reception of, 102–8, 165n5
Shoptaw, John, 130–31

Simmons, Dan, 47
Sloboda, John, 50–51
Snyder, Bob, 49–51
Soni, Vivasvan, 153n13
Sontag, Susan, 168n4
Spivak, Gayatri, 167n19
Stafford, Barbara Maria, 58–59, 63
Starr, Gabrielle, 19, 154n18, 158n16
Steiner, Peter, 165n7
Sterling, Bruce, 24–25, 29
Stonum, Gary Lee, 153n14

Terada, Rei, 147, 156n7
Tiffany, Daniel, 152n11
Time: chronological, 4, 9, 10, 20, 70, 99; historical, 97–99, 132; philosophy of, 3–4, 35–42, 44–46; as problem for art, 1–22, 26–28; psychology of, 3–4, 79–86, 106–8; subjective, 3–4, 9–10, 48, 60–66, 90–94
Traynor, Rebecca, 152n5, 163n25
Trungpa, Chogyam, 39–40
Turner, Mark, 19, 154n18, 155n1

Vance, Jack, 124, 166n7
Vatulescu, Cristina, 103, 165n5
Vendler, Helen, 43–45, 158n16
Vermule, Blakey, 1, 30–31, 57, 75, 151n1
Vincent, John, 122, 166n5

Walton, Kendall, 151n3
Wellbery, David, 168n8
Williams, Raymond, 87
Wimsatt, W. K., 33
Wolfson, Susan, 159n20
Wood, Michael, 69, 162n17
Wright, Erik Olin, 73

Yeats, William Butler, 6, 128, 166n10

Zinberg, Norman E., 163n27
Zunshine, Lisa, 19, 63, 75, 154n18